Teaching and Development of Marathi

ENCYCLOPAEDIA OF TEACHING LANGUAGES IN INDIA SERIES

Teaching and Development of Marathi

Edited by

S.R. SHARMA
M.A.,LL.B., M.Ed., Ph.D.

ANMOL PUBLICATIONS PVT LTD
New Delhi - 110002

ANNMOL PUBLICATIONS PVT LTD
4374/4B, Ansari Road
Daryaganj, New Delhi-110 002

First Edition 1993

ISBN 81-7041-788-0

PRINTED IN INDIA

Published by J. L. Kumar for Anmol Publications Pvt. Ltd., New Delhi and Printed at Chetna Printers, Maujpur, Delhi-110053.

Preface

The newly independent countries usually called by the name of developing societies or the third world countries mainly of the Afro Asian and Latin American countries had attained their freedoms in the wake of the World War II from colonialism. The newly attained freedoms had brought with them problems of political, economic and cultural nature. Apart from political instability and economic backwardness, these countries had to face the problems arising from the cultural imperialism of the West. The colonial masters had imposed their languages on the peoples of these countries. The use of a foreign language in the administration and in the field of higher education had led to problems of a very long nature. In view of the multiplicity of languages being used in these countries, agreement on a common language had become a very tough problem. It became a real danger to the very existence of these countries. Most of these countries even after 45 years of their independence are still using a foreign language for purposes of administration and at the level of the universities.

It has been rightly observed that if political factors have played an important role in the development of national languages in many areas of Europe and with an extraordinary intensity between 1900 and 1937—they have assumed a still greater importance in the multilingual new states of Asia and Africa since the Second World War. The importance of language for the people of these states can be ascertained from the fact that language often serves as one of the most important symbols of identification and distinction. However, the political importance of language varies to a certain extent with the differences in the multilingual pattern that can be discerned in these states.[1]

There are situations where a variety of languages may exist, each with its substantial literary tradition. This situation can be found in India, Pakistan, Ceylon and Malasia. Language has been defined as the totality of utterances that can be made in a speech community. It has been said that language as a complex of communicative symbols is inextricably related to social activity. Of the media of communication, language is the most versatile. In analysing the linguistic phenomena within the wider context of politics and society, the role of language in the speech communities and the relationships among these communities in the social and political evironments are usually emphasised.

People's love for their own language is as old as recorded history. But the political affirmation of language loyalty and the political manifestation of language rivalry have assumed salience in a relatively recent period of history. The invention of printing, the spread of education to the middle and lower classes, Humanism and the Reformation, and the increasing participation of the general population in national politics have been some of the decisive factors in the placing of a premium on language loyalty and its expression in the politics of nationalism. These developments in the European scene gradually persuaded some Romantic thinker to believe that language is the most important identifying characteristic of peoples and therefore it should be the obvious criterion of national political boundaries. Modern scholars however take into account the vast complexities in the relationship between language and political community.

Language is not a static factor. Although language loyalty has often been characterised as a primordial loyalty,

1. Jyotirindra Das Gupta Language Conflict and National Development Berkeley, University of California Press, 1970, pp. 14-30.

when the dynamic development of language is considered, it will be found that language loyalty is a variable, dependent at times on important political factors.

Both in Europe and elsewhere the transformation of traditional societies into modern political communities has been accompanied by corresponding linguistic modernisation.[2] One important feature of the traditional societies is that they show extremes of internal linguistic diversity in the sense that in such societies, administration, religious affairs, literary activity, and ordinary communication tend to be carried on in different languages. Thus, in a traditional society classical or foreign languages may be employed for administration and religious affairs, whereas the local populations generally speak a variety of unofficial and sometimes unwritten languages or local dialects. Low literacy and the considerable efforts needed for language training tend to favour polarization of power in a small elite, and internal linguistic diversity symbolises extremes of social and political stratification. With the advancement toward modernity the gap between the literary languages and the popular native tongues tends to be reduced. Standardisation of language advances, and with increasing literacy such standard languages become more accessible and the distance between the variants within the language gradually diminishes.

In Europe, the processes of linguistic modernisation followed from about the eleventh to the nineteenth century, and similar processes can be detected in the contemporary modernising stages of Asia and Africa.

As more and more people broke away from the old ways of their relatively isolated existence and restructured themselves in new economic patterns, in dynamic status systems, and in participative political frameworks, they needed more efficient media of commucation. Thus was the ground prepared for the emergence of standard languages and a decrease in the distance between the variants of the same language.

2. *Ibid.*

Language is the index of the stage of development of a society. The rise of the power of the industrialised nations of the west was inextricably linked to a developed language whether it was English, or French, German or Russian. It has been historically proved that the issue of development of a language becomes more political and less academic in due course. The newly independent countries of Asia, Africa and Latin America had inherited provincial languages and there was very little meeting point amongst these languages. The prophets of doom had confidently predicted the disintegration of most of the newly independent states on volatile issues like the language issue. This will have to be admitted that political stability has eluded many countries so far, they had to depend on the languages of their colonial masters. The continuance of a foreign language for the official purposes of the polity of these countries has been responsible for creating serious differences among various political and social groups and have become sources of tensions and the ultimate disintegration of these countries.

Language has long been recognised as an important social phenomenon. Long before the modern intellectual discipline of linguistics was taken up by the modern universities of the world, it had also been recognised that language could be planned and given direction to according to the changing social situations of given times and spaces.

There should be no theoretical objection to the planning of languages in response to the demands of social change, especially at time when independent sovereign nation states and planned social economy are recognised to be the major social objectives of vast numbers of men and women.

Some attention has been given in recent years to the problem of linguistic diversity in India and its relation to the development of regionalism. There is, however, disagreement on almost every aspect of the problem. Some analysts believe that the growing use of regional languages will only obstruct communication between the various sectors of the population and impair the proper functioning of the central government. While as others are confident that the difficulty will be overcome and that the development of Hindi as a national language will counteract the regional tendencies. The disagreements are not confined to matters of interpretation and policy making; they touch on almost every aspect of the basic data, such as existing languages and dialects, the areas in which they are used, number of speakers and even connotations given to the basic terminology.

At the time of its independence in 1947, India had inherited English language from its colonial Masters, the Britishers and it was being used as a link language throughout India for official purposes and at the university level. India is a very old civilization and Sanskrit has been its principal language out of which many languages had developed. A very old language Tamil also had developed in India over a period of 2000 years. But its spread was mainly confined to some parts of South India only. The political leadership of the country, though had decided during its freedom struggle that Hindustani, a language very close to Hindi would be adopted as a national link language made provisions in the Constitution that Hindi would be finally adopted as a national language and it would be enriched through the continued use of words from other Indian languages especially from Sanskrit, adopted a very cautious approach in regard to the switchover from English to Hindi and in fact some times gave the impression that it was indulging in appeasement of the people from South and East to keep the country united, since it has not been possible so far to switch over to Hindi from English and English has been retained as an associate language. Sufficient research has not been made in this field on the basis of which it could be said that India has a powerful language, which could match its economic development.

Language Commissions were appointed to make suitable recommendations for the adoption of Hindi as a national language, Parliamentary Committees were constituted to review the recommendations of the Official Language Commission.

Official Language Act was passed, later amended and Three Language Formula for the study of the three languages at the secondary level was evolved and adopted, and the debate in the National Parliament and State Legislatures it still continuing whether Hindi should be adopted as a link language and whether regional languages should be adopted as medium of instruction at the university stage or not ? It is interesting history and a subject of serious study.

Research in the field of languages in India has been mainly conducted by the Western scholars and the Indian scholars have either conducted research in the universities of the West or mainly using Western techniques of research and tools of analysis in India.

In India in its post independence period, the process of development was initiated on planned lines including the development of Indian languages. During this process of development of the languages, the role of the Indian Parliament, and the Government has been paramount.

This work is a unique study in the development of Indian languages in the post independence period. The editor has analysed the political, governmental and social forces which have been interacting with Indian languages and have consequently led to the development of a link language which is Hindi and the regional languages.

The whole study has been covered in 35 volumes and gives a chronological view of the political and governmental dimensions of the development of a link language and the regional languages in India. 15 regional languages as given in the Indian Constitution have been studied individually.

The editor acknowledges the assistance rendered by the members of the staff of the liberary of Parliament House of New Delhi. Special thanks are due to Dr. G.C. Malhotra, Joint Director, Mrs Arora, Executive Officer and Sh. Jagbir Singh, Assistant Librarian. The timely help in locating the material in the parliamentary debates provided an opportunity to me to compile the matter earlier.

My thanks are also due to the Publications Divisions, Government of India from whose books relevant information has been gathered.

My thanks are due to all the authors and editors of newspapers from where material has been taken.

Sita Ram Sharma

Contents

1

Introduction

The origins of Marathi literature are also found in the songs are Bhajans of saints of Hindu origins mainly.

Dnyanishwar of the thirteenth century, Nam Dev of the fourteenth century Ek Nath of the 15th century and saint Tuka Ram of the 17th century and saint Ram Dass of the same century are most notable among them apart from other saints and poets.

The later saints and literary men were not only poets, they were social reformers also and wrote about social exits and the removal of them. G.H. Deshmukh and jyoti Rao Phule wrote of the social degeneration of the society.

The first novel in Marathi Baba Pudmanji's Yamuna Paryatan (1857) was on social reform.

Similarly Poetry to keshavsut had an agitational role.

Narayan Waman Tilak wrote about the tender beauties of home and nature (1865-1919). Vinayak was an angry poet.

In Marathi drama names like B.P. Kirloskar, K.P. Khadilkar, . . . krishna Kolhatkar are prominent among those who were the pioneers in this sphere.

The contributions of Bal Gangadhar Tilak in the development of Marathi literature are unique. Tilak was not only a great political philosopher and activist, he was a great literary figure of his times. After his death in 1920, there was a void. Anti reformist and revivalist moralising became a common ferture of most writing, including that for the stage and journalism. The Gandhian politics had influenced Marathi educated etite but that also was preaching. Gandhian thought was attached both by the rightists and the leftists. Communism had its appeal for intellectuals in the beginning but ultimately it were the socialists led by Jawahar Lal Nehru who had the sway and they also were altimately absorbed by the Congress. These developments in the political field had their impacts on the Marathi writers.

The 1942 Quit India movement drew into its vortex the socialists too they were prominent in it in fact and when the Congress assimilated them, they added their colour to that multicoloured political melange.

Gradually concepts like prychoanalysis the new sex morality were adopted by the writers and led to the contemporary scene, which will be discussed in detail in the coming chapters.

The age of modern Marathi Literature begins from the end of the 18th century. For about this time two causes—the introduction of the art of printing in India and the contact with the western civilization and literature brought about by the all-absorbing rule of the East India Company—came into being which entirely changed the character of and gave a new impetus to Marathi literature. To describe, in detail, this modern age of Marathi literature is the main purpose of this historical work. But as a background to this subject it would not be inappropriate to give a brief account of the older Marathi literature. For, Marathi literature has a long pedigree, going as far back as the 10th century and the Marathi language traces its origin still further back. Let us, therefore, take a rapid survey of this long period of the origin and growth of Marathi language and literature. The Marathi language belongs to what the philologists call the Indo-Germanic family of the inflexional class of the languages of the world. The parent language of this family is conceived to be the spoken dialect (in their northern home, somewhere between Asia and Europe) of the Aryan race—the common ancestors of all Aryan people now scattered throughout the habitable part of this globe. The immediate offshoots of this conceived parent dialect in Asia are seen to be the two sister languages, the Avesta of the Zoroastrians or fireworshippers of old Persia and Assyria and the Ars or Vedic dialect of the Indian Aryans who came to the Punjab watered by the Indus and its five tributaries. This Vedic dialect or Ars language gradually grew into what came to be called the Classical Sanskrit language after Panini's time. The great grammarian Panini, who flourished about 700 B.C., determined and formulated the principles of this language. Since then the Sanskrit language became the perfect type of an inflexional language. It was this classical Sanskrit which first became known to Europe by the efforts of Sir William Jones, one of the servants of the East India Company, in the middle of the 18th century.

The Origin of the Marathi Language

Panini's Sanskrit language came to be the religious language of the learned people of India. Naturally the spoken language of the Aryan people who spread from the Punjab to the whole continent of India began to differ from this learned language. So, when Gautama Buddha, the founder of the great Buddhistic religion, had to enlighten the people about his new religious ideas he had to take recourse to the spoken language of the people. When, therefore, the teachings and sayings of Buddha came to be written down in the form of books, they were naturally expressed in the actual spoken dialect of the people so as to become easily intelligible to the general public. The language in which the religious books of Buddhism were written came to be called Pali. This language itself became a purely literary language and by the time of Asoka, the great patron and prophet of Buddhism who was instrumental in spreading Buddhism not only all over India, but even beyond India in all directions, the one spoken language of the people got split up into provincial languages which came to be called Prakrt and were regarded as separate languages. This fact is proved by the edicts of Asoka promulgated throughout the length and breadth of India. The language and script of these edicts show great variations and modifications according to the provinces in which the edicts were promulgated. These provincial variations grew in extent as time passed and about the beginning of the Christian era the provincial dialects practically became independent languages and came to have distinct names—the Paisaci, the Sauraseni, Magadhi, Ardha-magadhi and Maharastri. Just as Pali, the first form of spoken Prakrt, became the language of the religious literature of Buddhism, so Ardhamagadhi became the language of the religious literature of Jainism. During all this long period from Panini to the beginning of the Christian era, classical Sanskrit remained the language of the learned. So even the Buddhists and Jains had to learn Sanskrit and had to write books in that language in defence of their respective religious views. Also when they wrote on non-religious subjects they used Sanskrit as the common language of the learned. In Sanskrit dramas the practice of the poets was to use Sanskrit as the language of the higher characters; while they employed the several Prakrts and especially the Maharastri as the language of the inferior characters. So also popular songs introduced into dramas were written in Maharastri. At the time this would be a fair representation of the actual state of things in India, Sanskrit being spoken by educated people and higher classes and the several Prakrts being spoken by women and lower classes. Naturally Maharastri too became a literary language like Ardha-Magadhi and so from about the sixth century onwards literary works came to be written in both Ardha-Magadhi and Maharastri. Recent researches have brought to light many Maharastri literary works. As no spoken and written language remains the same for years together, this Maharastri itself underwent a gradual change and process of simplification to such an extent that the term Apabhramsa came to be applied to this modified Maharastri. Recent researches have discovered many a literary work in this Apabhramsa Maharastri. The literary works both in Maharastri and its Apabhramsa cover the period of about two centuries, from the 6th to the 8th century. The natural and inevitable process of change and modification in a living language, especially when it is used for literary purposes, must have taken place in the case of

Maharastra Apabhramsa. This led to the rise of the present 'Marathi' language.

Origin of Marathi Literature

This will show that the Marathi language is not directly descended from Sanskrit but it is connected with Sanskrit through Pali, Maharastri and Maharastra Apabhramsa. Such is the long pedigree of the Marathi language. Let us now proceed to consider the origin of Marathi literature. It is a well-known fact that the spoken stage of a language may continue for an indefinite period in a community. Such must have been the case of Marathi in the Marathi speaking community. But two important events or causes gave an impetus to the origin and growth of literature in the Maharastra country. The first great event was the rise of the Jadhava or Yadava family of Maratha Hsatriya caste to the position of power in Maharastra. A Prince of this family first established his dynasty at Sinnar in Nasik district and later on he transferred his capital to Devagiri when he became a suzerain ruler in Maharastra. The family became royal and renowned. It formed a stable and strong government for over 200 years. The Yadava dynasty adopted Marathi as the court lauguage. It also encouraged learning and learned men. The famous minister of this family encouraged Marathi language throughout his long period of administration which extended to the rule of two kings of Jadhava or Yadava dynasty. He is credited with the invention of the running hand for rapid writing called the Modi script in which all documents, state papers and private correspondence came to be written. Thus, the adoption by a powerful dynasty of the Marathi language as the court language gave a great impetus to Marathi literature during the 200 years in which the dynasty was the ruling power in Maharastra.

Religious sects and Marathi

The second great event of this period was the rise of two religious sects known as Mahanubhava Panth and Varkari Panth.

These sects were not schisms in Hindu religion like Jainism and Buddhism which developed into separate and independent religions; but they were rather reforming sects within the pale of Hinduism and had many characteristics in common. Both of them arose in the heart and home of Maharastra and at about the same time; both emphasized the value of devotion to and chanting the name of God as the best and easiest means of salvation and attainment of religious merit, the Mahanubhava sect selecting Krsna and Dattatraya and the Varkari sect selecting Hari and Vitthal as their special objects of devotion out of the Hindu pantheon. Both accepted the same religious books and regarded the Bhagavadgita as the gospel of their sects. Both of them made converts to their sects from all people irrespective of caste and creed. Both formed a kind of brotherhood, having a special badge of their creed in their dress and outward demeanour. Both of them inculcated simple living, prohibiting the use of meat and alcohol. Lastly, both these sects adopted the Marathi language as a vehicle for preaching their ideas to the people and thus gave a great and lasting stimulus to the growth of Marathi literature.

Though these two sects had many things in common and might possibly have made common cause in reforming the Hindu religion, their fate and fortune had totally different turns. While the Varkari sect rose in popular estimation and spread throughout the whole of Maharastra and especially among the lower strata of society, the Mahanubhava sect went out of favour in Maharastra and it had to find converts in far off places and provinces. The sect was denounced by the Varkari Panth as hypocritical and the term Mahanubhava got corrupted into Manbhava and this word actually came to mean Hypocricy. The Marathi saying 'You speak like a Mahanubhava but act like a scoundrel' indicates the inveterate prejudice and hatred against the followers of this sect engendered in the minds of the common people. Similar has been the fate of the Marathi literature developed by the two sects.

The writers of the Varkari sect came to be regarded as the

pioneers and founders of Marathi literature. In fact, the founders of the sect gave a tone and character to all subsequent Marathi literature which flowed on in a continuous stream down to the end of the 18th century. This stream of literature was, as it were, the overground current known and appreciated by the educated men till our own day; while the stream of literature produced by the founders and followers of Mahanubhava sect went underground and flowed on hidden from the general public.

Mahanubhava Literature

This underground current of Marathi literature was discovered by Marathi scholars like Messrs. Rajawade, Bhave and Candorkar only a generation back. These scholars made friends with Mahanubhava Mahants or religious heads and induced them to open the secret of their cipher alphabet. Thus they succeeded in bringing up to the surface the Mahanubhava literature long buried underground. This work is still being carried on and a great volume of Marathi literature anterior to and contemporaneous with the writings of Dnyanesvar and Mukundraj (till now regarded as the picneers and founders of Marathi literature) has come to light. So even in a brief review of old Marathi we must refer to this interesting chapter in its literary history.

According to the newly discovered Marathi literature, the founder of Mahanubhava sect was named Harpaldev alias Cakradhar. He was descended from a Gujarati Nagar Brahmin family. His father Visaldev was originally the minister of a Gujarat ruler but the kingdom was handed over to Visaldev as the ruler died childless. After the death of Visaldev Harpaldev came to the throne and ruled the kingdom for a long time. Towards the close of his life, however, he left his kingdom and became a recluse and came to Ruddhapur, a town in Berar, where he met a saint called Govind Prabhu. Govind Prabhu made him his disciple, gave him the title of Cakradhar and asked him to establish a new sect. Thus, Cakradhar became the founder of a sect which he called Mahanubhava Panth. He preached in Marathi and made disciples. Cakradhar did the work of spreading his sect from 1263 to 1271 when he finally retired to Badrikasram. He regarded Krsna and Dattatraya as his special objects of devotion. Of course he was against making images of these Gods. During the short period of 8 years Cakradhar made 500 disciples. They spread the new doctrine far and wide. Cakradhar did not himself write any book. But his actual utterances and sayings were collected together by his disciple Mahindrabhat. These works known as Acaryasutra and Siddhantasutrapath became the first religious books of Mahanubhava sect. He also wrote a life of Cakradhar named Lilacaritra. These works are in prose and may be regarded as the earliest known form of Marathi literature. Bhaskaracarya was also a disciple of Cakradhar and he wrote a poetic work called Sisupalavadha. This is the first Marathi epic having a literary claim. Thus the Mahanubhava sect gave a great impetus to Marathi literature both religious and secular. The sect spread far and wide. It was adopted by the Yadava rulers of Devgiri. Even after the fall of the Devgiri dynasty and the establishment of Mohammedan rule in Maharastra the Mahanubhava sect did not lose the royal favour as they were regarded as non-idolatrus by the Mohammedan rulers. So they secured privileges and concessions from these rulers such as exemption from taxes. But on account of this favour of the foreign rulers the Mahanubhavas lost the sympathy of the people. Moreover, from this time they began to write their literary works in a cipher alphabet the key to which was not explained to anybody except to the initiated people of their sect. Thus the whole Marathi literature developed by writers of this sect, whether it was religious or secular, remained a sealed book and continued as an underground current which was discovered only in recent times. But modern research has brought out more than a dozen Marathi works in prose anterior to the works of Mukundraj and Dnyanesvar regarded till now as the first literary writers in Marathi.

Varkari Literature

Mukundraj and Dnyanesvar are, like Castor and Pollux,

the twin stars of old Marathi literature. But tradition gives the palm to Dnyanesvar and regards him as the father and maker of that literature though the same tradition gives time precedence to Mukundraj. But there is not sufficient evidence to establish this point. For, while the time of Dnyanesvar is abolutely certain, he having given the exact year of the completion of his master-piece, the Dnyanesvari, that of Mukundraj is not equally certain. Here tradition seems the only evidence. If we look to internal evidence it points to a conclusion contrary to the tradition. For the language and style of Mukundraj looks a little more modern than that of Dnyanesvar. But as it is wellknown that the Dnyanesvari, the master-piece of Dnyanesvar, was modernised by Eknath, so the works of Mukundraj too may have been modernised by some unknown hand. Thus the argument based on the modern style of the texts of Mukundraj's works does not prove anything. The best way out of the difficulty is to respect the old tradition and regard Mukundraj as the older poet-saint. Mukundraj is credited with having written Vivekasindhu and Paramamrta. Both these are philosophical poems and are written in the Marathi Ovi metre. These poems give the Vedant doctrines of Sankaracarya but being written in the then Marathi language they were capable of being understood by the common people. But Mukundraj's works do not seem to have become very popular and hence Mukundraj did not come to be recognized as the father of old Marathi literature. That honour was reserved for Dnyanesvar.

The Father of Marathi Literature

Dnyanesvar was not only the father and maker of old Marathi literature but he was also the founder of a new religious sect in the Marathi-speaking country. His life and history are as interesting and impressive as are his literary works. So let us briefly refer to them here.

Dnyanesvar came of a devout Brahmin family living in Appegav in the heart of Maharastra. His father Vitthalpant had, from his youth, a tendency towards a recluse's life of solitude and meditation. Fortunately for Vitthalpant, he was married to a girl who was equally devout and so both of them pulled on every well. Rukmini was the name of Dnyanesvar's mother and like very Hindu lady she longed for a son and did penance for it. But Vitthalpant became more and more estranged from worldly concerns of life and pressed his wife to give him permission to become a formal and regular Sannyasi. Rukminibai, yielding to the incessant pressure of her husband, gave her consent though in the heart of her hearts she longed for a son. Immediately on getting permission, unwilling though it was, from his wife, Vitthalpant went straight to Benares and received the orders of a Sannyasi from a Svami by name Sripad. Soon after, the Svami happened to halt at Alandi on his way to Ramesvar. Rukmini the wife of Vitthalpant had come to stay at Alandi with her parents. She, while doing penance, fell at the feet of the new Svami who had come from Benares. The Svami gave her the usual benediction that she might get a son. Rukminibai seemed puzzled. So, the Svami made inquiries and came to know that the lady was the wife of Vitthalpant whom he had allowed to take the orders of a Sannyasi. Seeing her sorrow he went back to Benares and asked Vitthalpant to return home and perfrom the duties of the household and fulfil the wish of his wife, saying that in doing such a thing he would incur no. sin. In accordance with the request of his guru Vitthalpant returned home and resumed his life as a house holder. Rukminibai was glad to see her husband back, taking up again the duties of the household. Her desire to have a son was more than gratified by her having three sons and one daughter. All the children were brought up properly and soon the time for the thread ceremony of the sons came up. Here arose a religious difficulty. According to the orthodox view a Sannyasi has no caste and the sons of a Sannyasi are not entitled to the thread-ceremony. But considering the keen desire of the parents and sons, the local priests agreed to perform the ceremony provided the learned pandits and Sastris of Paithan pronounced such a course as being right and proper. The three sons, accordingly, went to Paithan. There Dnyanesvar proved his knowledge of the Sastras and his miraclous power by making a he-buffalo recite the Vedas. Seeing this knowledge and power of Dnyanesvar, the Pandits of Paithan gave the required permission. Then the thread-ceremony was duly performed. It was after this formal initiation into Brahminhood that Dnyanesvar began the writing of his famous exposition of the Bhagavadgita in Marathi verse. After the completion of this great work in 1290 A D. Dnyanesvar took his master-piece to Benares the great repository of the religious and philosophic learning of the Hindus. There the learned pandits examined Dnyanesvar with regard to his religious and philosophic knowledge and were astonished to see the young man a master of these abstruse sciences and capable of holding his own in discussions about them. They were also surprised to see his mastery over the Marathi language in which his exposition of the Bhagavadgita was written. Thus, Dnyanesvar came triumphantly out of the difficult ordeal and was able to attract disciples and followers. He soon returned home and laid the foundation of his Nath Panth or Bhaktimarga. Since he regarded Vitthal, the God of Pandharpur, as the symbol of Godhood and since he asked his disciples to make their annual pilgrimage or vari to Pandharpur, the sect soon came to be called the Varkari Panth, a name which all the followers of Dnyanesvar love so much. They soon had a badge of their sect, a garland of tulsi plant and a pink flag of devotion. The Bhavarth Dipika or Dnyanesvari (the name given by the public to the masterpiece), the exposition of the Bhagavadgita, became widely known and was widely read and recited.

The Dnyanesvari

The lucidity, the power of giving illustrations, the dialogue form, methodical treatment of the subject, mastery over the abstruse metaphysics and above all the wonderful and melodious vocabulary and rhythm—these unique characteristics of the Dnyanesvari mark the work as a master-piece in old Marathi literature. Hence, soon after its publication the book became the gospel of the new Varkari sect and verses from it were daily read and recited not only by the regular followers of the sect but also by the general public. But Dnyanesvar's devotional songs and prayers in simpler and plainer Marathi were chanted and recited both by the literate and the illiterate public. These fine devotional songs and prayers have maintained their popularity even to this day. Such is their melodious diction.

Besides these two works Dnyanesvar wrote a purely philosophical work called Amrtanubhava in Marathi. This work was evidently intended for the philosophically-minded people. It is very abstruse and difficult and though it is revered and respected by the followers of Dnyanesvar it is rarely read.

These three works constitute the sole literary output of Dnyanesvar. But they are the permanent ornaments of old Marathi literature and will remain so for generations together.

After these literary achievements Dnyanesvar died a premature death at the age of 22. But his literary work was carried on by his brothers and his sister though their total output is far less than and inferior to that of Dnyanesvar. It is interesting to see that the whole family was endowed with literary talent and all of them contributed more or less to the enrichment and refinement of old Marathi literature. Curiously enough, all of them died prematurely.

Namdev

The younger contemporary of Dnyanesvar was Namdev. He came of a family of Simpi (tailor) caste. Namdev's family joined Dnyanesvar's new sect. This indicates how the sect appealed particularly to the lower classes and castes of Hindu society. That the teaching of Dnyanesvar was permeating even the lower strata of society is proved by the fact that during the century following the death of Dnyanesvar saints and poets were found among all castes and they all prayed to Vitthal, made their annual pilgrimage to Pandharpur and wore the two famous badges of the sect. Namdev was converted to the new sect by Visoba Khecar, a Vani (grocer) by caste, who had become the disciple of Sopandev, the brother of Dnyanesvar. Thus the tradition of handing on the secret teaching of the sect from the preceptor to the disciple was followed. Namdev's conversion to Dnyanesvar's sect was a great asset. As Namdev was not a learned Brahmin like Dnyanesvar, his

Marathi verses were written in the simple and terse language of the masses. So they appealed more to them than the comparatively learned writings of Dnyanesvar. Namdev's songs and prayers became more popular as he established the practice of pilgrimage to Pandharpur and as the increasing number of Varkaris heard his songs sung by himself. By his long life also Namdev contributed to the spread of the new devotional literature of the Varkari Panth in the nooks and corners of the Marathi-speaking country.

Dnyanesvar and Namdev between them cover a full century in which Marathi literature was influencing the life and conduct of the people and was in turn influenced by them.

Rapprochement between the Sects

Between Namdev and Eknath, another famous saint and poet, there is a gap of about 200 years For according to tradition Namdev died in 1350 A.D., while Eknath was born in 1548 A.D. During this long period, the Mohammedan power was in the ascendant in Maharastra. Consequently there was no encouragement for Marathi literature as there was in the time of Mukundraj and Dnyanesvar and for a short period after them. But the Varkari Panth was not much disturbed and so the literary tradition was continued. No poet of outstanding merit arose during this period though there must have been lesser lights keeping the literary flame a-glow but giving only a dim light. However, during this period two great saints whose fame has continued even to these days did arise in Maharastra. Their names are Nrsimhasarasvati and Janardan Svami. Both of them were highly respected by the public of their time. A few songs and prayers are regarded as their composition. But it is obvious that they did not shine in the literary field at all. A disciple of Nrsimhasarasvati wrote a work called 'Gurucaritra'. This work describes the origin and history of the three-faced god Dattatraya. The curious thing about this book is that though the author did not attain any fame or name as a literary man his work came to be regarded as a gospel of Dattatraya worship. This worship became very popular and hence the work itself became sacred and it was itself worshipped as a symbol of God. Even now many orthodox Brahmins worship this book. Another feature of the period seems to be the cessation of estrangement between the Mahanubhava and the Nath or Varkari sects. As stated before these two sects began their career at the same time. At first there was a rivalry between them. Later on the Mahanubhava sect became discredited because of its having secured undue concessions from the Mohammedan rulers. But during the period that elapsed between Namdev and Eknath, the Mahanubhava sect lost its privileged position and so there came a rapprochement between them. Hence many followers of the Varkari sect became Mahanubhavas and gave their compositions to that sect. Mahanubhavas, from the beginning, were worshippers of Dattatraya. So this worship became the common tie between them and the new worshippers of Dattatraya adopted Guru-caritra as a sacred book of the new sect.

Eknath

Now comes on the stage of Maharastra a great saint and a greater poet, Eknath. The life of Eknath is both interesting and ennobling and so it is worth telling it here briefly. As referred to above, Eknath was born in 1548 A. D. He came of a devout Brahmin family. From his early boyhood he had a yearning for devotion to God. He was left an orphan, his parents having died suddenly and prematurely. So he was brought up by his grand-father Cakranarayana. Immediately after his thread-ceremony Eknath began the usual studies of a Brahmin and being a precocious boy he soon became well-versed in the usual lore. He had a desire to be a disciple of the famous Saint Janardan Svami and so he went to Daulatabad and learnt at the feet of the famous Svami. Eknath here studied the two philosophical books of Dnyanesvar, the Dnyanesvari and the Amrtanubhava. He was greatly influenced by these books and he began to hold in great reverence the author of these books. From them he received his inspiration to write in the Marathi language and add to its literature. Janardan Svami seeing the brilliant intellect of his disciple encouraged him to write and teach the people what he had imbibed from Dnyanesvar's works. According to the advice of his guru, Eknath at once began his career as a poet. First he composed an exposition of a small work called Catusloki Bhagvata. It was so well done that Janardan Svami asked Eknath to take up the more difficult work—the exposition of the famous eleventh chapter of the great Bhagvat. This exposition is known as Eknathi Bhagvata. This is Eknath's literary master-piece as Dnyanesvari is that of Dnyanesvar. This work of Eknath is the second great literary work in old Marathi. It is read by thousands of men and women who regard it as a sacred book like the Gurucaritra.

Eknath's Narrative Poetry

Having done what his guru had told him to do, Eknath went on writing work after work. For he had developed a simple flowing style and he was a great story-teller. He made use of the two great Sanskrit epics, the Ramayana and the Mahabharata and took out from them interesting and instructive stories and episodes as subjects for his famous poems. These became more popular than his great philosophical work, the Eknathi Bhagvata. The object of these poems was the entertainment and instruction of people both young and old, men and women. For these poems contained exciting incidents from the lives of the mythological heroes depicted in the two great epics. This poetry of Eknath belongs to the class of narrative poetry. Its purpose is, therefore, secular instruction and innocent entertainment. Eknath went on bringing out poem after poem till his death. Thus he became the founder of secular narrative poetry in Marathi. One important task of Eknath remains to be mentioned. He revised the Dnyanesvari and brought out a correct and intelligible version of it. During the long period since the death of Dnyanesvar, the Marathi language underwent great changes even though it was being used by many a poet. Consequently the language of the Dnyanesvari became obscure and unintelligible. Moreover, through the ignorance and negligence of scribes the text of the Dnyanesvari got corrupted. Eknath published a fine version of the famous poem. This is the version that peogle of these days have regarded, and do still regard, as the original Dnyanesvari.

Kknath, the Social Reformer

So far I have given an account of the literary works, great and small, of Eknath. I must now refer to his teaching and especially to the courage with which he put his teaching into practice—a courage which appeals even to modern minds. Eknath taught the oneness of God and all-pervading nature of the God-head. He taught that God created all human beings, nay, all animate and inanimate creatures. So all are the creation of God. As such all men are the children of God. There is nothing like superiority and inferiority among men. All are equal and hence all should be regarded as brothers and treated with love and sympathy. To help the needy and the poor, to remove the grief and sorrow of the afflicted and, above all, to love all mankind, was the main burden of Eknath's teaching. Eknath not only taught these ennobling views of his but he actually practised them. Let me recite one or two incidents in Eknath's life with regard to this. Eknath was regarded as a radical reformer by orthodox Brahmins who detested his views. And though he performed all the religious rights he was boycotted by them. Once the Brahmins refused to come to his house to partake of the food prepared on the occasion of his father's death anniversary day. Eknath gave all the food to the Mahars (untouchables) who were looking at the food with longing eyes. On another occasion he actually went to the house of an untouchable and partook of the food prepared by his family. On a third occasion he brought home a dirty crying child and taught people a lesson of kindliness by removing the child's dirt. Thus Eknath was a fine example of the famous Marathi saying, 'Bole taisa cale tayaci vandavi paule.' (He who acts up to his teaching should be revered and worshipped). After leading such a noble life Eknath died in 1599 A.D. at the age of 52. Though in his lifetime he was persecuted and boycotted by the Brahmins, he was highly respected by the general public and especially by the so-called lower classes of Hindu society and his name became coupled with that of Dnyanesvar as a great saint and poet of Maharastra.

Muktesvar

The practice of writing secular narrative poetry started by Eknath was continued and developed by Muktesvar, the grandson of Eknath by his daughter. Muktesvar was born in 1608 A.D. As his father led rather a wayward life Muktesvar was brought up by Eknath and was taught early in his life to read Sanskrit and Marathi. He must have particularly studied the works of Dnyanesvar, Namdev and his grandfather. He seems to have been influenced greatly by the works of his grandfather; he must have been fired with the ambition of emulating, nay excelling, him. So he began his literary career by composing Ramayana early in his youth. As a narrative poem it is not a very successful production. Its style is still crude and uncouth. But the narration is good and it shows here and there flashes of his poetic genius. But his Mahabharata is a work of his mature genius. It is deservedly regarded as the best example of a great narrative poem in old Marathi literature capable of being very well compared with any English narrative poem. Muktesvar is reputed to have brought up his narrative to the very end of the Mahabharata comprising 18 Parvas. He wrote the whole poem giving in his own style and manner the story of the great Sanskrit epic. But unfortunately only four Parvas are available now. What became of the remaining Parvas is a mystery. But recently two more Parvas—the Sauktika and Santi Parvas—have been discovered. So in time others may be found. Of the available Parvas the Adi Parva (the first Parva) is by far the best of Muktesvar's production. It shows the poet at his best. His power of vivid description, his capacity to appeal to the several sentiments of the reader, and his clear, sweet and vigorous style are to be seen in every verse of the poem.

Muktesvar wrote many smaller poems and miscellaneous pieces also. He is reputed to have written an exposition of the Bhagvata in the Ovi metre. But unfortunately that also is not available at present.

Muktesvar lived to a fairly old age and died in 1660 A.D.

Minor Poets

There were two or three lesser lights who contributed to the growth of the old Marathi literature and who, therefore, deserve mention even in this brief narrative. They are Ramavallabhdas, Sivakalyana and Lolimbraj.

Ramavallabhdas came of the rich family of an official of the Daulatabad ruler. His original name was Tukopant. While still young Tukopant had to go to attack an enemy of his ruler. He routed the enemy's army and in the loot accidentally came across an exposition of the eleventh chapter of the Bhagvata. He regarded this as a gift of God and began to read the book daily. He was greatly influenced by the teachings of the book. He soon met a saint by name Lakmidhar who initiated him into his order and named him Ramavallabhdas. He wrote several works which are more in the style of Dnyanesvar than in that of Muktesvar. Consequently his inferior expositions of the Bhagavadgita, Sankarabhasya and Bhagvata remained comparatively unknown and unpopular.

Sivakalyana, a contemporary of Ramavallabhdas, returned to the more popular poetry i.e., narrative poetry and he composed a great poem on the tenth chapter of the Bhagvata in which the amorous doings of Krsna with the Gopis are described in detail. Some parts of this great poem border on the obscene and the vulgar. Still the poem is a readable one.

Lolimbraj came from Junnar near Poona. His great work is on a medical subject though it is in verse. He also wrote a poem on the tenth chapter of Bhagvata. He composed many devotional songs and prayers which are sweet and melodious.

Tukaram

In the history of old Marathi literature Tukaram occupies a unique position. The poets considered so far may with some plausibility be considered to be mere translators or adaptors of Sanskrit poems who had no real poetic talent. But Tukaram was a man of true genius. All his poetry was original and came out of his own wonderful inspiration. Unlike all other poets and saints of Maharastra, Tukaram was a poet of introspection both individual and social. He looked into his own mind and into the social mind with his keen intellect and found out the failings and foibles both in himself and in the society of his time. He mercilessly exposed and ridiculed them with a view to remove and correct them. By satire, by ridicule, by cajolery and by supplication, he tried his best to reform the society of his time. Thus he was a radical reformer of social customs and ideas. He had a righteous indignation against the prevailing hyprocrisy and vices of his time, and in his poems he earnestly implored his countrymen to reform their way of life. Terseness, clarity, vigour and earnestness are to be seen in every line of Tukaram's verses. Hence they touch the very heart of the reader and wean him unconsciously from the evil ways of living. The influence of Tukaram over the men of his time was wonderful and even now that influence has not waned. Thus Tukaram comes under the class of saints and teachers who have been prophets of all ages. Tukaram and Socrates, though born at different times and in different countries, so curiously resemble each other in their life and conduct, that a theosophically minded reader will say that the soul of Socrates entered the body of Tukaram for the purpose of self-improvement and ultimate salvation.

Tukaram and Socrates

Both of them came to be recognized as great saints; both of them gave all their time and energy to public benefit, having no thought of their self-interest; they entirely devoted themselves to the teaching of the people of their respective countries; they never thought of their bodily comforts or concerns, being fully absorbed in things divine; both were devotees of the one true God; both hated hypocrisy and ritualism from the bottom of their hearts and exposed and ridiculed them in public. Like the similarity in their mental life there was a wonderful similarity in their surroundings and circumstances. Both of them came from what was regarded as a lower stratum of society; for Socrates was the son of a stone-cutter while Tukaram was the son of a grocer. Both of them by their intrinsic merit and good work attained the highest position in their respective societies. Both of them led a very simple life not caring for the pleasures and luxuries of life; they never became recluses but had wives and children; both had wives who were notorious termagants, the wife of Socrates excelled in this respect, so much that her name Xanthippi, came to be a common name for a termagant. Lastly, both of them were persecuted by the orthodox people of their respective countries. Socrates had to drink a cup of hemlock by way of punishment for his supposed crime of teaching heterodoxy to young men. The Hindus of Tukaram's times were a tolerant people and though they persecuted him and made him give up his teaching and writing in a heterodox way, they did not go to the length of any further punishment. However, in one or two respects these two saints differed from each other very widely. Socrates never wrote a single line. His teaching was all oral—given in conversation with the young and the old. His conversation was so interesting and inspiring that the people of Athens, especially the young, were attracted and Socrates was always surrounded by groups of young men. Fortunately what Socrates said in his conversations was taken down and carefully preserved by his devoted disciples, Plato and Xenophon. But such was not the case with Tukaram. He too spent all his life in giving public discourses and in them composed ex-tempore songs and verses; but he carefully wrote them down or dictated them to his disciples. So Tukaram's writings are all available in his own or his disciples' handwritings. In another important respect too, Socrates and Tukaram differed from each other. Socrates was impressed by the prevailing ignorance of his people and all his energy was devoted to the removal of this ignorance. He was a great believer in the method of knowledge, both secular and religious, and it was his firm conviction that such double knowledge led to the salvation of man. But Tukaram was a great believer in devotion to God as the true path of salvation. He felt that the people of his time went wrong because they did not know the true way to salvation. This true way, according to Tukaram, was heart-felt devotion and annual pilgrimage to Pandharpur.

After this long-drawn comparison between Socrates and Tukaram let me now briefly refer to the life and career of Tukaram.

Life of Tukaram

Tukaram was born at Dehu, near Poona, in 1608 A. D. He was a Sudra by caste but Vaisya by profession. Tukaram's ancestor Visvambhar was a devotee of God Vithoba of Pandharpur and had built a temple for the God at Dehu. Thus the worship of Vithoba was an established practice in the family and so Tukaram, from his early boyhood, had taken to the worship of Vithoba. At the age of 13 Tukaram lost his parents and his elder brother became a recluse and left the house, and so the young Tukaram had to shoulder the burden of the whole family with his two wives and children and his younger brother. For some time he carried on his profession in an efficient way. But days of difficulty and adversity came. There was a great famine in the land. Tukaram lost his cattle and there was nothing to eat. His wife and some other members of the family died of starvation. Under the weight of this great calamity Tukaram turned more and more to the worship of Vitthal. He began to like solitude and meditation and so he went to a hill near his village and there spent days and nights in study and meditation. His forgot all about his family and its difficulties. He second wife and sons searched and him and brought him home. But he could not be made to take interest in the household concerns. He became more and more absorbed in study and meditation. Soon after, he felt inspired and from that time began to compose songs and verses and began the practice of giving public kirtans (sermons). His exposition of radical views, his exposure of failings and foibles of the people about him, his earnest appeal to people to give up hypocrisy and turn to the worship of God Vitthal as the simple and sure means of salvation, were so impressive and instructive that his name spread far and wide, attracting people to his discourses from far and near. His fame reached the ears of Sivaji, the founder of the Maratha Svarajya, and once Sivaji came to his discourse incognito and was so much impressed by Tukaram's teaching of resignation and retirement from worldly affairs, that Sivaji was prepared to give up his great effort of founding the Hindu Empire. But when Tukaram came to know of this evil effect of his teaching on Sivaji, he purposely requested Sivaji to attend his discourse again. In this discourse Tukaram dwelt at length upon the sacredness of the duty of rulers to their subjects and upon the necessity of devoting all their energy to the good of the subjects and suggested that such disinterested performance of duty was the way to salvation for persons like Sivaji who occupied a high rank in society. This earnest, inspiring and impressive appeal of Tukaram went home to Sivaji's heart and he returned to his kingly duties with greater zeal and energy. Such is the wonderful power of persuasion possessed by inspired saints!

A Miracle

Thus Tukaram became a great poet and saint. He made verses suitable to the occasion on the spur of the moment. But all this wonderful power and influence of Tukaram raised against him a host of enemies from the selfish orthodox camp. He was persecuted by them and was made to throw all his verse books into the Indrayani, a river adjoining Dehu. Tukaram got depressed and for thirteen days prayed to Vitthal. On the fourteenth day the verse-books arose out of the river, dry! This is one of the miracles reported about Tukaram. This miracle silenced Tukaram's enemies and many of them became his staunch followers and disciples. But after this Tukaram began to see that his physical powers were waning and he felt that this was a divine call for him to go to heaven so as to be near his God at all times. This was probably a prognostic of his coming end. Another miracle reported about Tukaram is that he ascended heaven in a baloon with his physical body. It appears that Tukaram suddenly left his village and was no more to be seen. He, therefore, must have voluntarily taken a jala-samadhi (plunge in the river) and got drowned. As his body was never discovered he was supposed to have gone to heaven in person. Such is probably the explanation of the strange story of his physical ascension to heaven which became current among the people.

Radras

Some enthusiasts of Marathi literature, have cried up Ramdas, the poet and saint, to the skies. They regard him not only as a poet-saint but also as a great statesman and the political guru of the great Sivaji. According to them Sivaji was really influenced by Ramdas as regards his political goal and that he every now and then consulted Ramdas and acted up to his advice and so the sole credit of contributing to establish the Maharastra Svarajya belongs to Ramdas. How far this extraordinary claim is substantiated by the internal evidence of the writings of Ramdas or by the external evidence of contemporary writers, we shall discuss when we come to consider his writings and his doings.

It is a fortunate thing that we know more about the life of Ramdas than of any other poet-saint of his time. But these details are supplied by his followers a century after Ramdas' death. So they must be accepted with great caution. But in the first place let me refer to the account of his life which is indeed interesting. His life seems to be divided into four periods in which is discovered a continuous development of his character.

Life of Randas

Ramdas was born in 1608 A.D., at Jambgav on the Godavari river in a part of the Maharastra country which is now included in the Nizam's territory. His father was Suryajipant Thosar and his mother Ranubai. Both of them were very pious and virtuous. The original name of Ramdas was Narayana. He was regarded by his followers as an avatar of Maruti, the servant of Rama who was the hero of the Ramayana. Hence Narayana began to call himself Ramdas (literally, the servant of Rama) and later on he came to be called Samarth meaning powerful. According to the orthodox Hindu custom, Suryajipant wished to marry Narayana to a suitable girl when Narayana was 12 years of age. Everything was ready and while the priests, performing the marriage ceremony of Narayana, were reciting auspicious verses (mangalastake), each verse ending with the word attention (savadhan), Narayana suddenly bolted, to the surprise and astonishment of the assembled gathering. Here the first period of Narayana's life ends and the second period of preparation far his life's work begins. Narayana or Ramdas, (the name permanently adopted by him), went straight to Pancavati and there practised religious penance along with the acquisition of the old and the new learning for full twelve years. This was the second period of his life. In the third period Ramdas travelled over the length and breadth of the whole of India and visited all places of worship from Benares to Ramesvar and from Dvaraka to Jagannathpuri, acquiring varied experience and knowledge of the customs and ideas in the different parts of the country. By these long travels covering a period of twelve years Ramdas made a thorough preparation for the work of his life : he made up his mind to establish a new sect of the worshippers of Rama, the hero of the Ramayana. Thus ended the third period of his life. So, after attaining years of maturity Ramdas returned home and met his mother and told her and his brother his future plan of life. Then he moved about trying to find out a suitable place to found his math for the new worship. At last he selected Caphal in the Satara district as a suitable site and there built a temple of Rama and Hanuman and gathered about him. An annual festival of Rama was celebrated by Ramdas who got the necessary money by begging. Soon Ramdas felt the need of writing an authoritative book for his new sect for the worship of Rama and hence he betook himself to a retired place in the Sahyadri range, (the Western

Ghats), leaving the management of his math to his disciples. In this place of confinement. Ramdas lived for full ten years and completed his contemplated authoritative work. This work is calld Dasbodh (teaching of the servant of Rama). This is a great book. It is Ramdas' masterpiece and it deservedly ranks as an inspiring and impressive literary work in the Marathi language. It is on the authority of this book that the enthusiasts of Marathi literature regard Ramdas as a political guru of Sivaji and a prophet of Maharastra. I shall come to this work immediately, but let me bring to an end the story of Ramdas' life. While Ramdas was confined to his place of retirement his disciples went to Raja Sivaji and gave him information about their guru and his new math. Sivaji was impressed by the account and he sanctioned a cash grant of 200 hons (gold coins) to the math. After Sivaji had conquered the Satara and Parali forta and their surrounding country he remembered that Ramdas lived near about and hence expressed a desire to meet him. By this time Ramdas had returned to his math. So he was glad to receive Sivaji Raja at his math. Sivaji was so much impressed by the imposing personality of Ramdas and his wonderful conversational powers that he made up his mind to become his disciple and expressed his desire to that effect. Ramdas and his disciples were delighted to secure such a royal patron for their new math. Accordingly Ramdas himself initiated Sivaji into the regular order of his disciples and taught him the characteristic mantra of his sect. It was when Sivaji made Ramdas his spiritual guru that he presented him with the fort of Parali which thenceforth came to be called Sajjangad (the fort of the good) and gave grants of land for the expenses of the math. This took place in the year 1672 A.D. Thenceforward Sivaji paid visits to Ramdas and particularly consulted him about his contemplated coronation at the Raygad Fort. Soon after his coronation Sivaji led a successful expedition to the Karnataka and returned home with laurels. But he did not live long to enjoy the kingdom won with such super-human efforts. He died of gout at Raygad in 1680 A.D. Ramdas was extremely sorry to hear about the death of his great disciple. He felt his loss very much. Ramdas did not survive Shivaji long but died full of years in 1682 A.D., after having attained as great a name and fame as that of Dnyanesvar and Tukaram.

Ramdas wrote many miscellaneous poems, songs and verses and wrote also some narrative poetry. One small lyrical but instructive poem named 'Verses addressed to the mind' (Manace Sloka) is very popular. Even now every Hindu boy and girl especially of the higher castes daily recite these verses. They are no doubt ennobling and inspiring. But the Dasbodh is, par excellence, the masterpiece of Ramdas and his whole teaching is contained in that famous work. So let me give some idea of that book to my readers.

Dasbodh—the Masterpiece of Ramdas

The Dasbodh of Ramdas is divided into ten books—each book consisting of several chapters. Chronologically the great work is made up of two parts. The first seven books form a complete whole having a beginning and an end. Obviously it was composed at one stretch and there is a continuous line of thought in it. This part expresses in simple, terse, vigorous language the thoughts of Ramdas about human life and its destiny, and about the nature of man, the universe and its creation by God. In fact, it gives in brief outline the philosophy of retirement and the way to attain true salvation by simple devotion to God, beginning with the service of a spiritual preceptor. It gives, in the allegory of a person, the life of a typical householder, from his youth to his old age. It shows how he begins his youthful life in sexual pleasure, but soon loses all his wealth, then his wife; owing to the pressure of his relatives and friends he marries a second time and the young wife quarrels with him. His house is looted by a Mohammedan and his wife is kidnapped. Thus he ends in misery. Such a picture of the dark and painful side of human life is depicted with a view to make a person disgusted with family life and earnestly to appeal to him to seek salvation by retirement from such a miserable existence. In short, this part or the Dasbodh is similar to the writings of other saints and poets and shows Ramdas to be a follower of the same pessimistic school of thought to which all other saints of

Maharastra belonged.

Doctrine of Worldliness

The second part of Dasbodh appears to have been composed piece-meal. There is no continuous line of thought and there is much repetition. The same pessimistic view of life is depicted as in the first part. But another strain of thought is to be met with here and there. In this new vein of thought Ramdas becomes a teacher of the optimistic view of life. He now maintains the high dignity of human life. He exhorts people to do their allotted work and duty with zeal and earnestness. He tells men to have ambition and to become famous by doing great things. He now speaks openly of the tryranny of the rulers and asks people to take to political and military life and make a name for themselves. In this part he refers to the country and the patriotic duty of serving it. He now praises the life of the householder and exhorts men to serve their neighbours and to help the needy and the poor. It is this part of Ramdas' teaching that appeals to modern educated men with western ideas. And some of the enthusiasts of Marathi literature have cried up these teachings of Ramdas and they have tried to show that Ramdas was a great statesman and inspirer of the youth of Maharastra. As a further evidence of this, these enthusiasts point out that Ramdas established maths throughout the length and breadth of Maharastra and even in the southern Maratha country as far as the river Kaveri. In each village there was to be a temple of Maruti and a gymnasium for physical and military training. Further, Ramdas formed a secret order of bachelors and these bachelors took vows to do political and social work for the uplift of the country. All this may be true but it does not prove what the enthusiasts try to prove thereby. At most, the above facts show that Ramdas was a more practical man than the other poet-saints. He had come to see the futility of the usual advice of the saints during the course of his long travels. So he made a change in his former teaching. He gave advice to people which was more practical that they should lead a life of usefulness by serving the society and the family. He further taught that self-improvement was equally a means of true salvation of the soul. For promulgating these new doctrines Ramdas established his maths and formed his bachelors' order so as to have an unfailing supply of public teachers to preach morality and patriotism. Ramdas saw that the Varkari Panth did not appeal to the higher classes of Maharastra. In order to attract them he established local centres of worship by way of the new temples of Rama and Hanuman and by providing gymnasia for physical training—a feature which especially attracted the younger minds to his sect.

Ramdas as the Guru of Sivaji

Now let me refer to another point of controversy before we take leave of Ramdas. This point is about the true relationship between Sivaji and Ramdas. That Sivaji became a disciple of Ramdas and accepted him as his spiritual guru is an undoubted fact. This is proved by gifts of a permanent nature made to Ramdas and his math and by the gift of the Parali fort near Satara for the residence of Ramdas. The real question is, when did this take place? Those who want to establish that Ramdas was a political as well as a spiritual guru of Sivaji try to prove that the date of their meeting was about the year 1647 A. D. while the actual date proved by documentary evidence is 1672 A. D. The date of the meeting is obviously put back purposely by the followers of Ramdas in order to enhance the influence and prestige of Ramdas. To me the true relationship between Sivaji and Ramdas appears to be very well illustrated by the confluence of the two rivers the Ganges and the Yamuna. Both these rivers take their rise from the sacred Himalaya mountain; both of them run for a considerable part of their course parallel to each other, fertilising and enriching the country on their banks; their confluence takes place at Allahabad and then being united they take one name, the Ganges, and this united river joins the Bay of Bengal. So both Sivaji and Ramdas were born in Maharastra, both of them did their allotted work and benefitted the people of Maharstra—one by freeing them from bondage and tyranny and the other by teaching them their duty to serve the society. They met and became related as disciple and spiritual guru and after doing good to their country and its people in their respective spheres left this worldly theatre. So both of these great men of Maharastra are to be regarded as its makers.

As is natural with an inspiring teacher like Ramdas he gathered about him and in his maths a large number of disciples among whom there were a few ladies also. All of them revered Ramdas and regarded him as an avatar of Maruti. It is to this blind belief that many of the miracles attributed to Ramdas are to be traced. It is said that Ramdas assumed the form of Maruti now and then, that he could fly through the air for miles and miles, that he revived the life of a dead child and that he once fed the whole army of Sivaji by giving them a feast when apparently there was nothing in his hut. In this age of science and enlightenment no one can believe in such miracles. But they are uniformally attributed to many of the great saints of Maharastra. Many disciples of Ramdas have described these miracles wrought by him in their verse compositions in which biographical details of the life of Ramdas are given.

Literature Under Maratha Rule

Ramdas died towards the close of the 17th century. The 18th century marked the rapid expansion of the Maratha empire and towards the close of that century the empire showed signs of decline and fall. There was no need for religious propaganda. For the Mohammedan Empire having crumbled to dust, the domineering and aggressive attitude of the Mohammedan religion and its followers waned. The Hindus could hold their own in the possible struggle between the two religions. In fact, both learnt by bitter experience to live and let live. This change in the political conditions of India and of Maharastra is reflected in the Marathi literature of the 18th century. Like the improvement of political condition this century also saw the highest development of Marathi literature and towards its close signs of decline began to manifest themselves. But during the rising tide a host of Marathi writers came forward. They now formed a class by themselves. They were not dominated by religious zeal nor were they themselves saints or spiritual guides. The need for such men having disappeared no supply was forthcoming. But according to the growing and improving taste of the people pure poets arose to give disinterested delight to their readers by secular poems and versified stories from the two epics. They found also new material for their poems in the heroes and warriors of the previous generation and of their own time, a subject that inspired them.

Vaman Pandit

A foretaste of this 18th century poetry is given by the learned Vaman Pandit although he is a younger contemporary of Ramdas. He was born at Bijapur about the year 1615 A.D. He was a precocious boy and learnt both Sanskrit and Persian when he was quite young. But he had to leave Bijapur for good, for fear of being forcibly converted to Mohammedanism. He went to Benares, visiting places of pilgrimage on his way. At Benares he devoted himself exclusively to the study of Sanskrit and in a few years became proficient in the main Sanskrit sciences. He now despised his own mothertongue, Marathi, and was proud of his Sanskrit learning. So he went from place to place, defeating the local Sastris and Pandits in debate and winning laurels everywhere. After completing his northern tour Vaman Pandit turned to Maharastra and there met Ramdas. The latter severely expostulated with him for despising his mothertongue and exhorted him to apply his genius and learning to the service of Marathi literature. This was a turning point in the life of the great Pandit. He now seriously applied his mind to the study of old Marathi poets and naturally received inspiration from them. Thus he became proficient in Marathi as he already was in Sanskrit. The first use that Vaman Pandit made of his double proficiency was to translate the philosophical Sanskrit works into Marathi. First and foremost he translated the Bhagavadgita verse by verse into fine and flowing Marathi and called it 'Samasloki Gita'. This is a literal translation of the original work. But Vaman Pandit was not satisfied with the translator's roll. He wanted to emulate Dnyanesvar, the father of old Marathi literature. Hence he began an extended exposition of the teachings of the Bhagavadgita and soon completed that great work. He called it the 'Yatharth Dipika' (true commentary) as opposed to the 'Bhavarth Dipika' (suggestive commentary) which was the alternative title of the Dnyanesvari. This is no doubt a great work of Vaman Pandit. His great learning, his mastery of the Marathi language, his power of establishing his view after refuting opposed views, and lastly his persuasiveness in bringing home to his readers the obscure and difficult points in the teachings of the Bhagavad-gita are manifest on every page of his great commentary. Vaman Pandit wrote another philosophical work named 'Nigamasara'. This gives the substance of the Vedas in fine clear Marathi. He also wrote many small philosophical pieces. Having thus given to the Marathi—speaking public the benefit of his Sanskrit learning, Vaman Pandit devoted all his energy to writing secular narrative poetry so as to give disinterested delight to young and old. For the young people he selected beautiful incidents in the very interesting life of Sri Krshna. In these poems Vaman Pandit seems to have pandered to the vulgar taste of the common people. Some pieces in this class of poetry are certainly vulgar and obscene. But they are few and far between in the whole volume of his writing. Finally he adapted into fine and flowing Marathi verse the most popular Sanskrit poems, Bhartrhari's Satakas (three poems consisting of 100 verses each) and the famous 'Gangalahari' (Waves of the Ganges) of Jagannath. Vaman Pandit's adaptations of these famous Sanskrit poems are so well done that no one reading the lucid verses of Vaman Pandit can ever detect that these poems are adaptations. They read like original poems of the author.

Vaman Pandit combined in himself erudite learning and poetic talent— . . . . combination indeed. He died a fairly old man about the year 1678 A.D.

Raghunath Pandit

Raghunath Pandit is another Marathi poet in whom the same learning and poetic talent a rare combination is met with. The output of his genius is one short but beautiful poem with two others doubtfully attributed to him. Very little is known about Raghunath Pandit. Till recently there was a great dispute among Marathi scholars about his name, profession, date and place of birth. But some light is now thrown on these points by recent researches carried on in connection with the editing of the great poem Nala-Damayanti Svayamvar. It is now nearly settled that the real author of Nala-Damayanti Svayamvar was born at Tanjore in Karnatak where Sahaji, the father of Sivaji, carved out a Jahagir for himself and his eldest son Vyankoji. When Sivaji founded his new Kingdom and formed his cabinet of eight ministers, Raghunath Pandit who was occupying an important office at Tanjore was brought from there and made one of the ministers with the title Panditrav. He was entrusted with the management of the religious endowments of the State. Thus Raghunath Pandit's career seems to cover a long period and is coeval with that of Sahaji and Sivaji. He is said to have survived Sivaji and then returned to Tanjore. As stated above the only great work which undoubtedly belongs to Raghunath Pandit is Nala-Damayanti Svayamvar. Two more works i.e. Ramdasvarnan and Gajendramoksa are attributed to him. But they are much inferior to the famous poem which is undoubtedly his masterpiece. It is a short poem of about 269 verses in varied metres. But this poem is a real gem in Marathi literature and will ever remain the favourite of the Marathi reading public. The story of Nala is taken from Mahabharat. It is in itself a romantic love story and it is very beautifully rendered into verse by the poet.

Sridhar

The next poet to be noticed is unlike the two learned Pandits Vaman and Raghunath. This poet's work is similar to that of Muktesvar and to the secular narrative poetry of Eknath. His name is Sridhar. He was born in the year 1678 at the village of Nazra near Pandharpur. His father was a Brahmin and Svami. So Sridhar too followed the example of his father and became a Sannyasi at the age of

14 and made Pandharpur his home, leaving it at times to go out on holy pilgrimage from place to place. His early efforts. at writing poetry were confined to smaller pieces like Sivalilamrta, Jaimini Asvamedha, Brahmottarakhand and Pandurang Mahatmya. These are fairly good poems, simple in style. But his fame and popularity are due to his three great poems Pandav-Pratap, Harivijay and Ramavijay. These are in fact Sridhar's poetical adaptations of the three great Sanskrit works Bharat, Bhagavat and Ramayana. Though Sridhar's poems are adaptations they read almost like original poems. Simplicity. sweetness of diction, lucid flow of narration and the nobleness of the themes have earned for these works such a height of popularity as is unequalled by the writings of any other poet. His thrilling descriptions and suggestive similes add charm to his poems. Like Dnyanesvar, Eknath and Ramdas, Sridhar was an advocate of Marathi language and literature. He courageously told his audience that the Prakrt language was in no way inferior to Sanskrit and that the former was as capable of expressing all kinds of thoughts and ideas as the latter. Finally his object in writing in Marathi was to educate the masses and especially women. This object of Sridhar has been completely fulfilled. All his poems are constantly read and recited by the public. They have served as sources of entertainment and instruction to the women folk of Maharastra. Ever since their publication these three great poems of Sridhar have remained the most popular poems among the Marathi-speaking people, affording delight and noble instruction to young and old, men and women alike. Sridhar died at the age of 50 in the year 1728 at Paithan.

Madhvamuni

To the same class belongs a number of minor poets some of whom became better known than others. But it is necessary to consider them here as their works show how Marathi poetry was becoming varied both in style and subject matter and how it dealt with secular and original subject and stories. Madhvamuni is the first poet of this series. But his name is not much known nor are his poems familiar to the people. But he was the preceptor of the more famous poet Amrtray and as such deserves some notice. Madhvamuni lived at Paithan and at Aurangabad. His birth date is not known but he died about the year 1753. He wrote a poem named 'Dhanesvar' (Lord of Money). This is quite a secular story of a stingy man. It is written in Ovi metre. Another poem of his has been recently discovered but a part of the manuscript is not recovered as yet. But even the available part gives a good idea of the poem. It seems to be again an original story. It is named, 'Katha Cov rayaci' (story of King Cov). Pralhad Caritra, a fine short poem, is also attributed to him but whether it is really his or belongs to one of his disciples cannot be now ascertained.

Amrtray

Amrtray is a farfamed poet. As stated already he was the disciple of Madhvamuni. Amrtray was born in the year 1698. Though he was born and brought up in a village near Buldhana in Berar Province, he lived at Aurangabad and did his poetic work there and died in 1753. Amrtray is famous for introducing a new metre in Marathi named Katav. This is a forcible rapidly running metre, full of rhymes, very effective in didactic and narrative poems. When a poem composed in this metre is recited the audience is simply enraptured while the singer goes on repeating Katav after Katav with well-measured modulation of tone. Amrtray wrote most of his poems like the Durvasyatra, Draupadi-vastraharan and Dhruvacaritra in this favourite metre of his. He wrote in other metres also and some of his miscellaneous songs and padas are very popular.

Sohiroba

Sohiroba, much less known than Amrtray, was more a saint than a poet and in fact may be said to belong to the earlier generation of saints. Sohiroba was a Gaud Sarasvat Brahmin. He was born in 1714 at Banda in Savantvadi State on the western coast of the Bombay Presidency. Sohiroba's ancestors were hereditary accountants (Kulkarnis) and so in his early life he served the Savantvadi State in that capacity. Being tired of this worldly life he entered the order of a Sannyasi at the age of 35. He practised yoga and became a great Vedantin. He understood and realised the principles of the Vedant. He then went on a tour of holy places and visited the saints of the time. While travelling through the territory of Mahadaji Sinde in the course of his tour, Sohiroba was able to meet the great warrior Mahadaji through the influence of Jivaba Dada Baksi who was a Gaud Sarasvat Brahmin and held a high position in the service of Mahadaji. But this meeting proved an unhappy one. For, when Mahadaji who was fond of poetry was shown Sohiroba's poems, he did not seem to like them. But the large-hearted Sohiroba simply pitied Mahadaji.

This incident shows how Sohiroba was a real saint indifferent to worldly gain or position. Sohiroba died in the year 1789. The above rather detailed account of Sohiroba shows how all his poetical work was the outcome of his religious and Vedantic zeal. All his so-called poems have very unfamiliar names like Aksayabodha, Mahadanubhavesvari and Advayananda. That is why Sohiroba's name does not figure among the poets and his works are very little known. But among the learned they are valued.

Mahipati

Mahipati was as popular as Sridhar and Amrtray. He was born in the year 1715 at Tarabad a place about 40 miles from Ahmednagar. Hc belonged to the hereditary Desastha Kulkarni family. According in his early life he did that work under the Mohammedan king of Ahmednagar. Once he was so ill-treated by a mere servant of the king that he took a vow not to serve anybody thenceforward. He became a regular pilgrim and visited Pandharpur every year. There was a terrible famine once. Mahipati was so generous that he distributed all his grain to the poor and the starving. But, as a result, he became penniless and begged for his maintenance. He devoted all his time and energy to writing poetry. But his poetry is unique in the history of Marathi literature. It is not poetry so much as a biographical account of saints and poets. In fact, Mahipati, though retired from life, maintained his interest in life and especially in the lives of the saints of his time and of previous generations. He made use of his pilgrimages in collecting detailed information about poets and saints. Then he made use of the material in writing his unique biographical works in verse. Mahipati wrote in all four biographical poems or rather versified biographies. He gave very significant names to his works. They are Bhaktavijay (triumphs of devotees), Bhaktolilamrt (wonderful doings of the devotees), Santavijay (exploits of saints) and Santalilamrt (wonderful doings of the saints). In these four biographical works Mahipati has left a very precious heritage to the posterity of Maharastra. A great deal of what he now know of the poets and saints of Maharastra is due to these valuable works. The works show how a sense of reality and importance of having historical accounts in literature was growing in the minds of the people of Maharastra. This growing sense led to an entirely new class of fine literature in prose which began to make its appearance about this time and to which literature a reference will be made a little later in this brief and rapid survey of old Marathi literature. To return to Mahipati's works. His Santalilamrt was finished in the year 1757. It contains the lives of about 40 poets and saints. He wrote the Bhaktalilamrt in 1762. It contains the lives of about 60 poets and saints. Besides these biographical works Mahipati composed short hymns on the various religious holidays of the Hindus i.e. Haritalikavrat Rsipancamivrat, Anantavrat, Tulasimahatmya, etc. All these are commonly read by devout Hindu ladies on the respective holidays. Among his other works the following are worth mentioning: Kathasaramrta, Krsnalilamrta and Sanimahatmya.

Mahipati's writings are all in ovi metre. His style is entirely plain and simple. Mahipati often uses fine similes to illustrate his point.

Mahipati was a versatile and voluminous writer. Thus

he was the precursor of the age of Moropant to which we must now refer. He died in 1790 at the ripe age of 75.

Moropant

Now we come to the most versatile and voluminous writer among the poets of Maharastra. His name is Moropant, or as he liked to call himself in his famous devotional poem, Mayur (a peacock). Moropant is regarded as the greatest poet of Maharastra by the learned men i.e. the Puraniks and Kirtankars of the past and the present generation. But this view is not shared by men imbued with western ideas of literary criticism. They regard Moropant at a mere versifier with a facile pen and with a predilection for high-flown language full of figures of speech. They compare him with the English poet Pope who was highly thought of in his day but who has been regarded a mere versifier like Moropant by modern English critics. This led to a heated controversy about the position of Moropant among Marathi critics one school giving him the highest position, while the opposed school, giving him only a second rate or third rate position. As is usually the case in such controversies the truth lies between the extreme views, Looking to the vast volume of his poetry which contains many a fine passage scattered throughout his poems one cannot subscribe to the view that Moropant was a mere versifier and only a second or third grade poet. But it is equally true that Moropant did not reach the highest watermark of Marathi poetry. He undoubtedly had poetic talent which is unmistakable throughout his poetical work, but it is equally true that he was fond of the Marathi Arya metre and in his composition he overdid that metre which makes his poems a monotonous reading. Further, he was fond of acrostics and similar curiosities of versification. He actually wrote 108 Ramayanas in which all his feats of literary acrobatic art to be seen. But this predilection for superficial and meretricious beauties of versification detracted from the worth of his poems. Still there is no doubt that Moropant occupies a very high position among Marathi poets and he deservedly comes in to the category of the great poets of Maharastra. At any rate no poet of equal merit arose after his time and since his death a decline in Marathi poetry made its appearance.

Life of Moropant

With this preliminary discussion let me now refer to his life and character. Moropant came from a Brahmin family living at Panhala near Kolhapur in the southern Maratha country. He was born in 1729. His early life was spent at Panhala where he learnt at the feet of the Padhye Brothers, famous for their Sanskrit learning. Moropant, being a precocious boy, acquired proficiency in Sanskrit early and began to give such excellent discourses, both religious and secular, on topics derived from the Ramayana and the Mahabharat that his fame reached the ears of the great Jahagirdar and landlord of Baramati named Babaji Naik. The Naik was pleased to hear the fine puran of Moropant and he immediately took him under his service with an honorarium of Rs. 500 per year. Moropant went to Baramati and spent all his life there except for two years when he went to Kasi and other holy places in upper India and made occasional short pilgrimages to holy places near about his place of residence. At Baramati Moropant had only to give a daily discourse or puran and so he was free to devote the rest of his time to prosecute his studies in Sanskrit as well as in Marathi literature.

Early Poems

Moropant began to compose poems at the age of 25 and he carried on his literary activity for full fifty years till his death. His first poetical piece was written in praise of Sankar—his family God. But later on when a Brahmin presented to Moropant an image of Rama he regarded it as a gift of God and thenceforward he worshipped Rama till his death. After this Moropant wrote in rapid succession short but sweet poetical pieces especially for the entertainment and instruction of young people and in particular of girls. Striking stories were selected from the Ramayana and the

Mahabharat.

After these light poems Moropant took up the more serious work of his life and almost every year brought out at least one great poem. The first was an adaptation from the 10th chapter of the Bhagvat in which the early life of Sri Krsna was finely depicted, though its style was high-flown. This work is named 'Krsnavijay' (exploits of Krsna). Subsequently he completed the whole of the Bhagvat and called it 'Mantra Bhagvat' because he skilfully wove into his verses the great and famous mantra (religions formula) 'Namo Bhagavate Vasudevaya' (Salutation to God Vasudev). In this adaptation Moropant omitted the more abstruse and metaphysical parts of the original and dilated upon the narrative and anecdotal parts. Thus he tried to make his poem intelligible and interesting to the general public. Next, Moropant wrote at the desire and suggestion of his patron, the great poem 'Harivamsa'. This is a Marathi version of the Sanskrit poem of the same name. In this great work Moropant has narrated not only the early and later life of Krsna and his famous family but also the history of the Yadav dynasty to which he belonged. This work of Moropant is deservedly regarded as a fine fruit of his genius. Moropant had now attained the age of fifty. Still his powers were working with full vigour.

The First Marathi Epic

While Moropant brought out year after year his small and great poems in a continuous succession, he was all the while engaged in writing his master-piece, the version of the great Sanskrit epic Mahabharat. He took full ten years to complete this master-piece. It was finally published when he was 53 years of age. This is really the first epic poem in Marathi literature. It is written in the Arya metre. Moropant is seen at his best in this great work. His versatility, his varied knowledge, his mastery over the Marathi language, his power of vivid description, his capacity to rouse the several sentiments of his readers by narration of stirring scenes in stories and his dramatic skill in introducing striking in dialogues in the stories told—all these characteristics of a great poet are visible everywhere in this great epic of the Marathi language.

Moropant must have felt that his life's work was really over. Still he went on writing and he did not leave his work till his death.

After finishing this great poem Moropant amused himself by writing again lighter poetic pieces in the form of the several Ramayanas referred to already. Of course these hundreds of short poems show how facile his pen was and how he wielded it for his own amusement as well as for that of the Marathi-knowing public.

But the crowning pieces of Moropant's poetry have still to be noticed. They are really very short pieces. Amidst his vast and varied poetical work they are like a drop in the ocean. But they are original and unique. They came out of the depths of his heart. They are the highest water-mark of his genius. They prove without doubt that Moropant was a great poet with poetic genius. Both the pieces are devotional lyrics. One is called 'Symsayaratnamala' (A Garland of gems of Doubt) and the other Kekavali (Cries of a Peacock).

These poems are the gems of Marathi literature and they ever remain so. Moropant died in the year 1794 A. D., after having done his life's work and after having attained everlasting fame as a great Marathi poet.

It is a curious coincidence that the literary career of Moropant was coeval with the most critical period of Maratha History. Moropant was born during the reign of Sahu and Bajirav I and died just about the close of the rule of Savai Madhavrav. This period of about 65 years marked the rapid expansion of the Maratha Empire, the sudden and unexpected check that it received in the battle of Panipat and lastly the rapid recovery of that Empire. Thus Moropant was fortunate enough to live in the hey-day of Maratha supremacy. Soon after the death of Moropant signs of the decline and the fall of that Empire began to manifest themselves. Similar has been the fate of Marathi literature. Moropant's career marked the hey-day of Marathi poetry. But after his death a rapid decline of that literature began to manifest itself.

Imitators of Moropant

The extreme popularity of Moropant led to the rise of a host of imitators who followed his style and his forms of poetry. The history of the rise and the fall of the Maratha Empire too led to two new forms of literature referred to later on.

The whole period from 1794 A. D., the date of the death of Moropant, to the year 1818 A. D., the year of the commencement of the rule of the British East India Company over Maharastra, may be regarded as the closing period of the old Marathi literature and the beginning of the modern Marathi literature.

As already referred to there were hosts of imitators and servile versifiers who followed the example of Moropant and who were anxious to get fame and popularity similar to that of Moropant. These imitators and versifiers produced a great amount of literature but they could never attain real excellence. They could never catch the real spirit of Moropant's poetry. They mistook the superficial decorations of his poems as real beauty and thereby spoiled their writings. In fact, these imitators mark the decline of Marathi literature, though the running stream did not altogether stop. In fact it continued for some time after the modern literature had made its appearance under the influence of western culture brought into Maharastra by the all-pervading rule of the British East India Company over India and especially over Maharastra.

Let us then take a brief and rapid survey of this declining period of old literature as the concluding part of this long chapter which has made a survey of the old Marathi literature.

There is no doubt that even when the decline of Marathi literature was setting in and the stream was getting muddy, there were some writers who showed real poetic power. Unfortunately they had to prostitute their genius to satisfy the unhealthy and increasingly vicious taste of the public.

Ram Josi

The two exceptional writers of this period are Ram Josi and Anant Phandi. Ram Josi was born in Sholapur in the year 1762 A. D. In his younger days he was a mischievous boy. Moreover, he sought bad and vulgar company among the low class boys of the town and became enamoured of tamasas. These tamasas were something like operas in which, however, obscene and vulgar songs were recited by a boy dressed as a woman. The dancing and the dialogues were provided as the accompaniment. Young Ram took part in these tamasas and composed verses in the favourite metre of the people. Ram Josi's elder brother who was a renowned Kirtankar and puranik scolded him severely. Ram Josi left the house in anger and determined to show his brother that he too could perform kirtans and explain Puranas like himself. So he went to Pandharpur and there learnt Sanskrit, studied the Puranas and other Sanskrit and Marathi classical works. In a few years he came back to Sholapur and surprised his brother by performing Kirtans and Puranas in a charming manner. Having left the house in anger Ram returned home and showed what he was capable of. However, his predilection for tamasas and his association with low people continued as before. But fortunately for Ram Josi he met Moropant by chance. Moropant earnestly advised him to leave off his low degrading occupation and take to delivering Kirtans to the public. Ram Josi was impressed by the personality of Moropant. He had now passed his youth and was therefore disposed to hear the good advice of a great man. From that time he began to deliver Kirtans enrapturing his audience by singing moral songs and pieces of his own composition as well as repeating the Aryas of

Moropant. Just as the credit of revising Dnyanesvar's work and spreading it in that form far and wide belongs to Eknath, so the credit of popularising the Aryas of Moropant and of taking them into the nooks and corners of Maharastra belongs to Ram Josi. Ram Josi showed by his genius that the Lavni metre which was associated with vulgarity and low taste could be used for better purposes i.e. the entertainment and instruction of the public. He tried to improve the tone of the society about him by weaning them from the tamasas. His efforts were destined to bear good fruit. For when he died in the year 1812 A. D. the days of the Pesvai rule and its vulgar taste were numbered and better days were in store for the people of Maharastra. It is to the credit of Maharastra that Ram Josi tried his best to keep the purity and beauty of Marathi poetry amidst the vulgarising compositions of lower class poets that arose during the reign of Bajirav II according to the well known saying, 'As the Ruler, so the subjects.'

Anant Phandi

The second poet of lesser calibre than Ram Josi was Anant Phandi. He came from Sangamner in Ahmednagar district. He was born in the year 1774 A. D. He was a Yajurvedi Brahmin. His family were bankers by profession. But Anant Phandi did not take kindly to his hereditary profession. Like his contemporpry Ram Josi, Anant was a mischievous boy in early life. He took to low company and soon joined the then popular occupation of performing Tamasas. But he showed excellence in that art and become famous in that line. He had such an attractive delivery and such a wonderful power of composing appropriate Povadas, Lavnis and especially songs in a new metre called Phataka (whip) in which he excelled that the whole audience remained spell-bound throughout the opera. Of course these verses were calculated to please the low and vulgar taste of his vast avdience. But his fascinating style once not only saved his life and property but brought him a reward from unexpected quarters. Anant Phandi while returning from Malva to Sangamner was surrounded by Bhils who wanted to loot him. But using his presence of mind and conscious of the power of his lyre and his verse he composed extempore verses on the chief of the Bhils and sang them so finely that the chief and his followers were enraptured by them. So they not only returned his property which they had forcibly taken from him but gave him a gift in addition ! Such is the power of music ! But like Ram Josi, Anant Phandi was destined to be weaned from his low occupation and apply his talent for the higher entertainment and instruction of the public. This was done by the famous Ahilyabai, the Rani of Indore. She once happened to meet and here Anant Phandi. Being herself a pious lady she exhorted Anant Phandi to give up his low occupation and apply the God-given talent of composition to the good of the people. Anant Phandi was won over by her sweet words and thenceforward began to perform Kirtans in which he tried to impress upon men's minds the true spirit of devotion to God and the need of improving their character by leading a good life. Anant Phandi composed poems in the varied Marathi metres and used various subjects for his compositions. He also composed Katavs and Phatkas on contemporary events and incidents. He survived to witness the sad end of the rule of Bajirav II but he also saw with satisfaction that the people wished to have a chage of Government in Maharastra. Anant Phandi died in the year 1821 A. D. at the age of 77.

Patriotic Narrative Poetry

Now we come to the historical section of the old Marathi literature, a unique thing in the Marathi language. This consists of two parts, one being in the usual metrical style and the other in the new prose style. The first section is known under names of the Povadas, historical Katavs and Lavnis, metres introduced by the poets of the declining period of old Marathi literature. The other section consists of well-known Bakhars (chronicles) and public and private correspondence. Both these types of literature could only arise after the establishment of the Maratha Empire which inspired the bards and poets called by the special name of Sahirs to write and compose patriotic poems celebrating the stirring events and exploits which came about during the century of the rise and the fall of the Maratha Empire. It is to the lasting credit of these Sahirs that they did not merely praise the exploits of old and contemporary heroes with exaggeration but were faithful in the narration of events, and just as they described in a happy mood and manner the success of their warriors they told in mournful numbers the misfortunes and failures of their heroes. These latter incidents led them to compose tragic songs which excited the sympathy of the audience for the heroes of the past.

Of course the Povadas and Lavnis composed by the Sahirs were written as poetry and had, therefore, all the characteristics of poetry. In fact, they were all narrative poems in which fact and fiction were artistically mingled so as to entertain and rouse the public. They constitute, therefore, a unique but fine type of poetry in Marathi language.

Historical Literature

There were many famous names among these Sahirs. Many of them rivalled the popularity of the older poets. Their name is legion and it is not possible to refer to any of them individually. A reference to some of them will be found in one of the later chapters of this history. Similar is the case with the Bakhars. They began to be written after the foundation of the Maratha Kingdom by Sivaji and they continued with breaks to the beginning of the modern times. The last famous Bakharkar Malhar Ramrav Citnis who wrote more than one Bakhar lived about the year 1810 A. D. These Bakhars were all written for giving useful information about the history of the country to later generation. They were written in prose and there was no attempt at embellishment. They were mere recitals of events in simple language and they were not written with the scrupulousness with which the historical works in English literature are written. In fact, they only serve as valuable materials for future historians. But all the above Bakhars and ballads do come under literature in the wider sense of the term and thus form a part of the history of

Marathi literature.

But this cannot be said of the public and private correspondence discovered in modern times. For these letters and dispatches were never intended as literature which would be ready by future generations. They were written with the purpose of communicating news to the parties concerned. No thought was ever bestowed upon the language in which they were written. But now they have acquired the value of literature. For they reveal the thoughts, ideas and feelings of the people of those times. They show how the people spoke and communicated with each other. They indicate the manners and customs that obtained in the Maratha society of the time. Now all these things are expected from literature. Thus though originally they served a different purpose these letters and dispatches have now acquired the character of true literature. A reference to them will be made in their appropriate place.

DIVISION OF MARATHI LITERATURE INTO PERIODS

Broadly speaking Marathi literature made its appearance about the year 1000 A. D. in the heart of Maharastra though the spoken language must have preceded it by one or two centuries. This tiny little stream of Marathi literature broadened, in time, into a mighty river in which the character and sentiments, ideas and ideals of the Marathi-speaking people were reflected. This implies that Marathi literature has a long history of about ten centuries similar to that of English literature. In this long history there was never any break, though, with lapse of time and under varying conditions, the original character and spirit gradually changed, and in place of the old types, new types of literature made their appearance. In order to understand properly and to describe in detail these changes it is necessary to divide the history into different ages and periods.

For the purposes of exposition it would be convenient to divide the history of Marathi literature into two broad ages, and then into periods, for detailed exposition.

The first age extends from the year 1000 A. D. to the year 1800 A. D. and may be called by the generic name 'the old or ancient age'. An age of 800 years appears too long, so it will have to be divided into periods. The second age extends from the year 1800 A. D. to the year 1938 A. D. Comparatively this is a short age of only 138 years and it may be styled 'the modern age'. But this apparently short age is in no way inferior either is quantity or quality of literary production to the old or ancient age, which is apparently, of very long duration.

Characteristics of Old Marathi Poetry

Let us now proceed to find out the distinguishing features of the old or ancient age and the modern age.

To begin with all old poets (old literature was almost all poetical) composed their poems and miscellaneous pieces in the material from which restricts the poet's choice of words and rhythm. But even in the field of poetry they knew only two forms of poetry, the devotional—a form peculiar to Marathi literature—and the narrative. They were altogether ignorant of the more interesting forms of literature like the drama, the novel, the short story and the essay—forms to be found in all developed literatures. Secondly, the old poets had a very low opinion of human life. They looked only to its dark side, scarcely recognising that God, by his grace, gave to mankind noble feelings and sentiments by means of which they could make their life joyous as well as useful. In short, the old poets took a very pessimistic view of life and in their poetry that taught people to retire from life or at least to curb their passions and sentiments. Thus all their poetry became gloomy and uninteresting. Thirdly, the old poets had absolutely no sense of humour in them and hence they deprecated laughter. Their poetry is always grave and serious. It is on account of the absence of playful disposition that old Marathi poets could not develop many interesting forms of literature like satire, parody, ironical and humorous poetry. Lastly, the old poets altogether neglected to make use of their inner and outer experience, i.e., experience of the mental and of the natural phenomena. Thereby they lost a great source of poetry. For it is a well-known fact that individuals differ in their temperaments and tastes. Each man's experience is often different from that of another. This variety in human experience leads naturally to varied types of poetry. For each poet gives expression to what he sees, feels and thinks. It is due to this neglect of personal experience that old Marathi poetry is wanting in descriptions of natural scenery, and depicting the inner mind of man. There is also a kind of monotony and repitition in the old poetry. For, all poets depended for their subject matter and sources of information, upon the celebrated epics, the Mahabharat and the Ramayana and upon other Puranas and philosophical and semi-religious works. As all poets depended upon the same sources, they brought out poems dealing with the same themes, each poet using his fauourite metre to tell his story. That is the reason why there is so much of repetition and sameness in the old poetry. The different poems appear to be versions of the same thread-bare stories. The old posts did not make use of the ever changing and ever expanding experience of man. They remained satisfied with worn out material.

New Learning

Now modern poetry gave up all these distinguishing features which were in reality the defects of old poetry. Modern writers had the great advantage that they came to know the varied and varying store of English literature rich in all forms. The great treasure of Sanskrit literature was also open to them. The old poets studied Sanskrit but they learnt only Puranas and semi-religious books and neglected the lighter and more interesting literature such as dramas, novels, story books and the epic poems. But modern writers learnt with greater zeal and pleasure these literary works. Having such fine models before them and having learnt to use their individual experience, the modern writers began to produce poetry of a new type. So, modern poetry has developed distinguishing features diametrically opposed to those of old poetry. They can be gathered from the features of old poetry through the well-known principle that opposites imply each other.

Let us now turn to the causes which tended to produce modern Marathi literature.

In the first place the enlightened people of Western Europe, the British people, conquered within a century the whole of India and brought it under a uniform system of laws and administration. With this enlightened rule came perfect security of life and property—a thing which the country did not enjoy for very many centuries. Rapid means of communication were established and thereby the barriers of great rivers, big mountains and vast deserts were removed and the whole country became united and people of one province could freely and easily visit another province and could come into contact with its people. In fact, the face of India altogether changed since the advent of the British rule in India.

More important causes than those mentioned above came into being slowly and gradualy.

Contact with the West

Western education, western culture, direct contact with a progressive civilization and acquaintance with and study of English and Sanskrit literature—all these combined to produce a revolution in society. New ideas, new experiences and a better and a brighter outlook on life were produced in the minds of men.

The last but not the least of these causes was the introduction of printing in India. This happened about 1800 A.D. This new invention produced a revolution in Europe. Its introduction into India produced a similar effect. Books could be rapidly and easily printed and thousands of copies could, in no time, be distributed throughout the length and breadth of the country.

All the above-mentioned causes combined to produce a ferment in men's minds. Such a ferment necessarily found expression in literature and thus the modern period in Marathi literature began from the year 1800 A.D.

Periods of Old Literature

It now remains to point out the minor periods in the two major periods considered so far.

As stated before, the age of old Marathi literature consists of about 8 centuries. It naturally gets divided into three periods.

The first period begins with Cakradhar and Dnyanesvar, the founders of the two contemporary religious sects—Mahanubhava and Varkari and ends with Eknath. This may be called the early period. The second period begins again with Eknath. For he is a joining link between the two periods. It ends with Moropant. This may be called the middle period. But this period shows the highest water-mark of old Marathi literature. The third period begins with the imitators of Moropant and ends with the Sahirs, though the muddy waters of the stream of literature pass on as an under current even into the great and growing modern age which begins from 1800 A.D. This period may be called the declining period of the old Marathi literature.

Periods of Modern Literature

The modern age though consisting of only 138 years has to be divided into several periods. For, in this age, short though it is, almost all the forms of literature in verse and prose like drama, novel, short story and essay, and like history, biography and popular science came gradually into being. Moreover the volume of literature produced year by year assumed vast proportions. For purposes of exposition, therefore, it becomes necessary to form periods of very short duration. It is very difficult to designate these periods by significant names, on account of the varied literature produced in each, though I have made an attempt to assign names. The periods with their names are as follows :

Period			
Period	I	1800 to 1818 A.D.	External attempt.
,,	II	1818 to 1836 A.D.	Indigenous attempt.
,,	III	1836 to 1856 A.D.	Translations.
,,	IV	1856 to 1866 A.D.	Status of Marathi in the University.
,,	V	1866 to 1876 A.D.	The Romantic novel.
,,	VI	1876 to 1896 A.D.	Makers of classic Marathi.
,,	VII	1896 to 1912 A.D.	Great novelists.
,,	VIII	1912 to 1918 A.D.	Literature for a variety of tastes.
,,	IX	1918 to 1928 A.D.	Newer forms of literature.
,,	X	1928 to 1938 A.D.	Recent phenomenal growth.

Conclusion—Future of Marathi literature.

2

G.A. Grierson on Marathi Language

G.A. Grierson in his first linguistic survey of British India has given the following account-of Marathi language.

THE SOUTHERN GROUP

MARATHI

The Southern Group

Like the Mediate Group of Indo-Aryan vernaculars, the southern one is a group of dialects, and not of languages. It includes only one language, viz., Marathi.

Area in which spoken

Marathi with its sub-dialects occupies parts of three provinces, viz., the Bombay Presidency, Berar, and the Central Provinces, with numerous settlers in Central India and the Madras Presidency. It is the principal language of the north-western part of His Highness the Nizam's dominions and of Portuguese India. The area in which it is spoken is, roughly speaking, 100,000 square miles.

Political Boundries

On the west, Marathi is bounded by the Arabian Sea, from Daman in the north to Karwar in the south. The northern frontier follows the Daman Ganga towards the east and crosses Nasik, leaving the northern part of the district to Khandesi. It thence runs along the southern and eastern frontier of Khandesh, through the southern part of Nimar,

Betul, Chhindwara, and Seoni, where the Satpura range forms the northern boundary. The frontier line thence turns to the south-east, including the southern part of Balaghat and almost the whole of Bhandara, with important settlements in Raipur. The Halbi dialect occupies the central and eastern part of the Bastar State, still farther to the east.

From the south-eastern corner of Bhandara the line runs south-westwards, including Nagpur and the north-western corner of Chanda, where it turns towards the west through the district of Wun, leaving a narrow strip in the south to Telugu. It then continues towards the south, including the district of Basim, and into the dominions of His Highness the Nizam, where it again turns westwards to Akalkot and Sholapur. The frontier then goes south-west wards, in an irregular line, including Sholapur and Kolhapur, to the Ghats, and thence to the sea at Karwar.

Linguistic Boundaries

Marathi has to its north, in order from west to east, Gujarati. Khandesi, Rajasthani, Western Hindi, and Eastern Hindi. To the east we find Eastern Hindi, Gondi, and Telugu. Halbi, which is separated from Marathi by Chhattisgarhi and Dravidian languages, merges into Oriya in the east through the Bhatri dialect. In the south we find, proceeding from the east, Gondi, Telugu, and Kanarese.

Dialects

The dialectic differences within the Marathi area are comparatively small, and there is only one real dialect, viz., Konkani. There are, of course, everywhere local varieties, and these are usually honoured by a separate name. On the whole, however, Marathi is a remarkably uniform language.

Three slightly different forms may conveniently be distinguished, the Marathi of the Dekhan, the Marathi of Berar and the Central Provinces, and the Marathi of the Central and Northern Konkan. The last two forms of the language have some characteristics in common, and these are also shared by the rustic dialects of the Dekhan, such as the form of speech current among the Kunbis of Poona.

In the southern part of the district of Ratnagiri the Konkan form of Marathi gradually merges into Konkani, through several minor dialects.

Several broken dialects are spoken in various parts of the Marathi territory, and will be dealt with in connection with the various forms of that language. In the northern part of the coast strip belonging to Marathi we find some smaller dialects, such as Kathodi, Varli, Vadval, Phudgi, and Samvedi, which in several points agree with Gujarati-Bhili. The Khandesi dialect of Khandesh, which has hitherto been classed with Marathi, has in this Survey been transferred to Gujarati. It contains a large admixture of Marathi, but the inner form of the language differs, and its base is a Prakrit dialect more closely related to Sauraseni than to Maharashtri which latter Prakrit is derived from the same base as modern Marathi.

Further towards the east we find some broken dialects, such as Katiya, Halbi, Bhunjia, Nahari, and Kamari, which have been so largely influenced by Marathi that it has been found convenient to deal with them in this connection, though they are no true Marathi dialects.

Nnmber of Speakers

Marathi, including its dialects, is the home tongue of several districts which are not included in the present Survey, such as the Portuguese territories and part of His Highness the Nizam's dominions. The numbers of speakers of such districts must be added to the figures returned from the various districts within the scope of this Survey.

Speakers of Marathi in those districts of Central India and the Central Provinces over which the Peshwa and Holkar formerly held sway have been included among the total of those who use the Dekhan form of Marathi as their home language. The details will be found under the different forms of Marathi; the total number of speakers of the various forms of the language within the Marathi territory is as follows :

Marathi of the Dekhan	6,193,083
Marathi of Berar and the Central Provinces (including the Nizam's dominions)	7,677,432
Marathi of the Konkan	2,350,817
Konkani (including Portuguese territories and Madras Presidency)	1,559,029
Total	17,780,361

These figures include the speakers of broken dialects in the Konkan and the Central Provinces. The figures for the Nizam's dominions, Portuguese India, and the Madras Presidency have been taken from the reports of the Census of 1891.

Marathi and its dialects is also, to some extent, spoken outside the territory where it is a vernacular. At the Census of 1891 Marathi and Konkani were separately returned. The figures for those districts where Marathi and Konkani were spoken as foreign tongues were as follows :

Marathi spoken abroad in	Number of Speakers
Ajmere-Merwara	1,604
Andamans	913
Assam	85
Bengal and Feudatories	909
Burmah	565
Coorg	2,621
Madras	123,530
Mysore	65,356
Punjab and Feudatories	551
Quettah	1,340
Rajputana and Central India	11,072
Sind	9,265
United Provinces and Feudatories	7,414
Total	225,225

Konkani has been returned for the purposes of this Survey as spoken by 20 settlers in Chanda. The other figures which follow have been taken from the reports of the Census of 1891 :

Where spoken	Number of speakers
Mysore	4,166
Rajputana	47
Chanda	20
Coorg	2,129
Total	6,362

By adding together all these figures we arrive at the following total for Marathi and its dialects :

Marathi spoken at home		
Dekhan	6,193,083	
Berar and Central Provinces	7,677,432	
Konkan	2,350,817	
	16,221,332	
Marathi spoken abroad	225,225	
Total Marathi		16,446,557
Konkani spoken at home	1,559,029	
Konkani spoken abroad	6,362	
Total Konkani		1,565,391
Grand Total		18,011,948

Origin of Marathi

The Prakrit grammarians tell us that at a very early period there were two principal languages spoken in the Ganges and

Jamna valleys, Sauraseni in the west and Magadhi in the east. Between both was situated a third dialect, called Ardhamagadhi, which must approximately have covered the territory within which the modern dialects of Eastern Hindi are spoken. These dialects were recognised as the most important forms of speech in Aryavarta, i e., the country to the north of the Vindhya range and the River Narmada. To the south of Aryavarta was the great country called Maharashtra extending southwards to the Kistna, and sometimes also including the country of the Kuntalas which broadly corresponds to the southern part of the Bombay Presidency and Hyderabad. The language of Maharashtra was considered to be the base of the most important literary Prakrit, the so-called Maharashtri. The South-Indian author Dandin (sixth century A.D.) expressly states that the principal Prakrit was derived from the dialect spoken in Maharashtra. And the oldest work in Maharashtri of which we have any knowledge was compiled at Pratishthana, the capital of King Hala on the Godavari. There is, accordingly, no doubt that the Indian tradition derives the so-called Maharashtri from the vernacular of Maharashtra, or, in the terminology of the Prakrit grammarians, the Maharashtra Apabhramsa, from which latter form of speech the modern Marathi is derived.

The opinion of the Indian grammarians has not been universally adopted by European scholars, and it will, therefore, be necessary in this place to go into detail in order to explain my reasons for adhering to it.

The arguments generally adduced against the derivation of Marathi and Maharashtri from the same base are of two kinds. In the first place it is argued that Maharashtri and Sauraseni are simply two varieties of the same dialect; in the second place it is pointed out that Marathi in several respects agrees with eastern vernaculars which must apparently be derived from a Magadha dialect and not from the old language of the Saurasena country. It will be seen that both arguments are in reality one and the same, and that if it could be shown that Maharashtri was a quite distinct dialect which differed from Sauraseni and approached the eastern Prakrits, the analogy which certainly exists between Marathi and eastern vernaculars could no more be adduced against deriving Marathi and Maharashtri from the same base.

It will, therefore, be necessary to put the supposition of the identity of Maharashtri and Sauraseni to the test.

Our knowledge of the Prakrits is to a great extent based on the Prakrit grammarians who were not content to describe the various vernaculars which furnished the base for the literary Prakrits, but who also tried to systematise them, and often seem to have constructed general rules out of stray occurrences or phonetical tendencies. The literary Prakrits in this way came to differ from the spoken vernaculars. They were not, however, mere fictions, and the more we learn about the linguistic conditions of old India, the more we see that the differences stated to exist between the various Prakrit dialects in most cases correspond to actual differences in the spoken vernaculars.

On the other hand, the description given of the various Prakrits by the grammarians is not complete, and must be supplemented from the Prakrit literature. This literature is considerable and it makes it possible to get a good idea of two dialects, the so-called Maharashtri and Ardhamagadhi. Sauraseni is less known, though we are able to understand the principal features of that dialect. With regard to Magadhi we are almost entirely confined to the rules given by the grammarians.

Professor Pischel has, in his masterly Prakrit Grammar, collected the materials from the grammarians and from the literature and rendered it a comparatively easy task to define therelationship between the different Prakrits.

Classification of the Prakrits

Three different classifications seem to be possible, according to the features which we choose as our starting points.

Northern and Southern Group

In some features Sauraseni agrees with Magadhi as against Maharashtri and Ardhamagadhi. The principal ones are the treatment of single consonants between vowels, and the formation of the passive and of the conjunctive participle.

According to the Prakrit grammarians every Sanskrit unaspirated mute consonant between vowels, if not a cerebral, is dropped in the Prakrits and a faintly sounded *y*, or, in the case of *p* or *b*, a *v*, is substituted for it. This *y* is not, however, written in other than Jaina manuscripts. It seems certain that this rule of the grammarians was a generalisation of a phonetical tendency and did not exactly correspond to the actual facts of the genuine vernaculars. The tendency to drop consonants in such positions must, however, have been strong, as we find its results largely prevalent in modern vernaculars. Compare Marathi kumbhar, Sanskrit kumbha-(k)ara, a potter; Marathi tale, Sanskrit ta-da(g)a, a tank; Marathi suy, Sanskrit su(ch)i, a needle; Marathi nenno, Sanskrit na-(j)anami, I don't know; Marathi bi, Sanskrit bi(j)a, a seed; Marathi sam(bhar), Sanskrit sa(t)a, hundred; Marathi pay, Sanskrit pa(d)a, a foot, and so on.

The Prakrit grammarians make one important exception from the rule. A *t* between vowels becomes *d* in Sauraseni and Magadhi, but is dropped in other dialects. Thus, Sanskrit gata, Sauraseni and Magadhi gada, Maharashtri and Ardhamagadhi gaa, gaya, gone. A *t* between vowels is very common, and, especially, it occurs in numerous verbal forms. The result is that its different treatment gives a very marked character to the two groups. There cannot, however, be any doubt that this difference is one of time and not of dialect. The *d* is the intermediary stage between *t* and the dropping of the sound, and there can be no doubt that a *d* was really often pronounced in the vernaculars on which Maharashtri and Ardhamagadhi were based. For not only does the oldest Prakrit grammarian Vararuchi (ii, 7) allow the change of *t* to *d* in Maharashtri in certain words, but the manuscripts freely write *d* in Maharashtri, a confusion which it would be difficult to explain if the distinction made by the grammarians corresponded to the actual facts in the spoken vernaculars. This point cannot, therefore, be made the basis of a classification.

The passive is formed by adding the suffix ia in Sauraseni and Magadhi, but ijja in the other dialects. Thus, Sanskrit kriyate, Sauraseni and Magadhi kariadi, Maharashtri and Ardhamagadhi karijjai, it is done. This distinction between the two groups has been inferred from the practice of the best manuscripts. There are, however, numerous exceptions, and forms ending in iyyadi, which is a variant of ijjadi, seem to occur in Magadhi verses. This point cannot therefore be urged.

There remains the formation of the conjunctive participle which usually ends in ia in Sauraseni and Magadhi and in una in Maharashtri and often also in Ardhamagadhi. This latter dialect has, however, several other forms. Thus, Maharashtri hasiuna, Sauraseni and Magadhi hasia, having laughed. The subsequent linguistic history of India shows that we are here face to face with a real distinction between the north and the south. The *u*-form has survived in Marathi, in some Rajasthani dialects, and in Oriya, while other languages use forms derived from the old participles ending in *ia*.

A division of the Prakrits on account of this distinction cannot, however, seriously be maintained, and Sauraseni and Magadhi differ in so many points that it is out of question to bring them into close connection with each other.

Eastern and Western Groups

Dr. Hoernle, in his Comparative Grammar of the Gaudian Languages divided the Prakrit dialects into a western group, *viz.*, Sauraseni-Maharashtri, and an eastern *viz.*, Magadhi. These two groups differ in pronunciation and in the formation of the nominative singular of masculine *a*-bases. The western group changes every *s*-sound to a dental s, the eastern to a palatal *s*; the western substitutes *j* for every initial *j* and *y*, the eastern prefers *y*; the western possesses both *r* and *l*, the eastern only *l*; the nominative singular of masculine *a*-bases ends in *o* in the west and in *e* in the east. Ardhamagadhi agrees with the west in all points excepting the last one, the nominative singular of masculine *a*-bases usually ending in *e*, but also, in old texts in *o*.

This last test point, the termination of the nominative. must probably be eliminated from the features which distinguish the east from the west, for the most eastern Prakrit dialect of which we havy any knowledge, the so-called Dhakki, which must have been based on the dialect spoken in Dacca, forms the nominative in *o*; thus, puliso, a man. This dialect also differs from Magadhi in the treatment of *s*-sounds. It possesses a dental *s*, corresponding to *s* and *sh* in Sanskrit, and a palatal *s*, corresponding to Sanskrit *s*; thus, dasu, ten; pulisassa, Sanskrit purushasya, of the man. Dhakki also seems to use *j* like the western Prakrits. Thus, jampidum, Magadhi yampidum, Sanskrit jalpitum, to talk.

There thus only remains one of the test points in which the east differs from the west, the use of *l* and *r* respectively. I do not think that this point is of sufficient importance to base a classification on it.

Final classification of the Prakrits

The division of the Prakrits into a western and an eastern group is based on the supposition that Sauraseni and Maharashtri are essentially the same dialect. Since this theory was first put forward our knowledge of the Prakrits has advanced very far, and we now know that the two are radically different. They differ in phonology, in the formation of many verbal bases and of many tenses, in vocabulary, and in their general character. Sauraseni has, on the whole, the same vocabulary as classical Sanskrit, while Maharashtri is full of provincial words; the inflexional system of Sauraseni has nothing of the rich variety of f ns which characterizes Maharashtri. If we add the points of disagreement adduced above, the wide divergence between the two dialects cannot be doubted. The relation between them can be compared to that existing between classical Sanskrit and the Vedic dialects, on the one side the correct and fixed speech of the sishtas, or educated classes, on the other the ever fluctuating, richly varied language of the masses.

In these characteristics Maharashtri agrees with Ardhamagadhi. The close connection between those two Prakrits is so apparent that it has always been recognised. Several scholars have even gone so far as to identify them. Nobody would do so at the present day. There can, however, be no doubt with regard to the close relationship between them, and they may safely be classed together as forming one group as against Sauraseni.

Ardhamagadhi is the link which connects Maharashtri with Magadhi. This latter Prakrit is very unsatisfactorily known. It seems to comprise several dialects, but we are not, as yet, able to get a clear idea of them. In phonetics they seem to have struck out independent lines of their own. There are, however, sufficient indications to show that they had more points of analogy with Maharashtri and Ardhamagadhi than would appear at the first glance. I pass by some points of phonology, and shall only draw attention to a few facts which seem to show that Magadhi is based on a dialect, or on dialects, which had an inflexional system characterized with the same rich variety of forms as in Maharashtri and Ardhamagdhi.

Magadhi has preserved traces of the old dative of *a*-themes, which has been throughout replaced by the genitive in Sauraseni. Thus, vinasaa, Sanskrit vinasaya, in order to destroy. Such forms are, however, perhaps only correct in verses. There are two forms of the genitive singular and three forms of the locative singular of *a*-bases; thus, puttassa and puttaha, Sanskrit putrasya, Sauraseni only puttassa, of the son; muhe, Sanskrit mukhe, in the mouth; kuvammi, Sanskrit kupe, in the well; kulahim, Sanskrit kule, in the family. Sauraseni has only forms such as kute.

The Atmanepada form of verbs, which in Sauraseni is confined to the first person singular, is used more freely in Magadhi; optatives such as kareyya, I may do, occur in Magadhi as well as the Sauraseni forms kaream or kare; imperatives such as pivahi, drink, are used in addition to piva, Sanskrit piba, but not so in Sauraseni.

A suffix corresponding to the illa, which plays a great role in Maharastri and Ardhamagadhi, but not in Sauraseni, must have been common in Magadhi, as the modern vernaculars clearly show. Compare also Magadhi gamelua, Sanskrit gramya, boorish.

Such instances might be multiplied if we could draw the Magadhi of the inscriptions and Pali into the scope of our inquiry. The preceding indications are, however, sufficient to show that the general character of the Magadhi dialects was more closely related to that of Maharashtri and Ardhamagadhi than that of Sauraseni. We seem therefore to be justified in dividing the Prakrits into one inner grorp, viz., Sauraseni, and one outer comprising Maharashtri, Ardhamagadhi, and Magadhi. This latter group shows great variety in its dialects, but has throughout the same character of inflexional richness.

There cannot, then, any more be any objection to the derivation of Maharashtri and Marathi from the same base, and we must return to the Indian tradition and to the conclusion that Maharashtri and Marathi are based on the same form of speech just as the two names, Maharashtri and Marathi, are two different forms of one and the same word.

Marathi and Maharashtri

It is now permissible to draw attention to several points in which Marathi agrees with Maharashtri. When similar forms also occur in other modern vernaculars, especially in the east, this fact is only in accord with the remarks above. Even Western Hindi forms can often be adduced which agree with Marathi and Maharashtri as against Sauraseni. This is partly to be explained by assuming that Western Hindi is derived from various sources. Though it is, in its general character, a Saurasena dialect, it has also assimilated elements from other, say outer, forms of speech. Maharashtri was, moreover, once the dialect of lyric poetry all over India, and it must necessarily have exercised an influence on other dialects, such as that spoken in the home of the present Western Hindi.

Maharashtri has been preserved in two slightly varying forms, the chief language of Prakrit literature, and the dialect of the non-canonical literature of the Svetambara Jains. This latter form of the language is usually called Jaina Maharashtri, and was perhaps based on the vernacular spoken in Surashtra, the modern peninsula of Kathiawar, before the present settlers entered it. The difference between the two forms of Maharashtri is, however, of comparatively small importance and need not trouble us in this connection.

In comparing Marathi with Maharashtri, we cannot base our inquiry on the vocabulary. In the first place we know too little of Sauraseni and Magadhi, and in the second place, the vocabulary of modern Aryan vernaculars does not differ to any considerable extent. A comparison of the inflexions will also yield but a small result, the modern system being quite different from that prevailing in the old Prakrits. It will hence be necessary to base our conclusions on those facts in which the old Prakrits are known to differ from each other, and where the same difference can be traced down to modern times. We shall begin with some phonetical features.

Vowels

Long vowels are occasionally shortened in Maharashtri. Thus, in the common word kumaro, Sanskrit and Sauraseni kumaro, a boy. Compare Marathi kumar, which is not a poetical form. Other dialects have kuwar and kuwar.

Haridra, turmeric, often becomes haliddi or haladdi in Maharashtri. Compare Marathi halad, dative haldi-la, rural

Hindi halad, haldi, hardi.

The Sanskrit vowel *ri* is sometimes differently treated in the old dialects. Thus, Sanskrit krita, Maharashtri and Ardhamagadhi kaa (compare Magadhi, Ardhamagadhi kada), but Sauraseni usually kida, done; Sanskrit ghrita, Maharashtri and Ardhamagadhi ghaa, but Sauraseni and Magadhi ghida, clarified butter. Similarly we find Marathi kele, i.e., kaya-illaam, done, while ghi, clarified butter, according to Molesworth is scarcely used in Marathi and must be considered as a Hindi loan-word.

Consonants

Soft consonants are occasionally hardened in the Prakrits. Thus, Maharashtri machchai and majjai, Sanskrit madyati, he grows mad; Maharashtri vachchai for vajjai, Sanskrit vrajati, he goes Compare Marathi matsne (Hindi machna), to swell; Konkani votsu, to go.

The aspiration has been transferred in the Maharashtri and Ardhamagadhi ghettum, Sanskrit grahitum, to take. Sauraseni has genhidum. The base occurring in the Maharashtri and Ardhamagadhi forms has only survived in Marathi. Compare ghetle, taken.

Dental consonants are much more commonly cerebralised in Maharashtri, Ardhamagadhi, and also in Magadhi, than in Sauraseni. Compare Maharashtri and Ardhamagadhi dasai, Sanskrit dasati, he bites; dahai, Sanskrit dahati, he burns; dola, an eye (compare Sanskrit dola, oscillating); dollai, Sanskrit dolayate, he swings; dohalaa, Sanskrit dohalaka, the longings of a pregnant woman. Similarly we find Marathi dasne, to bite; daho (poetical), heat; dadzne, to be hot; dola, an eye; dohla, longings of a pregnant woman, etc. Similar forms occur also in other dialects.

We may add stray forms such as Sanskrit kshetra, Maharashtri and Ardhamagadhi chhetta, Marathi set, but Sauraseni khetta, Hindi khet, a field; Maharashtri kira, Marathi kir, but Sauraseni and Sanskrit kila, forsooth; Sanskrit gardabha,

Maharashtri gaddaha, Marathi gadhav, but Sauraseni gaddaha, Hindi gadha, an ass; Sanskrit panchasat, Maharashtri pannasam, Marathi pannas, while other modern vernaculars have forms such as Western Hindi pachas.

Nouns and Pronouns

The termination of the nominative singular of masculine a-bases was *o* in Maharashtri and Sauraseni. The same is the case in old Marathi, thus, ravo, a king; nandanu, a son. The final *u* in the latter form is directly derived from an older *o*.

The genitive of *i*-bases, with which old in-bases were confounded, ends in issa and ino in Maharashtri and Ardhamagadhi, but only in ino in Sauraseni; thus, aggissa and aggino, Sanskrit agneh, of the fire; hatthissa and hatthino, Sanskrit hastinah, of an elephant. The form hatthissa directly corresponds to Marathi hathis.

Verbs

With regard to pronouns we may note that the typical Maharashtri forms majjha, my; tujjha, thy, have survived in Marathi madzha, my; tudzha, thy.

The Marathi verb shows something of the same rich variety as the Maharashtri one.

Thus we not only find the old present, future, and imperative, but also some traces of the precative.

Compare—

dekhe	indriya	adhina	hoije,	tai	sitoshna-te
see	of-senses	dependent	he-may-become,	then	cold-and heat

pavije	ani	sukhaduhkhi	akalije	apana-pe;
he-will-get	and	with-pleasure-and-sorrow	he-will-bind	himself;

'See, if a man is dependent on his senses, then he will feel cold and heat and become subject to the feeling of pleasure and sorrow' (Dnyanesvari, ii, 119). Such forms have usually been explained as passives, by assuming that the old passive can also be used as an active. The explanation given above seems, however, in some cases preferable.

The old passive survives in forms such as labhne, to be got; disne, to appear, and so on. In old poetry, however, a passive formed with the characteristic *j* is in common use; thus, vadhijati, they are killed; kije, it is done. Such forms have been confounded with the remains of the old precative, and both were probably felt to be identical. In modern Marathi only the forms mhanje, it is said, namely; and pahije, it is wanted, have survived.

It is of importance to note that such forms correspond to the Maharashtri passive ending in ijjai, while Sauraseni has iadi.

Marathi infinitives such as maru, to strike, are directly derived from Maharashtri forms such as marium, to strike. The participle of necessity, which ends in avva in Maharashtri, tavya in Sanskrit, has survived in most modern dialects, sometimes as a future or an infinitive, as in eastern dialects, sometimes as a present participle passive as in Sindhi. Marathi, as well as Gujarati, uses forms derived from this participle as infinitives, but has also retained it in its original meaning of a future participle passive. Thus, Marathi mya karave, Maharashtri mae kariavvam, it should be done by me, I should do.

The Marathi conjunctive participle in un, old Marathi u and u-nia, i.e. u+nia, is derived from the corresponding Maharashtri from ending in una and um, and has nothing to do with the Sauraseni form which adds ia. Thus, Sanskrit kritva, Maharashtri karituna, karium, Marathi karu, karunia, karun, but Sauraseni karia and kadua.

We may add the frequency with which the sufix illa is used in Maharashtri and probably all eastern Prakrits, just as its modern representative *l* in Marathi, and, lastly, the use of the emphatic particle Maharashtri and Ardhamagadhi chea, chia, chcha, Marathi chi, ts, Chhattisgarhi ech, but Sauraseni jeva, Gujarati and Rajasthani *j*.

Such points of agreement cannot fail to add strength to the conclusion that Maharashtri Prakrit was based on the vernacular of the Maratha country, which is the direct source from which modern Marathi is derived.

Place of Marathi in reference to other Indo-Aryan vernaculars

Marathi is the only modern vernacular which has been derived from the old Maharashtra Apabhramsa. That latter form of speech had a distinct character of its own. Though being of the same general kind as the eastern vernaculars, it differed from them in several points and sometimes agreed with Sauraseni, especially in the pronunciation of certain sounds. The modern representative of the old Maharashtra Apabhramsa is Marathi, and it is, therefore, to be expected that that form of speech occupies a somewhat independent position, sometimes agreeing with the languages of the outer, and sometimes with those of the inner group. That is also the case. Moreover, the conservative character of Marathi has tended to make this independence greater than it was, and at the present day Marathi is a language with very well marked frontiers, and does not merge into any of the neigbhouring forms of speech. The border line between Marathi on one side and Gujarati, Rajasthani and Western Hindi on the other, is very sharply marked. In the west we see that Gujarati Bhili and Khandesi gradually become more and more influenced by Marathi. But even when such dialects assume the linguistic form of Marathi, as in the case of Vadval, Varli, etc., they retain the character of mixed forms of speech and are no real connecting links. Similar is the state of affairs in the east. The Halbi dialect is not a connecting link between Marathi, Chhattisgarhi and Oriya, but a mechanical mixture of all these three languages, spoken by a tribe whose language did not originally belong to the Indo-Aryan Family.

Relation of Marathi to the inner Group

It has already been stated that Marathi in some points agrees with the languages of the inner group. The principal ones are as follows :

The pronunciation generally. In Konkani, however, we find some features which agree with the state of affairs in the east. Thus Konkani possesses the short *e* and *o* sounds and pronounces the short *a* like the *o* in 'hot'.

Marathi has two *s*-sounds, a dental *s* and a palatal *s*. This latter sound is used before *y* and before *i*, *i*, and *e*, which vowels are usually pronounced almost as *yi*, *yi*, *ye*, respectively, a state of affairs which is not in accord with the principles prevailing in the east. The palatal pronunciation of *s* is, therefore, due to the combination of *s* and *y*, and quite different from the Bengali *s*, which has another origin as the eastern Prakrits clearly show. Some Marathi dialects only know the dental *s*.

The pronunciation of the palatals as ts, dz, respectively, also occurs in some eastern dialects, and in Kasmiri. A similar pronunciation is common in several dialects of Gujarati and Rajasthani. Exact parallels to the Marathi pronunciation of *s* and of the palatals are only found in Telugu. Such points do not, therefore, prove a closer connexion between the pronunciation of Marathi and of eastern vernaculars.

On the other hand, *v* and *b* are distinguished as in Gujarati, Panjabi, Sindhi, and, partly, in Rajasthani. Marathi has a cerebral *l* like Rajasthani, Gujarati, Panjabi, and also Oriya.

With regard to the inflexion of nouns and verbs, it should be noted that Marathi has three genders like Gujarati and some rural dialects of Western Hindi.

The nominative singular of strong masculine bases ends in *a* as in the east and in some dialects of Western Hindi, but in *o* in Konkani. The nominative plural ends in *e* as in Western Hindi.

Marathi possesses a separate case of the agent and, in consequence thereof, uses the passive construction of the past tense of transitive verbs. The verb is put in the neuter singular if the object is accompanied by a case suffix. In the Konkan, however, it agrees with the object also in such cases, just as it does in Gujarati and Rajasthani. Konkani also agrees with Gujarati in possessing a separate form of the nominative singular of the personal pronoun of the first person; thus Konkani hav, Gujarati hu, I.

The nominative singular masculine of demonstrative and relative pronouns ends in *o* as in Western Hindi, like the nominative of masculine a-bases in Maharashtri.

Marathi uses an n-suffix to form a verbal noun, as does also Western Hindi. The same suffix, however, also occurs in Eastern Hindi, and Marathi has also a *v* infinitive like Gujarati and eastern vernaculars.

None of these points are of sufficient importance to prove a closer connexion between Marathi and the languages of the inner group. They are partly due to the conservative nature of the language, as in the case of the preservation of a separate case of the agent, and they are partly of the same nature as those features in which Maharashtri agreed with Sauraseni.

Relation of Marathi to the Outer Circle

In other points Marathi agrees with the languages of the outer circle. The points of analogy in pronunciation have already been noted, and it has been stated that they are of relatively small importance. On the other hand, the preceding pages dealing with the relationship between Marathi and Maharashtri will have revealed many facts which show that the phonetical laws of Marathi often closely agree with those prevailing in the east. Of greater importance, however, are several points of analogy in inflexion.

All weak a-bases in Marathi have an oblique form ending in a; thus, bap, a father, dative bapa-la. The same form also occurs in the east. Thus, Bihari pahar, a guard, oblique pahra. The eastern vernaculars do not, it is true, use this form regularly. Its existence is, however, of sufficient importance to be adduced in this place. Marathi also shows the origin of this form. In addition to the oblique base ending in a, it also, dialectically, uses a form ending in as; thus, in the Konkan, bapas-na, by the father. Bapas directly corresponds to the Maharashtri from bappassa, of a father, and it is evident that bapa has the same origin, the change of ss to h being already found in Maharashtri.

The termination of the second person singular of verbal tenses ends in *s* as in Bengali, Bihari, and Eastern Hindi. Konkani, however, uses *y* like Kasmiri, and in Berar and the Central Provinces the second person is usually formed like the third person without an *s*.

The past tense has different forms for the three persons, as in eastern dialects. The personal suffixes are the same as in the case of the old present, and it is, therefore, doubtful whether Marathi possesses the so-called pronominal suffixes which play so great a role in many outer languages. The *s* which is, in some dialects, added to the second person singular of all verbs, may perhaps be such a suffix. In a similar way we sometimes find a *t* added to the second person plural, and an *n* to the third person singular. Compare forms such as kariles, it was done (by thee); sangillan (Konkan and Berar), it was said (by him). Such forms are, however, only occasionally used, and the whole question about pronominal suffixes must be left open so far as Marathi is concerned.

The past tense is formed by adding an l-suffix as in the east. This feature pervades the whole conjugational system and gives a peculiar colour to the language which is entirely wanting in the inner group. Gujarati, it is true, forms a pluperfect participle by adding an l-suffix. This seems however, to be one of these points in which that language has been influenced by the vernaculars formerly spoken in its present home. The l-suffix must be derived from the Prakrit suffix illa which played a great role in Maharashtri, Ardhamagadhi, and probably also in Magadhi. It is a secondary suffix, added to the old past participle passive, and it is, consequently, originally not necessary. We also find that it is occasionally dropped, not only in the east, but also in Marathi dialects; thus, Chitpavani mayra and marila, it was struck. On the other hand, this suffix is used in a much wider way in Konkani. The oldest instance of its use in the modern way is the Ardhamagadhi anilliya, brought.

The future is formed by adding an l-or n-suffix. This form has been compared with the l-present in Bihari. An l-future also occurs in Rajasthani and some northern dialects. The base of the Marathi future is identical with the habitual past, the old present. Sometimes, however, the two differ; thus Nagpuri nidzo, I used to sleep, but nidzal, I shall sleep; Karhadi marsi, thou wilt strike (the corresponding form of the habitual past does not occur in the materials available). It is, therefore, perhaps allowable to conclude that the Marathi future (and past habitual) has preserved traces of two old forms, the present and future. Maharashtri future forms such as karihisi, thou wilt do; karihii, he well do, would regularly become karis and kari in Marathi.

The most important points in which Marathi agrees with eastern vernaculars are thus the oblique form of weak a-bases, the termination of the second person singular of verbal tenses, the distinguishing of the various persons in the past tense, and the l-suffix of the same form. These points are of sufficient importance to justify us in stating a closer relationship between Marathi and the languages of the east. It should, however, be borne in mind that all these characteristics can be explained from the features of Maharashtri Prakrit.

In many points Marathi differs from all other Indo Aryan vernaculars. We may mention the almost universal use by nouns of a distinct oblique base; the dative in s; the genitive suffix tsa; the possessive pronouns madzha, my; tudzha, thy; the numeral pannas, fifty; the conjunctive participle ending in un (compare, however, Oriya), and so on.

General conclusion

The position of Marathi as compared with other Indo-Aryan vernaculars may, therefore, be defined as follows. In some points it has developed peculiar forms of its own; in others it agrees with the languages of the inner group, more especially, in pronunciation; and in important points of inflexion it forms one group with the eastern vernaculars of the other circle.

In the Konkan there are important points of agreement with Gujarati, a fact which may perhaps be accounted for by the supposition that the Marathi-speaking inhabitants of the Konkan once occupied the modern Gujarat, and only settled in the Konkan after having lived for some time in the neighbourhood of the Gujaratis. The tradition according to which their original home was Trihotra may be a faint recollection of such a migration.

Marathi Literature

The Maratha country has long been famous for its literature. The Vaidarbhi Riti, the literary style of the Berar school of Sanskrit writers, was highly praised by Dandin, as far superior to the artificial style of the east, the Gaudiya Riti. The old Maharashtri lyrics fully justify this praise, and later poets such as Rajasekhara proudly mention Maharashtra as Sarasvati-janma-bhuh, the birth-place of the goddess of eloquence, where the sweet and serene, the graceful and agreeable nectar of poetry is found. We cannot in this place give even a rapid survey of the Prakrit and Sanskrit literature connected with Maharashtra. We must be content to give a short account of the later literature in Marathi.

The revival of literature in the Maratha country is, just as is the case else where in India, closely connected with the religious renaissance which can be traced from the time of Sankara down to the present day. The oldest Marathi literature is, therefore, religious. It is due to the wish to make the religious thoughts and ideas of the old Sanskrit literature accessible to those who were not masters of any language other than their own vernacular. Sanskrit works were, therefore, translated and free paraphrases were made. The bulk of Marathi literature is of this description, and like its prototype, it is written in verse. Prose compositions are later, and have not played the same role.

For the history of Marathi literature and the development of the Marathi language it is of importance to note that almost all its poets have come from the Dekhan and the country round Paithan. The Konkan and Berar do not claim a single name of importance.

The beginning of Marathi literature seem to be connected with the Vishnuite reformation inaugurated by Ramanuja (beginning of the twelfth century). To him Vishnu was the 'Supreme Deity, endowed with every possible gracious attribute, full of love and pity for the sinful beings who adore him, and granting the released soul after death a home of eternal bliss near him.'

The same religious devition to Vishnu, or, as he calls him Vithoba, meets us in the Abhangs of Namdev, who is considered to be the first Marathi poet. He was a tailor from Pandharpur, and probably fiourished in the middle of the thirteenth century. Most of his works have been lost, but some of his stanzas have found their way into the Adigranth of the Sikhs, and they can still impress us with his devotion to God, for whom he longs 'as the Chakravaka longs for his mate or a child for its mother.'

A contemporary of Namdev was Dnyanoba, or Dnyanesvar who wrote a paraphrase of the Bhagavadgita in the Ovi metre. He lived at Alandi, north of Poona, and his work, the Dnya nesvari or Bhavarthadipika, is dated Saka 1212=1280 A. D. This work is very highly esteemed among the Marathar. It is penetrated by deep religious feeling, but is also pervaded with the barren philosophy of later Hinduism.

The poet Mukundaraya probably belongs to the same age. His best known work is the Viveka-Sindhu, or Ocean of Discrimination, which is strongly influenced by orthodox Vedantism.

The next important poet whose works have been preserved is Ekanath, a Rigvedin from Paithan, who died in 1609. His favourite metre was the Ovi, but he also wrote Abhangs. His principal works are based on Sanskrit originals and are devoted to the praise of Vishnu. His Ekanathi Bhagavata is based on the 11th Skanda of the Bhagavata-Purana, and has been printed in Bombay. He further wrote the Bhavartha-Ramayana, the Rukmini-Svayamvara, the Svatmasukha, etc., and also composed works in Hindostani. He was a contemporary of Shahji, the father of Sivaji, and is spoken of as an ardent student of the Dnyanesvari.

His daughter's son was Muktesvar, who was born in 1609, and lived at Paithan. He is often spoken of as the master of the Ovi metre, and his principal works are paraphrases of Sanskrit originals. He wrote part of a Mahabharata, a Bhagavata, a Satamukha-Ravanakhyana, and, according to tradition, also a Ramayana.

We have now come down to the time of Sivaji, the founder of the Maratha power. This national hero, who is usually known as a rude the treacherous warrior, was himself influenced by the growing marathi literature, and its greatest poet courted his favour. He sat as a pupil at the feet of Ramdas (1608-1681), the son of a Kulkarni in Jamb at the Godavari, who spent his life in devotion to Rama, and hence changed his name Narayan to Ramdas. Sivaji is said at one time to have offered him his whole kingdom, but Ramdas declined the offer, and continued till his death to live as an unmarried devotee. The principal work of this author is the Dasbodh, on religious duties, and he also wrote numerous Abhangs and Slokas.

Tukaram (1608-1649) was born at Dehu, a small village to the north of Poona,. and his father is said to have been a Sudra. By profession he was a wandering reciter of Kathas or religious stories and legends, and he is considered to have brought the Abhang to the highest perfection. His poetry is devoted to the praise of Vithoba. Religious longing and devotion, affectionate love and moral purity, are the keynotes of his verses, many of which are also remarkable for the sincere consciousness they exhibit of the idea of sin,—an expression of religious faith rarely met with in older literature, but which was in later times imitated by poets such as Mahipati.

A contemporary of Tukaram was Vaman Pandit (died 1673), Rigvedin from Satara, who studied in Benares, and also wrote in Sanskrit. His style is heavy, and the predilection for yamakas and other artificial embellishments show the growing influence of the Sanskrit Kavya. He wrote a commentary on the Bhagavadgita in the Ovi metre, called the Yatharthadipika, and numerous works based on the Mahabharata, the Ramayana, the Bhagavata, and so on.

Sridhar (1678-1728), the most copious of all Maratha poets, was a Brahman from the neighbourhood of Pandharpur. His works mostly based on the Sanskrit epics and on the Puranas, and are highly popular. Some of the titles are Ramavijaya, Harivijaya, Pandavapratapa, Sivalilamrita, and so on.

Amritaraya, who was a Desastha Brahman, lived in Aurangabad about the middle of the eighteenth century. He was renowned as a sighrakavi, and wrote also in Hindostani. His works are partly based on the Puranas, and are partly of a more metaphysical description. They abound in various kinds of alliterations. Like Tukaram he used to perform recitations.

A younger contemporary of Amritaraya was Moropant or Mayura Pandit (1729-1794), a Karhada Brahman from Baramati in the Poona district. As a boy he acquired considerable proficiency in Sanskrit, in which language he also wrote some poems. His Marathi works are largely influenced by Sanskrit poetry. He used all the artificial apparatus of Sanskrit rhetoric, and freely introduced Sanskrit words into his Marathi. His works, which include a Bharata, a Bhagavata, several Ramayanas, a Mayurakekavali, and so forth, are held in high estimation among his countrymen, but are less palatable to European taste.

Mahipati (1715-1790), Desastha Brahman of the Rigvedins from Tahrabad near Paithan, was an imitator of Tukaram, but his chief importance rests on the fact that he collected the popular traditions about national saints, and put them in a poetical form. His various works, such as the Bhaktavijaya, the Bhaktalilamrita, the Santavijaya, the Santalilamrita, are usually described as the Acta Sanctorum of the Marathas. They are partly based on older works by Nabhaji and Udbhavachidgan, but partly also on oral tradition, and narrate the miraculous life and doings of older deified poets such as Dnyanoba and Tukaram.

There are, besides, a great many minor poets, such as Chintamani, Raghunth (end of eighteenth century), Prabhakara and others, who mainly based their poems on the Puranas, the Mahabharata, and the Ramayana. It is not, however, possible to enter into details.

Almost all the Marathi poetry mentioned on this and the preceding pages is religious. Erotic lyrics have, however, also been highly appreciated by the Marathas from the earliest times. We possess a precious testimony to this leaning of the national mind in the famous Sattasai of Hala. In modern Marathi the erotic poetry is principally represented by the so-called Lavanis, small ballads usually put into the mouths of women, and often of a rather scandalous description. Among the authors of Lavanis we may mention Anantaphandi (1744-1819), a Yajurvedin from Ahmadnagar, who also mis-used his poetical genius in lavishing praise on Baji Rao, the last Peshwa, and Ramjosi (1762-1812), a Desastha Brahman from Sholapur. In this connection we may also mention the Nauka Kridan of Visvanath, and the Anangarang of Kalyana Mala.

The feats of the national heroes from Sivaji and downwards, have furnished materials for numerous Pavadas, or war-ballads, mostly by nameless poets, which are sung everywhere in the country. Lastly, the numerous proverbs current among the Marathas should be noticed. A good selection has been published by Manwaring. See Authorities below.

The prose literature in Marathi is of much smaller importance. It embraces narratives of historical events, the so-called Bakhars; moral maxims such as the Vidur Niti; folk tales, such as the Vetal Pantsvisi, the Simhasan Battisi, the Suk Bahattari, and so forth. In modern times a copious literature of prose works has arisen, mainly translations from English, and several journals and newspapers in Marathi are published, chiefly in Bombay and Poona.

Authorities

A—Early references

Maharashtra as the name of a country, does not seem to occur before the sixth century A. D., when it is mentioned by Varahamihira in his Brihat Samhita, v. 64. The reference to the language of Maharashtra as the base of the principal Prakrit in Dandin's Kavyadarsa, i, 35, belongs to about the same time.

The name was also known to the Chinese pilgrim Hiuen Tsiang, to Albiruni, and to Ziau-'d-din Barni. See the references in Yule's Hobson-Jobson, s. v. Mahratta.

The first reference to Maharashtri as the name of a language seems to be in Vararuchi's Prakrit Grammar, the date of which cannot be ascertained. Other grammarians simply use Prakritam, i. e., the Prakrit language, instead.

Later authors, such as Ramatarkavagisa and Kramadisvara, mention a dialect called Dakshinatya as a form of Apabhramsa, i. e., in this connection, as one of the vernaculars of India. Dakshinatya is, in the Sahitya Darpana stated to be identical with Vaidarbhika, the vernacular of Berar. Dakshinatya is usually mentioned together with Magadhi and Ardhamagadhi and Professor Lassen was therefore inclined to class it with those dialects. We are not, however, told that Dakshinatya has any characteristics of its own. On the contrary, Markandeya expressly states that Dakshinatya is not a separate dialect, lakshanakaranat, because it has no characteristic marks of its own. Ii is therefore, impossible to base anything upon the names Dakshinatya and Vaidarbhika. They may, or may not, correspond to the modern Dakhini and Varhadi, the dialects of the Dekhan and Berar respectively. Modern Marathi is, at all events, so old that the mention of Dakshinatya and Vaidarbhika can refer to it. The oldest Marathi inscription of which anything is known, goes backe to about A. D. 1115-8, and an inscription of some extent is dated A. D. 1207. Compare Epigraphia Indica, Vol. i, pp. 343 and f.; Vol. vii, p. 109. It should be mentioned that a reference to the dialect of the Dakshinatyas, or Southerners, occurs in the Mrichchhakatika, where we are told that it was no distinct form of speech. On account of their knowledge of various aboriginal languages the Dakshinatyas are said to speak as they thought proper. The passages which might be expected to illustrate this dialect are, however written in Sauraseni.

The first mention of the Maratha country in Europe seems to be found in Friar Jordanus' Mirabilia Descripta (c. 1328). The passage containing the reference has been reprinted in Yule's Hobson-Jobson, l. c., and is as follows :

> c. 1328. "In this Greater India are twelve idolatrous Kings, and more . . . There is also the Kingdom of Maratha which is very great."—Friar Jordanus, 41.'

The same authority also reproduces the earliest mention of the Marathi language of which I am aware. It has been taken from John Fryer's—A New Account of East India and Persia, London, 1698, and it is dated 1673. It is as follows :

> '1673. "They tell their tale in Moratty : by Profession they are Gentues."—Fryer, 174.'

Other old references to the Marathas and their country will be found in Hobson-Jobson. They may here be left out of consideration, and we shall turn to early mentions of the language.

The Konkan form of Marathi was early dealt with by Portuguese missionaries, who called it the northern dialect of Konkani. A paraphrase of the contents of the Gospels in that language by Francisco Vas de Guimaraens, was printed in 1659, and a grammar by an unknown missionary was completed in the seventeenth century. See the authorities quoted under Konkan Standard below, p. 65.

The Konkani dialect was described at a still earlier date. The old references will be found among the authorities dealing with that form of speech. See p. 166.

Marathi itself began to occupy European scholars early in the eighteenth century. It was considered to comprise two dialects, Balabande and Marathi. In reality, however, these are only the two common characters used in writing Marathi, Balabande corresponding to the Balbodh and Marathi to the Modi character.

Marathi does not seem to be represented in the translations of the Lord's Prayer published by Joh. Chamberlayne in 1715. La Croze in a letter to Theophilus Siegfried Bayer dated November, 1731, mentions Marathi as Marathica lingua, also called Balabande. He rightly remarks that the written character is identical with Devanagari. See Thesaurus epistolicus Lacrozianus, Vol. iii, Lipsiae 1746, p. 64, where a specimen of the written character is given. La Croze derives the alphabet from Hebrew.

In the same work, Vol. i, Lipsiae 1742, p. 338, is printed a letter from Benj. Schultze, the well-known author of one of the first Hindostani grammars, who for some time lived as a missionary in Madras. The letter is dated the 28th January 1734, and it contains the incidental remark that Schultze had sent specimens in the Devanagari and Balabande languages to Europe. We learn from other sources that he furnished translations of the Lord's Prayer into Marathi. His manuscripts were preserved in Leipzig, and afterwards published in several collections, for the first time in the Orientalisch-und Occidentalischer Sprachmeister of Johann Friedrich Fritz. This book which was printed at Leipzig, 1748, was an enlarged reprint of a similar work by Johann Heinrich Hager, published in Leipzig, 1741, which is, in its turn, based on older collections by Andreas Muller. The Sprachmeister was, however, revised by the Danish Missionary Benj. Schultze, just mentioned, who added 15 Indian specimens from his own collections. It accordingly contains the Modi character on pp. 94 and ff. which is called Marathicum Alphabetum. On pp. 120 and ff. some remarks on Hindostani, taken from Schultze's Grammatica Hindostanica, have been printed. We are here told that the Balabandish and Marathish language is a daughter of the Dewanagara language, that is of Sanskrit. P. 124 gives the Balabandu, i.e., the Balbodh character. On p. 206, we find the first ten numerals in Marathi figures. Between pp. 212 and 213 is inserted a comparative vocabulary called Tabula exhibens harum linguarum affinitatem et differentiam. The fifth and sixth columns in this table contain some words in Marathi, with the headings Marathice and Balabandice, respectively. The two columns are identical. Column 9 contains the same words in Konkani, Cuncanice. To the Sprachmeister is annexed a collection of versions of the Lord's Prayer. It includes the Lord's Prayer in Goanica, p. 85; Balabandeca, p. 90; and Marathica, p. 93, all by Schultze. The Sprachmeister furnishes the materials for the mention of the 'Marathica' and 'Balabandeca' languages in the Alphabetum Brammhanicum sev Indostanum universitatis Kosi. Romae, 1761, p. ix. This work, which was published by the Congregatio de Propaganda Fide, was soon followed by the Grammatica Marasta, Rom., 1778, and a Catechismo da Doutrina' Cristam, Rom., 1778, in Portuguese and Marathi.

From about the same time is Iwarus Abel's Symphona symphona, sive undecim Linguarum orientalium Discors exhibita Concordia, Tamulicae videlicet. . . Marathicae, Balabandicae. . . Cuncanicae. . . Kopenhagen, 1782.

Lorenzo Hervas y Panduro, a Spanish Jesuit from Galizia, also dealt with Marathi in his huge cyclopedia Idea del Universo, Cesena, 1778-87. The twentieth volume has the title Vocabulario poliglotto con Prolegomeni sopra piu di cl Lingue, Cesena, 1787, and contains a comparison of 63 words in 154 languages. The Marathi portion is printed on p. 163. The ensuing volume, the twenty-first, is a collection of versions of the Lord's Prayer in more than 300 languages and dialects. The title of this part is Saggio prattico delle Lingue con Prolegomeni e una Raccolta di Orazioni Dominicali in piu di trecento Lingue e Dialetti. It contains a Marathi version on p. 143, and a Goanese one on p. 145, both after Benj. Schultze, and also, on p. 146, another Marathi version, after the Catechism, mentioned above.

Some Marathi words are also given in the Russian publication Glossarium comparativum Linguarum totius Orbis, St. Petersburg, 1787. They were reprinted by Franz Carl Alter in his book Ueber die Samskrdamische Sprache, Vienna, 1794.

A short review of the older works will be found in Adelung's Mithridates. See below.

The Scriptures were partly translated into Marathi by the Serampore missionaries. The New Testament and the Pentateuch were published in 1807; the prophetic books in 1821. A Konkani translation of the Bible appeared at Serampore in 1819.

The list of authorities which follows does not include the works mentioned in the preceding pages. It should be compared with the shorter lists printed below under Konkan Standard and Konkani.

Written Character

Marathi is usually written in the so-called Balbodh or in the so-called Modi character. Balbodh, lit. 'teachable to children' is identical with Deva. nagari, and has been described in Vol. v. Part ii, pp. 7 and ff. It is used in almost all printed books, and also, to a great extent, in private transactions and letters. The Modi character is almost totally confined to the latter kind of writing.

The forms of the vowels given above are only used at the

beginning of words or syllables. When the vowels follow a consonant they are expressed by means of secondary signs in the same way as in the Devanagari alphabet. For the sake of teaching these signs the alphabet is disposed in Barakhdis, or series of twelve letters, each containing a consonant combined with all possible vocalic sounds.

In Konkani the Kanarese and also the Roman alphabet are often used for the printing and writing of the dialect. Compare below p. 167. The Kanarese letters have been described in Volume IV under Kanarese.

Grammar

Mr. Beames has justly pointed out that Marathi has 'a very decided individuality, a type quite its own, arising from its comparative isolation for so many centuries.' The vocabulary chiefly consists of Tadbhavas of different age. The loans from Persian are comparatively unimportant. On the other hand, old Tadbhavas have, since the revival of Marathi literature, to some extent been replaced by Sanskrit loan-words. Thus, we now find prasad, favour, instead of the pasay of Dnyanoba's poetry; gambhir deep, instead of his gahiru; nath, a lord, instead of his nah, and so on. The general character of Marathi has been described by Mr. Beames as follows :—'Marathi is one of those languages which one may call playful—it delights in all sorts of jingling formations and has struck out a larger quantity of secondary and tertiary words, diminutives, and the like, than any of the other tongues.

Pronunciation.—The short a is pronounced like the u in English 'but'. In Konkani, however, it assumes the open sound of o in 'hot', as is also the case in Bengali. Thus, votsu, to go. A short a is inherent in every consonant which is not combined with any other vowel. In poetry this short a is always pronounced. Thus, ghar, a house, is pronounced ghara, Such a word is, therefore, said to be disyllabic. In the same way gharas, to a house, is said to a have three syllables, and so on. On the other hand, in everyday speech the final short a of a polysyllabic word is not pronounced. Thus, ghar, a house; bahin, a sister.

In a word of three syllables, which ends in a vowel other than a, a short a in the penultimate is slurred; thus, tsalni, a sieve. In words of four syllables a short a in the antepenultimate is silent; thus, karvat, a saw. In a word of five syllables a short a in the second syllable, and, if the word does not end in a silent a, in the penultimate is silent. Thus, sarkhavat, resemblance; vartavla, an extra payment. The short a in compound words is dropped in the same cases as in the uncompounded word. Thus, vi-sarla, he forgot; kalkal-ne, to be agitated.

These rules are observed in the Konkan, in the northern part of the Dekhan, Berar, and the Central Provinces. In the Dekhan south of Poona every short a is fully sounded, though the educated classes try to conform their speech to the Poona standard; thus, visarala, he forgot. A final a is, however, in most cases silent. This tendency to pronounce the short a is probably due to the influence of the neighbouring Kanarese. It is most strongly developed in Kolhapur where even the short final a is often fully sounded; thus, dona, two. Similar is the case in the dialect of the Saraswat Brahmans of Karwar. See below, pp. 188 and ff.

Short and long a are often interchangeable with e, more especially in the termination e of neuter bases, of the instrumental and of verbal forms, and in the termination en of the future. Thus, ghare, ghara, and ghara, houses; bapa-ne and baba-na, by the father; sangitle and sangitla or sangitla, it was said; mhanen, mhanan, or mhanan, I shall say. The a forms are not admitted into literature or into the language of the educated classes in the Dekhan, but are quite common in the Konkan, Berar and the Central Provinces.

Short i and u as final vowels only occur in loan-words such as mati, intelligence; bhanu, sun. In the dialect of the Saraswat Brahmans of Karwar, however, final i and u are quite common.

I and u are always long in the penultimate of words ending in a silent a; thus marit, striking; lakud, wood; us, a sugar-cane. They are short when they are followed by a full nasal sound; thus, unt, camel. These rules, however, only apply to the language of the educated classes.

When a word is inflected or ends in a long vowel the long i and u of the penultimate are shortened or changed to; thus, marit, striking, marita or marta, while striking.

A long a is apparently also shortened under the same conditions, though it is written as long, thus, hatas, written hatas, to the hand; kanas, written kanas, to the ear. In such cases a has the sound of a in Italian ballo.

E is commonly pronounced as ye; thus, yek and ek, one. This form is common everywhere with the exception of Poona and the neighbourhood. Literary forms such as yene, to come; yethe; and ethe, here, etc., show that the pronunciation of e as ye has been common all over the Marathi country. E is commonly interchangeable with ya; thus, te, or tya, veles, at that time. Compare sam-bhar, for syam-bhar, and sem-bhar, hundred.

The Anusvara is commonly written before surd consonants in order to denote the nasal corresponding to the consonant. Thus, unt, a camel; mandi, a thigh. Such nasals occur before soft mutes, and also, if the preceding vowel is short, before hard mutes. In other cases the Anusvara coalesces with the preceding vowel to a nasal vowel which is indicated by means of the Anunasika. Thus, at, inside; bhovai, an eyebrow. In Sanskrit words the Anunasika before r, s, sh, s, and h is pronounced as a nasal v, and before y, l, and v as a nasal y, l, v, respectively. Thus, savsar, the world; savhar, destruction of the universe; sayyog, junction.

The Anunasika is often dropped, or, when it is considered necessary to pronounce it distinctly, in order to distinguish between forms which would otherwise be confounded, replaced by n. The latter pronunciation is especially used in honorific words such as tyanla, to him (honorific plural). Thus, gharat, in the house; tya-ne, by him. In the Southern Konkan, however, the nasal pronunciation is very marked.

The gutturals, dentals, and labials are pronounced as in Sanskrit.

The palatals are pronounced as in Sanskrit in words borrowed from that language and from Hindostani, and in Marathi words before i, i, e, and y; thus, chand, fierce; jama, collected; chikhal, mud; bapa-che ghar, the father's house; majhya gharat, in my house. Ch is also pronounced in the same way in char, four. This form is derived from Prakrit chattari and chauro probably through the steps chaari, chyar; compare ghodyas from ghodaassa, ghodaas, to a horse. The numeral 'forty' is usually pronounced tsalis. In other cases the palatals are pronounced as ts, tsh, dz, dzh, respectively. In the Konkan this pronounciation is also common before e. Thus, tsakar, a servant; dzane, to go; dze (Konkan), which.

Jn is pronounced as dny, or, in the Konkan, as gy; thus, dnyan or gyan, knowledge. The sound only occurs in borrowed words.

The cerebrals are usually pronounced as in Sanskrit. The cerebral d after vowels is, however, pronounced as an r in the Central and Northern Konkan, and as an r in some dialects in Berar and the Central Provinces, and probably also elsewhere. Thus, ghoda, ghora and ghora, a horse. We may compare the change of d to l between vowels in Maharashtri-Prakrit; thus, Sanskrit tadaga, Maharashtri talaa, Marathi tale, a tank. In some rustic dialects in Berar d is, in a similar way, often confounded with l; thus, ghola, a horse; dzavad, near. The cerebral n is often confounded with the dental n, though both have a different origin, thus, pani instead of pani, water. It has often been stated that the cerebral n is more common in the Konkan. This statement, however, only applies to the Konkani dialect, where the two sounds seem to be correctly distinguished. In Nagpur every dental n is said to become cerebral. All the specimens forwarded for the use of this Survey, however, give a dental n in all places.

Marathi possesses a cerebral as well as a dental l-sound. The former is derived from a single l between vowels in Prakrit, the latter from a double ll; thus, kal, Maharashtri Kalo, time; phul, Maharashtri phullam, flower. The cerebral l is pronounced by putting the tip of the tongue against the palate and allowing the air to pass on both sides. On the coast, from Thana to Rajapur, the cerebral l has become dental, and in Berar and the Central Province it is often pronounced as an r or as a y. Thus, mali, mali, mari, and mayi, a gardener.

The consonant v has a sound between v and w. It is produced by bringing both the lips (not only the lower one as in English) in contact with the upper teeth, the rounding of the lips being less than in pronouncing a w. Before i, l, e, y, and h it sounds almost like a v, while in other positions it approaches the sound of w. A final v coalesces with a preceding vowel to a kind of diphthong; thus, gav, a village, pronounced almost as gao or gav. Before i. i, and e, a v has a tendency to be dropped. Thus, we find isto and vistav, fire; is and vis, twenty, yel and vel. time. Such forms occur all over the Marathi country, especially in rustic dialects.

Marathi has two s-sounds, a dental s and a palatal s. The latter is used before i, i, and e, and y, and in loan-words from Sanskrit and Persian. Thus, simply, a caste name; sil, a stone; set, field; syam, blue. Similarly sam-bhar, instead of syam-bhar or sembhar, hundred. Dialectically every s is changed to s. A cerebral sh only occurs in borrowed words such as sesh, rest; soshne, to dry up. It is pronounced as an s.

Aspirated letters have often lost their aspiration, thus, hat, Prakrit hattha, hand; madz, Prakrit majjha, waist; sangne, Prakrit samghai, to say. In the Southern Konkan and Dekhan, where Marathi borders on Karnarese, disaspiration is almost the rule.

Nouns.—Nouns may end in a short silent a, or in a long

vowel, including e, with or without nasalisation. A few nouns end in ai, o, and au. Final i and u only occur in borrowed words such as kavi, a poet; mati, intelligence; dhenu, a cow.

The bases of nouns are weak, when they end in a short inherent a, or strong, when they end in a long vowel or a diphthong. Thus, weak, ghar, house: bhint, wall : strong, ghoda, horse; moti, pearl. The long final of strong bases is derived from contradiction. Thus, ghoda goes back to a Prakrit ghodau; moti to a Prakrit mottiam.

Gender—There are three genders, masculine, feminine, and neuter. The neuter is used to denote inanimate beings, and also animate beings in the plural where both the natural genders are included, or the gender is left undecided; thus, manse, people. In the Konkan the neuter singular is commonly used to denote females before the age of puberty; thus, chedu, a girl. In the plural the neuter is often used as a honorific feminine; thus, bai-saheb ali, the lady came.

Strong bases ending in a are, if they are not borrowed words, masculine. The corresponding feminine and neuter terminations are i and e, respectively; thus, mulga, a boy; mulgi, a girl; mulge, a child.

Number—There are two numbers, the singular and the plural. Of masculine nouns only those ending in a, which take e instead of a, change for the plural. Thus, bap, father, fathers; but ghoda, a horse; ghode, horses.

Most feminine nouns add a in the plural; thus, jibh, a tongue, plural jibha; ghodi, a mare, plural ghodya; bayko, a woman, plural bayka. Compare borrowed words such as katha, a tale, plural katha.

Most feminine nouns ending in a short silent a form their plural in this way. They are derived from Prakrit bases ending in a; thus, jibh, a tongue, goes back to a Prakrit jibbha. In Prakrit there was also a large class of feminine nouns ending in i. This final i must be dropped in Marathi, and these old i-bases, therefore, look exactly like old a-bases. Thus, jibh, a tongue, Prakrit jibbha; muth, a fist, Prakrit mutthi. These two classes are, however, distinguished in declension, and the old i-bases form their plural, not in a, but in i; thus, bhint-i, walls; vel-i, creepers, etc. To this class belong many verbal nouns which in the nominative are identical with the verbal base. Thus, bhet, a meeting, from bhetne, to meet; thev, a deposit from thevne, to deposit, and so forth.

Some feminine nouns ending in u do not change in the plural; thus, daru, liquor and liquors.

Neuter nouns ending in e form their plural in i, all other neuter nouns add e; thus, tale, a tank, plural tali; ghar, a house, plural ghare; moti, a pearl, plural, motye, and so forth.

Words ending in i and u do not change in the plural; thus, kavi, a poet, poets; dhenu, a cow, cows.

Case—Cases are formed by adding postpositions, not, however, to the base, but to a modification of it called the oblique form. There are, besides, some remains of the old synthetic cases of the Prakrits. The most common of those old forms is a dative ending in s; thus, bapas, to a father. Bapas is derived from Prakrit bappassa, the genitive of bappo, a father, the genitive having replaced the dative in all Prakrits. The origin of the form has, however, been forgotten, and s is now used exactly like other dative suffixes and is added to the oblique base of all nouns; thus, mulgyas, to daughters. The original force of a genitive can still be seen in the Konkan where this form in s is often used as an oblique base. See p. 66 below.

An old locative occurs in forms such as ghari, in the house; paya, at the feet. It is very common in poetry. In the Konkan we find another old locative in the word ger, in the house.

An old instrumental ends in e, plural i and hi; thus, kumare, by the boy; kauli, by the crows; isvarehi, by the lord (honorific plural). Such forms are mostly confined to poetry.

The oblique form of borrowed words ending in i and u ends in i, plural i, and u, plural u, respectively. Thus, kavi, a poet, obl. sing. kavi; dhenu, a cow, obl. plur. dhenu.

Masculine bases ending in a and neuter bases ending in e change a and e to ya, plural ya in the oblique form. Thus, ghoda, a horse, obl. sing. ghodya, obl. plur. ghodya; tale, a tank, obl. sing. talya, obl. plur. talya. E is often substituted for ya, thus ghode-la, to the horse. Radza, a king, often rejects the y of the oblique form in writing; thus, raja-kade, to the king. The same is also the case in other words after palatals, the y being only seen in the palatal pronunciation of the preceding consonant.

All other masculine and neuter bases add a, plural a in the oblique form. Thus, bap, a father, obl. bapa, (plur. bapa; moti, a pearl, obl. plur. motya.

Masculine bases ending in u, however, usually retain the u; thus, tsaku, a pen-knife, obl. plur. tsaku. In other bases ending in u the oblique form often also ends in a or va; thus atu, a grandson, obl. natu, nata, and natva. Bhau, a brother, usually forms bhava. Many neuter bases in u, especially all diminutives, add u, plur. ya; thus, kardu, a kid, obl. kardu; plur. karde, obl. kardya. In the Konkan both masculine and neuter u-bases often add va, plur. va; thus, ladu, a cake, obl. ladva.

The oblique singular of feminine nouns ending in i, u, and o is like the base; thus, gadi, a cart, obl. gadi; bayko, a wife, obl. bayko. Old i-stems ending in a silent a take i; thus, ag, fire; obl. agi. Old a-stems ending in a silent a and borrowed words ending in a form the oblique base in e; thus, jibh, tongue, obl. jibhe : katha, a tale, obl. kathe. The same is often the case with feminine u-bases in the Konkan, and feminine i-bases in Konkani. Thus, dzalu, a leech, obl. dzalu and dzalve; rani, a queen, obl. ranye. In female names ending in a the polite oblique form ends in a; thus, Yamuna-kade, to Yamuna. The oblique plural is the nasalised plural base; thus, gadya, carriages, obl. gadya.

In Berar and the Central Provinces the nasalisation of the oblique plural is often dropped and a hi, i or ha may be added. Thus, papa-hi-kade, to the fathers.

An old oblique plural ending in n occurs in compounds such as paisan-paisa, every pice; gharan-ghar, every house.

The usual postpositions will be found in the Skeleton Grammar. It should be noted that the dative is also used to denote the object of transitive verbs when it denotes a person, or, else, when it is emphasised, as is also the case in connected languages; thus, tya-ne Rama-la hakun dile, he drove away Rama; hya naskya ambya-la kay mi khau, what, shall I eat this rotten mango ?

Adjectives.—Adjectives are not inflected unless they end in a, in which case they form their feminine in i, and their neuter in e. The plural then ends in e, fem. ya, nent i, and the oblique form in ya or e; thus tsangla manus, a good man; tsanglya bayka, good women; tsangli mule, good children. The oblique form is used before inflected nouns. The genitive in tsa is such an adjective; thus, bapa-chya gharat, in the father's house; tsanglya mulgyas, to good girls. The suffix tsa is also used to form ordinary adjectives from nouns; thus, ghartsa belonging to the house.

Verbs—Verbs are quoted in the form of the verbal noun ending in ne; thus, karne, to do. The old, present tense, which is used in poetry to denote all times, has developed into a habitual past; thus kari, I used to do. In the negative it expresses unwillingness in the past; thus, to gharat dzai-na, he house-into would-not-go. The imperative and the future are likewise old forms; thus, karin, I shall do; bar, do. All other tenses are formed from participles. The present participle is used in the formation of present tenses, the past participle passive forms the past tense, and a present conjunctive is formed from the future participle passive; thus, mi uthto, I rise; mi uthlo, I rose; mi uthava or mya uthave, I should, or may, rise.

The tenses formed from the present participle are all active, and the subject of the sentence is also the subject of the verb and agrees with the latter in number, person, and gender; thus, to karto, he does; ti karte, she does. This construction is called by Native grammarians the kartari prayoga, the Active construction.

The past participle has a different meaning in intransitive and in transitive verbs. In intransitive verbs its meaning is an active one. Thus, gela, Sanskrit gata, means 'gone,' 'having gone.' The past tense of intransitive verbs is accordingly used in the Active construction; thus, mi uthlo, I rose.

The past participle of transitive verbs is passive. Thus, while vachit means 'reading,' vachila means having been read,' 'read.' The boy reads a book' is mulga pothi vachito, but 'the boy read a book' must be expressed 'a book was read by the boy,' mulgya-ne pothi vachili. Here the verb agrees in number, person, and gender with the object. This construction is called the karmani prayoga, or Passive construction and is used in all cases where the object is uninflected.

In other cases the participle is put in the neuter gender, and the object of the verb is put in the dative. Instead of 'I killed him' we thus say 'a killing was done by me with reference to him,' mya tya-la marile. This is called the bhave prayoga, or Impersonal construction. It is used when the object is inflected, that is, in most cases where the object of a transitive verb is a person. In the Konkan, however, the passive construction is often also used in such cases.

The future participle passive or participle of necessity never has an active sense. Thus, tsalave means 'to be gone,' eundum; and marave, which is to be killed, interficiendum. The tenses formed from this participle of intransitive verbs should accordingly be expected to be used in the impersonal construction; thus, mya uthave, it is to be risen by me, I should rise. A tendency exists, however, to forget the passive force of the participle, and thus we often find the active construction, the participle agreeing in gender, number, and person with the subject. Thus, to uthava, he may, or might, rise; ti uthavi, she may rise, etc. In the case of transitive verbs either the passive or the impersonal construction is used. Thus apradh na karava, sin should not be committed; mya vatsave, I should read.

The preceding remarks will have shown that transitive and intransitive verbs differ in construction in the past tense and in subjunctive. There are, however, same transitive verbs which take the active construction in their past tense. Such verbs are tarne, to pass over; padhne, to study; pavne, to obtain; pine, to drink; bolne, to speak; mhanne, to say; lene, to put on; visarne, to forget; sikne, to learn; samadzne; to understand; harne, to loose, etc. Thus, to bollo, he said; ti dhada sikli, she has learnt her lesson.

The Marathi verb is generally stated to have two conjugations. The first comprises intransitive verbs and such transitives as use the active construction, the second most transitives. Verbs ending in vowels and h form their present tense after the first conjugation. Verbs ending in h form their past tense after the second conjugation, while the past tense of vocalic roots is irregular.

Both conjugations agree in the formation of most tenses. The differ in the following particulars. In the present and past participles and in tenses formed from them an i is inserted between the base and the suffixes in the second conjugation, while verbs following the first insert an a. Thus marit, striking; uthat, arising; marila, struck; uthla, arisen. Similarly the characteristic vowel of the habitual past and the future is i in the second, and e, or, dialectically, a, in the first conjugation. Thus, mi karin, I shall do; mi uthen, or uthan, I shall arise.

The two conjugations are howev r, continually confounded, not only in poetry, but also in the current speech of the people, especially in Berar, tne Central Provinces, and the Konkan.

The terminations of the various persons will be found in the Skeleton Grammar on pp. 30 and f. It should, however, be noted that the difference between the second and third persons has a strong tendency to disappear. The details are as follows.

In the singular the second person usually takes the form of the third person in Berar and the Central Provinces. Thus, tu ahe, thou art; tu gela, thou wentest. In Konkani the second person usually ends in y; thus, tu asay, thou art.

In the plural the second person often has the same termination as the third in Dekhan and Konkani; thus, ahat, Konkani asat, you are; in Sholapur even ahot, we are. In Berar and the Central Provinces the second person plural of the past tense is usually like the third, and in Konkani also the first person plural takes the same form. Thus, Berar gele, you went; they went; Konkani gele, we went, you went they went.

A dialectical termination of the second person plural is v, which is found in a few cases in the Konkan, thus, hav and ha, you are; marsiv, you shall strike.

The third person singular often ends in n in the Konkan, Berar, and the Central Provinces, regularly only in the past tense of transitive verbs. Thus, tya na sangitlan, he said.

The verb substantive has in the Konkan a form different from that used in other districts, a being substituted for o; thus, mi hay instead of mi hoy, I am.

The present tense of finite verbs will be found in the Skeleton Grammar. Instead of the termination e of the first person singular neuter, however, we commonly find o in the Dekhan; thus, mi karito, I (neuter subject) do. The termination te used with a subject of the feminine gender is commonly replaced by ti in the Dekhan and tye in the Konkan. Thus, ti kariti, or karitye, she does.

In the Konkan, Berar, and the Central Provinces, the present tense is very commonly formed by adding the abbreviated verb substantive to the present participle without any change for gender. Thus, Konkan mi soditay, that is sodit-hay, I seek; Berar to, te, yete, he, she, comes; Nagpur te dzatet, they go.

The past and future participles passive are commonly used as verbal nouns. The past participle passive in such cases takes a subject in the nominative, in the same way as when it is used as a past tense. A postposition is afterwards added, the participle being inflected like an ordinary noun. Thus, tum-chi tsakri sodilya-var, your service left-on, on having left your service; tujhi ai varlya-pasun, thy mother dead-from, since your mother's death.

The future participle passive is used in the dative and genitive cases as an infinitive of purpose, a verbal noun, and a gerundive. Thus, bag pahvyas tsala, go to see the garden; vatsavya-che pustak, a book to read; mi maravya-tsa nahi, I am not to die.

The usual verbal nouns will be found in the Skeleton Grammar. Several other dialectical forms occure; thus, tsarava-la, in order to tend (Konkan, Berar, Central Provinces), formed from a base tsarav; kara-le, in order to do; tsaray-le, in order to tend (same localities), form a verbal noun tsar; tsarya-le, in order to tend (Berar), from a verbal noun tsare, and so on.

The conjunctive participle usually ends in un; thus, karun, having done. Besides this there is a form ending in on, corresponding to poetical forms ending in on, oni, oniya. It is occasionally met with all over the Marathi country; thus, nighon, having gone out.

Several forms of the transitive verb are, as has already been pointed out, in reality passive. There is, accordingly no necessity for a separate passive voice. Marathi has further preserved many verbal doublets, the one being intransitive or an old passive, the other an active verb. Thus, galne, to drop; galne, to strain : tsarne, to graze; tsarne, to cause tog raze, to feed : padne, to fall; padne, to fell: tutne, to be broken; todne, to break, etc. In other cases the passive is expressed in a periphrastic way; thus, tya-tsa uddhar hoil, he will be saved. The Hindi passive, formed by adding the verb 'to go, to the past participle passive, is used in business letters, and does not really belong to the language; thus, mi marila dzain, I shall be struck.

The potential verb is formed the future participle passive and is always used in the passive or the impersonal construction. Thus, ma-la uthavte, for me arising can be-done, I can rise.

Old passive forms are pahije, it is wanted; mhanje namely, lit. it is said. Other old passives only occur in poetry.

When the preceding remarks are brone in mind it is hoped that the principal features of the language will be easily understood from the short grammatical sketch which follows.

MARATHI IN THE DEKHAN

The form of Marathi spoken in the Dekhan very closely agrees with the preceding grammatical sketch. It is usually called Desi, that is the language of the Des, the country par excellence.

Territory where spoken

The frontiers within which this form of Marathi is spoken coincide with those given for the whole language towards the north. Towards the west it gradually merges into the Konkan form of the language in the hilly country which separates the Konkan from the Dekhan. It will be shown below that this latter form is largely influenced by Desi along the whole frontier line. On the other hand, similar dialects are also spoken in the Dekhan, thus, for instance, by the Kunbis of Poona. These mixed forms of speech will be dealt with in connection with the Marathi of the Konkan.

Towards the east, Desi merges into Varhadi in Buldana, where it occupies the western part of the district. Farther to the south the frontier line coincides with that given above for Marathi. It is not, however, possible to state how many speakers in Hyderabad should be assigned to Desi and how many to Varhadi.

The Dekhan form of the language is also spoken in the towns of Bijapur, the chief language of which district is Kanarese, and, to some extent, in Dharwar. In Baroda it is the language of the court, and is spoken by the following numbers in the different districts :

Baaroda	35,678
Navsari	10,674
Kadi	3,138
Amreli	2,338
Total	51,828

Number of Speakers

The revised figures for the districts where it is spoken as a vernacular were reported for this Survey as follows :

Bombay Town and Island	80,000
Thana	32,000
Nasik	520,000
Ahmadnagar	804,000
Poona	939,000
Bhor State	153,000
Sholapur	586,000
Akalkot State	26,000
Satara	1,159,500
Satara Agency (State Aundh)	55,000
,, ,, (State Phaltan)	59,500
Belgaum	265,000
Jat State	43,000
Kolhapur State	710,000

Dharwar	44,000
Dharwar (Kulwadi)	3,000
Southern Maratha Jaghira	265,350
Bijapur	27,680
Baroda	51,828
Buldana	270 000
Total	6,093,858

It is probable that much of this total in reality refers to a form of speech similar to that current in the Konkan. We know this to be the case with the Kunbis of Poona. The difference between the two dialects is not, however, so important that any serious disadvantage will arise from the whole total being put down as belonging to Desi.

The Desi form of the language is also to some extent spoken by the educated classes all over the Marathi territory, and by settlers from the Dekhan throughout India. In most cases no detailed figures are available, and the estimates forwarded from Janjira, Kolaba, and Ratnagiri have therefore been put down as belonging to the Konkan form of Marathi, though many of the educated classes speak pure Desi.

The speakers of Marathi in those parts of India where it is not a varnacular have been returned as speaking Marathi, without mention of sub-dialect. The figures will be found in the general introduction to the group. See above p. 2.

Standard Marathi in the Dekhan form, has however, been reported from several districts outside the territory where that dialect is spoken as a vernacular. The details, so far as they could be ascertained, are as follows.

In the Bombay Presidency Standard Marathi has been returned from Kanara and Savanur. The ensuing estimates of the number of speakers have been forwarded by the local authorities,—

Kanara	2,000
Savanur	800
Total	2,800

In Berar, where a slightly different dialect is current in most districts, settlers from the Dekhan have brought the Standard form of the language with them. It has only been returned from Akola and Ellichpur, and the numbers of speakers have been estimated as follows :

Akola	5,000
Ellichpur	250
Total	5,250

One thousand of the speakers in Akola and all in Ellichpur have been returned as speaking 'Dakhini Marathi.' They are stated to be immigrants from the south. The western part of Buldana belongs linguistically to the Dekhan, and the speakers of Marathi in that district have been included in the total given above on p. 32.

In Central India Marathi, in the form which this language assumes in the Dekhan, is the court language in the Indore State, and it is also spoken by Dakhini Brahmans and Marathas in the Sajapur district of Gwalior and in Bhopal. The revised figures are as follows,—

Indore	77,000
Gwalior	1,000
Bhopal	3,300
Total	81,300

In the Central Provinces the language of Poona and surrounding districts is sometimes called Punekari. Almost all the speakers are found to the north of the Satpura plateau, in the Saugor and Narbada territories. These districts once belonged to the Garha-Mandla dynasty of Gonds, but were finally handed over to the Peshwa in 1781 and thence for some time formed part of the Maratha principality of Saugor. Though the Bhonslas of Nagpur afterwards held sway over the country from 1791 till it was annexed by the British in 1818, the Marathi of those districts is still the Dekhan form of the language. The number of speakers has been returned for the use of this survey a follows :

Hoshangabad and Makrai	5,500
Narsinghpur	600
Jubbulpore	2,250
Damoh	1,500
Chanda	25
Total	9,875

By summing up the figures given in the preceding pages we arrive at the following total for the Dekhan form of Marathi.

A. Spoken as a vernacular		6,093,858
B. Spoken abroad—		
Bombay Presidency	2,800	
Berar	5,250	
Central India	81,300	
Central Provinces	9,875	
	99,225	99,225
Total		6,193,083

POONA

The specimens received from Poona very closely agree with the grammatical sketch on pp. 30 and 31. Marathi is spoken all over the district, without great dialectical differences, by the bulk of the population. The two specimens which follow have very few peculiarities. The form mi is used in addition to mya as the case of the agent of the personal pronoun of the first person; thus, mi pap kele ahe, by-me sin done is. Transitive verbs add s in the second person singular of the past tense; thus, tva, or tu, kardu hi dile-nahis, by-thee a-kid even was-not-given-by-thee; mothi jevnaval kelis, a great feast was-made-by-thee, thou gavest a great feast.

There are no instances of the use of the first person neuter and the third person feminine singular of the present tense. These forms end in te, te respectively, in Standard Marathi. Thus, yete, I (neuter) come; yete, she comes. The usual forms in the Dekhan are yeto, I (neuter) come; yeti, she comes.

In all other respects the specimens well represent the language of Marathi literature. A list of Standard Words and Phrases will be found below on pp. 395 and ff.

FREE TRANSLATION OF THE FOREGOING

Narayan Rao tried his best with many representations, but Govinda would not be moved. His mind was only set on learning the medical profession. And in those days there were not sufficient means for studying that science.

He (Narayan Rao) intended to get his only son employed somewhere when he had become educated after learning a little more English. In those days employment was easily got, and when once empolyed promotion was rapid. But Govinda had only one thing in his head. He intended, without learning any more English, to become an apprentice under a doctor in the neighbourhood and soon to be a medical practitioner himself. Narayan Rao even told him to learn a little more English and he promised him that he would than send him to the newly opened medical college, but in vain. At last having determined to satisfy his son he informed Doctor Damodar Rao of the boy's object and requested him to take him under his care. The doctor promised to do so, and teach him on condition that when he became able to practise himself, he should not carry on the business in that village.

ELSEWHERE IN THE DEKHAN

To the north and west of Poona Marathi is spoken as a vernacular by most of the Dekhan Hindus and Musalman Tambolis in Bombay Town and Island, and further in Thana, Nasik, and Ahmadnagar.

Bombay Town and Island is a meeting-place for all the different Marathi sub-dialects. The real home language is the Marathi dialect of the Central and Northern Konkan. The usual Dekhan form of the language is, however, spoken by about 80,000 people. It has no peculiarities of its own, and need not be illustrated by separate specimens.

The principal language of Thana is the dialect of Marathi which, with slight local variations, is spoken from Daman to Rajapur. It will be dealt with below, under the head of Konkan Standard. The usual Dekhan form of Marathi is spoken by Brahmans and other high castes. The number of speakers has been estimated at 32,000.

The principal language of Nasik is Marathi, shading off into Khandesi in the north. This latter language is spoken in the north, on the Khandesh border, where we also find a Bhil dialectd. It has hitherto been classed as a dialect of Marathi. The materials collected for the Linguistic Survey, however, show that it is rather a dialect of Gujarati, and it will therefore be dealt with in connection with that language. See Vol. ix, Part ii.

No specimens have been received of the Marathi dialect of Nasik. It is, however, almost certain that it does not materially differ from the form which that language assumes in the neighbouring Ahmadnagar. Specimens have been forwarded of two border dialects, spoken in the west of the district. They are the so-called Konkani, which is entirely different from Konkani proper, in the north, and Thakri in the south. The former is a Bhil dialect, and the latter will be dealt with in connection with the Marathi spoken in the Central and Northern Konkan. See below pp. 109 and ff. It is very probable that the current Marathi of Nasik, especially in the west, has some of the same characteristics. Above the hills, the difference between the two forms of speech is so unimportant that no inconvenience can possibly arise from the Nasik dialect being classed under the standard form of Marathi current in the Dekhan.

To the South of Nasik lies the district of Ahmadnagar, the principal language of which is Marathi. It is the usual Dekhan form of that language, and it is not necessary to illustrate it further.

Marathi is further spoken all over the Bhor State as the principal language. It is the usual Dekhan form and need not be illustrated by means of a separate speciman. We may only note that t is often added to the second person plural of the past tense of intransitive verbs. Thus, tumhi gelat, you went.

In Sholapur the same form of Marathi is the principal language in the north and the west.

Marathi is also the principal language of the northern part of the Akalkot State and of Pilio and Kurla of the same State. The language of the rest of the State is Kanarese. No specimens have been received, but there is no reason for assuming that the Marathi of Akalkot differs in any important points from that spoken in Sholapur.

The principal language of the Satara District, as also of the States Phaltan and Audh in the Satara agency is Marathi with the usual characteristics of the Dekhan. Of the 59,500 speakers in the Phaltan State about 56,000 are stated to be Kunbis. Their dialect does not, however, differ from that of the rest of the population.

The principal language of Belgaum is Kanarese. In the west of the district the bulk of the population speak Standard Maratihi. The figures returned for the different Talukas are as follows :

Gokak	4,000
Athni	40,000
Chikodi	85,000
Belgaum	82,582
Parasgad	4,000
Khanapur	48,381
Sampgaon	500
Total	264,463, or, in round numbers, 265,000.

The dialect of Belgaum closely agrees with that of Satara. The dental and lingual n are confounded. Thus, we find tya-ne and tya-ne, by him. The numeral 'one' is written yek, a state of affairs which is common in many parts of the territory in which Marathi is a vernacular. The conjunctive participle is sometimes slightly irregular. Thus, nighon, having gone out; yevun, having come. The verb hone, to become, forms the past tense dzahla, where Standard has dzhala. Such discrepancies are, however, not sufficiently important to make it necessary to give any specimen of the dialect.

In Jat and Daphlapur, Marathi is spoken on the north-western border and in a small district half-way between Jat and Karajgi, about Asungi and Jilyal. The dialect closely agrees with that of Satara.

Marathi is also the main language of Kolhapur. The dialect shows all the characteristics of the form of Marathi spoken in Satara. The tendency of pronounce the short a fully seems here to have been carried to an extreme. In other respects the dialect does not differ from that current in neighbouring disricts. The only peculiarity is that a ta is added in the second person plural of the past tense. Thus, ma-la kokaru suddha dile-nahita to-me-a-kid even has-not-been-given-by-you; eka medzavani tumhi det ahata, you have given a feast.

In the Southern Jaghir States Marathi is spoken in the North and East. Specimens have been received from Miraj, Sangli, and Kurundwad. They all exhibit the same form of the language as that current in Satara and neighbouring districts. The second person singular of the past tense of transitive verbs only occasionally adds s. The only other peculiarity which needs be mentioned is the preference shown for the word avagha, all.

Closely related is also he dialect exhibited in the specimens received from Ramdrug.

As in the neighbouring Belgaum dialect the past tense of the verb hone, to become, is dzahla, and not dzhala.

As will have appeared from the preceding remarks Marathi is remarkably uniform all over the Dekhan. In order to illustrate the widespread tendency to pronounce the short a fully it will be sufficient to give the first lines of a version of the Parable of the Prodigal Son which has been received from Kolhapur. The tendency has here been carried to the extreme.

MARATHI

(*State Kolhapur*)

Kona eka monushyasa dona mulage hote. Tyantila dhakata apalya bapasa mhanala, 'baba malamatte-tsa dzo bhaga ma-la yavaya-tsa to ma-la de.' Maga tya-ne apali jinagi tya na vatuna dili. Pudhe phar divasa lotale nahita to-tsa dhakatya ne ti sarva dzama-karuna eka dura-chya desa-chya marga dharila, ani tethe udhalepana-ne vaguna apala aivadza gamavila.

Standard Marathi, in the usual Dekhan form, is also spoken to a great extent in Janjira, Kolaba, and Ratnagiri, and it has influenced the speech of the educated classes all over the Konkan. No estimates are, however, available with regard to the proportion of the population in those districts which speak the Dekhan form of the language, and the reported figures have, therefore, been put down as all belonging to the slightly different form which Marathi assumes in the Central Konkan.

Marathi is also the principal language in the north western portion of the Nizam's territory, which does not fall within the scope of the present Survey.

The Marathi spoken in Berar and the Central Provinces differs in some respects from the form which the language has in the Dekhan, and it will, therefore, be separately dealt with below. The usual Dekhan form is, however, also spoken by a a considerable portion of the population in Buldana.

The District of Buldana is the meeting ground between the two forms of Marathi current in the Dekhan and in Berar respectively. The west of the district belongs to the former, and the east to the latter.

The first few lines of the Parable of the Prodigal Son which follow will show that the current dialect of Western Buldana in no important points differs from the usual Dekhan Standard. We may only note the frequent use of va instead of ani, and. A list of Standard Words and Phrases which has not been reproduced gives the forms amu-che, our; amhi ahont, we are; tumhi ahant, you are. These do not occur in the specimen.

FREE TRANSLATION OF THE FOREGOING

Once upon a time there were a fox and a vixen. One day they were strolling about and came to the house of a tiger. Said the vixen, 'here and nowhere else I will be delivered of my cubs.' When the fox heard this he said, 'O you hussy, when the tiger comes home in the evening he will devour you and your life will be at an end.' The vixen did not listen to him but entered the house of the tiger. The tiger returned in the evening, and the fox, when he had seen this, said to the vixen, 'why are the children crying.' Answered the vixen, 'they ask me to give them some tiger's flesh.' The fox answered, 'have I not already given you some?' When the vixen heard this she said, 'that has all been consumed.' The tiger heard this and ran away thinking that they would kill him. In due time the children grew up. Then the mother went with them to their own house, and they began to live there. When the tiger saw that they were gone he came back to his own house.

KONKAN STANDARD

Marathi is the principal language of all the coast districts of the Bombay Presidency, from Daman in the north to Rajapur in the south. The northern part of this territory from Daman to Umbargaon, is divided between Marathi and Gujarati, and the influence of the latter language is also felt farther south, the vocabulary being, to some extent, Gujarati. This element is not, however, strong.

In the south Marathi gradually develops into Konkani, the connecting links being Sangamesvari and Bankoti on one side, and Kudali on the other.

The Marathi spoken in the territory defined above is closely related to the language of the Dekhan. In some characteristic points, however, it differs, much in the same way as is the case with the Marathi of Berar and the Central Provinces.

It has already been remarked, and it will be shown below, that the dialects spoken by the Kunbis of Poona and the Thakurs of Nasik mainly agree with the Marathi of the Konkan. They will therefore, so far as materials are available, be dealt with in connection with that form of the language.

The Marathi of the Dekhan is the language of the literature and of the Government. Through the gradual spreading of education it more and more influences the dialects of the coast districts, and the specimens received from Kolaba, Janjira, and Ratnagiri, and professing to be written in Sangamadvari, one of the dialects of the Konkan, have proved to be in the usual language of Marathi literature. Most of them represent the speech of the educated classes, which is more or less influenced by the written language all over the Konkan.

Name of the dialect

The Portuguese missionaries, to whom we are indebted for a grammar of the dialect as spoken in Salsette, call it the northern diatect of Konkani. It is not, however, a dialect of Konkani, but a form of speech intermediary between that dialect and the Standard form of Marathi current in the Dekhan. It may conveniently be designated as the Konkan Standard of Marathi. This name cannot lead to confusion. It has long been customary to state that Marathi has two main dialects, one belonging to the Konkan, and the other current in the Dekhan. The Konkan Standard corresponds to the former, It must, however, be borne in mind that this dialect is different from Konkani, the language of the Southern Konkan.

Sub-dialects

The Konkan Standard has been returned under a bewildering mass of different names, partly denoting locality and partly caste or occupation. To the former class belong Bankoti, Damani, Ghati, Maoli and Sangamesvari; to the latter Agri, Bhandari, Dhangari, Karhadi, Kiristav, Koli, Kunbi, Parbhi, and Thakri. These so-called dialects will be separately dealt with below. In this place we shall consider them all as one form of speech, with slight local variations.

Area in which spoken

The Konkan Standard is the principal language of Thana, the Jawhar State, Kolaba, Janjira and the northern part of Ratnagiri. It is spoken by about. . .million people.

3

Development of Marathi Literature

Modern Marathi literature extends roughly over the last 150 years. During the seventy years, from 1875 to 1945, modern literary forms were established and a new orientation and content was given to literature. After 1945, the phase of contemporary literature begins.

In this seminar, our attempt will be to explore the significance of the concept of 'modernity' in the context of contemporary literature. How far this can be done in the context of Marathi literature? This is the specific question which we shall attempt to answer.

At the outset, one may say that 'modernity' as such is a concept which nas no limitations of location, period or language. Since human culture is a process of continuous renewal, 'modernity' and 'tradition' appeer as mutually interlocked aspects of a single life-process. At any and every cross-section of this process these two aspects inevitably coexist. Thus, at every stage of a culture, or of a literature, the most sensitive minds are aware of traditional values as well as of the new challenges of contemporary life. They seek to revivify some traditional values and also try to give a form and a concrete shape to contemporary sensibility. They succeed in giving a new synthesis in which the past and the present emerge together as a new entity, endowed with a new life and vitality. In this sense, every creative thinker and artist is fully aware of contemporary life and is 'modern'.

The words 'modern' and 'contemporary' may also be understood in another sense. By the modern period we may understand a specific period in human history. This period is marked with a breakdown of parochial and national cultures, and we witness a movement towards interaction of cultures on a world scale. In India, this period begins with the impact of Western culture on our traditional culture. In this historical concrete context, the terms 'modern' and 'contemporary' acquire a specific sense. They mean a new awareness of contemporary life, as modified by the East-West contact and conflict. The 'modern' Indian mind has to come to grips with the sensibility, the hopes and fears of the Western mind and also to re-discover the traditional heritage. The modern Indian Artist has to create a new synthesis, keeping himself fully aware of contemporary Indian life, as well as of the contemporary human situation.

In this essay, we will confine ourselves to certain aspects of Marathi literature in the light of considerations above. We will only indicate the central shifts in sensibility, motivating Marathi literature. We will also confine our remarks to Marathi poetry, because poetry as a literary form, may best reveal such shifts.

In Marathi literature, the 'modern' trend reveals the following concrete aspects:

(a) Universalism
(b) Critical approach to life
(c) Man at the centre
(d) Attempt to reach the rhythm of life

We shall briefly explain these aspects, with reference to Marathi literature. In the course of the explanations it will be necessary to refer to Marathi literature belonging to the pre-British period. It will also be necessary to use the concepts of 'religion' and 'culture'. We shall broadly follow the assumptions that 'religion' and 'culture' are neither identical nor mutually contradictory concepts, and further that 'modernity' can only be understood with reference to both the concepts. We will further assume that though social changes do not have a causal and direct effect on literature, still they are vitally relevant to the form and content of literary expression.

The starting point of our discussion may conveniently be the poetry of Keshavasuta (1867-1905). He lived the modest life of a teacher and died young at the age of 39. He did not evoke any appreciable contemporary response, and the full worth of his contribution to modern sensibility is still being assessed in this year of the centenary-celebration of his birth. His total literary output is small, consisting mainly of short poems. However, we have in his poems, a spontaneous, forceful and simple expression of the modern cultural awareness which was slowly shaping the intellectual climate of Maharashtra.

In Maharashtra, the impact of the West was severe and mainly negative. The upper strata of society keenly felt a sense of loss. The political and military power of the Peshwas was vanquished, and the cultural prestige of the upper castes was rudely challenged. The resulting anguish and bitterness created a sense of wounded pride and insularity. This explains why Brahmo Samaj (and the similar movement of Prarthana Samaj) could not take root in Maharashtra. Similarly, the influence of Tagore and Gandhi on our literary and social thinking was very limited. In a way, this explains why Keshavasuta was meagerly understood by his contemporaries and even by his successors.

We shall now proceed to explain the main concepts, in the context of Keshavasuta's poetry.

Universalism : The major contribution of Keshavasuta to modern Marathi literature is that he gave us a new awareness of universalism. His poetry breathes a new atmosphere. The parochial and sectarian 'Hindu' outlook is discarded. Man is understood in a new image. This is the image of Universal Man.

It will be remarked that the image of Universal Man was

ever-present in our ancient tradition. True, but the concept of universalism introduced by Keshavasuta was different in its bearing.

The traditional concept was 'spiritual', in a specific Indian sense. Man was a part of the Cosmos and, in a unique way, he could be identified with, even merged into, the One or the Many. Man, even gods, could be identified with animals and plants; alternatively, man could reach a state of absorption into the Absolute. In this Cosmic universalism, Man as man lost his identity. In fact, to lose one's identity or 'ego' was the highest spiritual achievement for man. It cannot be gainsaid that this spiritual universalism had its own merits and even sublimity. In the poetic utterances of Marathi saints, this universalism finds expression in the form of intense love, universal sympathy and a sense of beautitude and repose in tune with the Infinite. But, then one must clearly distinguish this universalism from the newly-felt universalism of Keshavasuta.

In the new awareness of Keshavasuta, universalism has a purely human context. All men are brothers, because they are men. In a sense, this modern universalism is alienation. Man alienates himself from all other entities; and also from the One, from the mysterious Cosmic Centre. It is this alienation that sets afoot the movement towards further alienation. Not only man, but each man, the individual, gets alienated. Hence the fear, the anguish and the predicament, which finds poignant and painful expression in contemporary post-1945 literature.

In a sense, alienation is the essential first step in all aesthetic creation. The human mind is normally immersed in the environment, as fish in water. We are normally not concious of our natural surroundings, of other people and of ourselves. The artist, however, steps out of this normal sense of identity. He stands alienated. This creates the tension that seeks resolution. The resolution comes through the creative effort; and the work of art embodies a new identification of the artist with his environment. The process of alienation is, therefore, the vital step which triggers the creative process. This, however, is not to be confused with the 'self-alienation' of artists or non-artists who lose their identity and sense of belonging. Such 'self-alienation' can not lead to artistic creativity. It will lead to aesthetic sterility and imitative pseudo-art, which often masquerades as ultra-modern art. The alienation, mentioned in the context of Keshavasuta must be understood as that which is vital to all art and not the sterile self-alienation which is often evident in contemporary Indian literature.

By modern 'universalism' in Marathi literature we mean, therefore, the poet's involvement into the *total human* situation. In the case of Keshavasuta this total involvement has two aspects : (a) the poet alienates himself from the religious, cultural and literary tradition in which he was born. His vision is not restricted by the horizon known to the Marathi tradition. He looks beyond. The Romantic British poets open a new world of beauty and feeling for him. He does not imitate them. This is evident from poems, which have allusive references to poems of the British poets. Even, in such poems Keshavasuta creates a new world of his own. Keshavasuta felt and practised a new universalism, a new awareness, which sought to embrace the aesthetic feeling of all men; and (b) the open all-embracing awareness of Keshavasuta also reached out in another direction : for him poetry is vitally united with graphic and plastic arts. In his poetry, we find, for the first time in Marathi literature, a realization that the poet, the painter and the sculptor are all engaged in the same task of creating artistic symbols.

He also realized that the poet was a seer, a person who gave a quasi-religious message. Poetry was a for him akin to religion, if not religion in its true essence.

Critical approach to life : We shall now pass on from universalism to another aspect of 'modernity' in modern Marathi literature, the deeply entrenched critical approach. In Maharashtra, we had a renaissance of which Justice Ranade (1842-1901) and later on Phule (1827-1890), Agarkar (1856-1895) and others were able pioneers. This renaissance was essentially a movement for religious, social and political 'reform'. The word 'reform' meant not mere superficial modifications, but revaluation. The rise of nationalism, in its extreme militant forms, pushed back the 'reform' movement; partly because some of the reformers were politically moderate, and partly because the extremists were in a sence revivalists.

This entire bankground of renaissance in Maharashtra must be borne in mind when we appraise the 'critical approach' in modern Marathi literature. This approach was, like that of the reformers, critical of tradition. Keshavasuta and Haribhau Apte (1864-1919), the novelists were with the reformers in their crusade against traditional social evils. But, it would be wrong to suppose that these men of literature were merely voicing slogans.

If we again take Keshavasuta as the most significant literary personality, we find that his 'critical approach' invaded not only tradition but also contemporary life. He said that social institutions must change, but added that Man is essentially free. His concept of human freedom implied that Man is his own legislator. Further, he conceived of Man as the 'Child of Nature'. His vision was the vision of 'Heaven on Earth'. Nature, as the hidden reality behind the phenomenal world of human sorrow, was for him the embodiment of Love, Beauty and Happiness. He saw in Nature the promise of Human fulfilment. It was, for the poet, a new religion of priti, charuta and ananda. Thombre, known as Balakavi later developed in his lyrics this poetic devotion to Nature.

This new awareness and quasi-religious faith made him critical, even bitter, against contemporary society. His criticism of tradition goes far beyond the attacks of remormers. In the far-reaching critical approach, he laid the basis for a new outlook on life, in all its manifold aspects. Later on, we find that Dr. S. V. Ketkar (1884-1937), the scholar who compiled the Jnanakosha in Marathi, and V. M. Joshi (1882-1943), the critic and the novelist, followed the lead given by Keshavasuta, and attacked the smug and facile modernism of the educated elite in their novels and essays. Anant Kanekar developed this critical approach, and gave it a new poignancy and content as a result of his acquaintance with Marx, Freud and Russell. The earlier humanism voiced the misery of the oppressed and called for a just social order; Kanekar voiced the self-confidence of the oppressed and their hope that they are the inheritors of the future.

The 'critical' approach to life is one aspect of 'modernity' which helped Marathi literature to develop those characteristics, which have acquired a new significance in contemporary literature. We shall return to this point, when we shall discuss the 'break' with the Keshavasuta tradition by Mardhekar (1910-1956) and by the contemporary writers.

'Universalism' and 'critical approach' are two aspects of 'modernity' which lead us to the central shift, that has given modern Marathi literature its vitality, as well as its contemporary precarious uneasiness. The central shift may be better stated as a shift of the vital centre. Now, Man is the vital centre. Literature has always concerned itself with Man, but now there is a new awareness that Man stands alone facing Nature, not merging with it. Keshavasuta made a final break with the past by asserting that 'Man has created the gods' and that 'Men are not born to conform to any laws; laws have to conform to human aspirations'.

Keshavasuta follows the European Romantic tradition and worships Nature as Mother, Beloved and Divinity. The ancient tradition of worship of Mother Goddess could have easily assimilated this new Romantic worship of Nature. But, Keshavasuta did not succumb to such an assimilation. He severed all ancient moorings. Man was now seen in all his naked weakness and strength, face to face with Nature.

This was a Copernican revolution, a shift of the vital centre. In ancient Sanskrit literature and also in traditional Marathi literature, the moon, the bee, the flower were friends of Man. The simili (upama) reinforced the bond between Man and such natural objects as could embellish the natural beauty of Man. But now such embellishment (alamkara) could only serve as an adjunct. Human and natural qualities were placed side by side; there was neither detachment nor fusion between Man and Nature.

The essential aspect of 'modernity' seems to be a simultaneous detachment and fusion between Man and Nature. As a self-conscious entity, man stands detached from the objects of his contemplation, i. e. from Nature. But as an artist, he seeks to be identified with it. Only such identification can give him an insight into the inner nature of things. This fusion with Nature is not, as in traditional literature, based on the desire for embellishment. It is a true participation in the creative processes of Nature. There is a give-and-take between Man and Nature, and as Coleridge put it 'O Lady! We receive but what we give, and in our life alone does Nature live'.

This new concept of Man at the centre of existence and face to face with the mysteries of Nature and also engaged in a process of participation and fusion with Nature's creativity is the core of 'modernity'.

It is this core that gives contemporary literature its unique orientation. The Romantic optimistic quasi-religious trend, represented ably by Keshavasuta, ran its course and found its own ripeness and exhaustion. Man, however, remained at the centre. Contemporary literature is an exploration of Man, who is at the centre of existence. Existence, however, is now without any internal cohesive force There is no moral order in Nature. Religious faith is dried up. The Romantic ideal of unity between Man and Nature is also found to be empty. This corrosive and self-frustrating awareness is all that is left of the heritage of ancient tradition and modern Romanticism.

This is only the negative side of contemporary literary sensibility. Positively, the artist is groping at the central problem of Man alienated from all other things. The problem of alienation helps to focuss all energies on the contemplation of Man as man. Human finiteness becomes a reality of which the artist becomes painfully aware. One may say that now, as never before in human history, the artist is wholly engaged with man. This is the central fact of contemporary life; and men in all fields of thought, feeling and action are engaged with the naked truth of human finiteness. Human hopes and endeavours have now been brought to earth, shorn of all illusions, nurtured in ancient and modern traditions.

We shall now take up that aspect of 'modernity' which is directly concerned with literature. 'Modernity' may be taken to be a return to the rhythm of language. It is in this sense that Keshavasuta, Apte and other modern Marathi writers ushered in a new era in our literature. They tried to bring both poetry and prose close to the language of common men, expressing their thoughts and feelings in Marathi. The spoken language of ordinary men, in their ordinary business of life, expresses the rhythm of human life. It is this rhythm that these writers tried to catch. This attempt to catch the rhythm of life is the most vital aspect of 'modernity'.

Here a digression may be fruitful. The beginning of Marathi literature in the past, i.e. in the thirteenth century, also marks a similar attempt to break away from the fetters of Sanskrit literary tradition. Sanskrit was the language of scholarly discourse and often employed in the royal court. It was, however, not the spoken language of the people in any part of the country. The literary tradition in Sanskrit was, therefore, elegant, full of embellishments, but far removed from the feelings of men.

The pioneers of Marathi literature could not break through the traditional pattern of faith, but they could boldly affirm the right and duty of the artist to express in the 'vulgar' language of the people. The influence of Jainism and of the Natha Cult had helped them to get over narrow orthodoxy. Cakradhar, the founder of the Mahanubhava Sect, and Jnaneshwar, the author of Bhavarthadipika, wrote in simple Marathi, and thus laid the basis for the future development of Marathi literature. The translation of the Bible in German and later on in other languages was an event which has great significance for European literature; the same may be said about the efforts of these Maratha saints.

In the modern period, Keshavasuta, Apte and others have again tried to revitalize the aesthetic sensibility of the Marathi-speaking people by going to the direct and simple rhythm of the Marathi language. They became conscious, and imparted that consciousness, of the innate beauty and power of the spoken word.

The same may be said about contemporary writers, who are trying to avoid the 'literary' styles and cliches which had accumulated in modern Marathi. During the period 1875-1945, dominated by Keshavasuta, Apte and others, the spoken language did come to be used. But there was a tendency still to keep 'literary' Marathi close to the speech of the learned. Contemporary writers have set their face against this hangover, and have tried to write in a language which is free from ornateness, artificiality and sentimentalism.

So far we have sketched some of the salient aspects of 'modernity', which have shaped our contemporary literature. We may thus briefly summarize the content of 'modernity' in the light of these aspects : universalism, a critical approach to traditional and contemporary life, a firm commitment to keep Man at the centre of attention and finally to reach to the rhythm of language and of life : these are the salient aspects which our writers have inherited from the pioneers.

Mardhekar may be said to be the pioneer of the later phase of the contemporary movement. We may now see how Mardhekar developed these aspects of 'modernity.' He was truly universal by education, temperament and aesthetic sensibility. He was firmly linked up as much with Marathi literary tradition as with European literary movements. Moreover, he was vitally interested in European painting, and this interest has influenced his work, both as an artist and as a critic.

His critical approach was deep and touched the past as well as the present. In fact, his attack on contemporary life was more bitter and penetrating than his criticism of the past.

The picture drawn by him of contemporary life is one of frustration, artificiality and drift.

He also kept the image of Man at the centre of this chaos. Man, both as an individual and as member of a group, feels lost today in meaningless conflicts. Can he redeem himself? Mardhekar has again posed this question, but does not give the answer which Keshavasuta gave. Romantic optimism is rejected as sentimentalism. But the question remains alive at the heart of his poetry. It is this question that one finds recurrently posed by some of our young poets.

Mardhekar gave the contemporary movement a new freedom in expression. He attempted to use spoken Marathi, the language currently spoken in urban centres, to express his new aesthetic feeling. He used images familiar to the industrial population. He often parodies the imagery and diction of the earlier poets. The result was first bewildering, and his poems were either offending to the elite or were not easily understood. But it was realised slowly that he was sincerely trying to catch the rhythm of contemporary life in a corresponding language.

The young poets of today are indebted both to Keshavasuta and Mardhekar, as also to all other writers in verse and prose; but they are not imitating any of these earlier writers. Among them one finds a new urge to experiment with language, imagery and concepts. Literary magazines, like Satyakatha and Abhiruchi played a great part in bringing contemporary poetry to the readers. The new generation of poets find that their creativity is cramped by these magazines. 'Little magazines' have sprung up, which cater to a small group and soon wither away. All this points to a new ferment

Within this experimental and chaotic situation, one may discern the following trends : (1) writers who are experimenting with what they call pre-verbal poetry or 'pure' poetry. Aruna Kolhatkar's 'Horse' is an example of such a poem; (2) others have an affinity to Rilke and other European poets—Dilip Chitre may be said to represent this trend; (3) some poets are deeply concerned with such metaphysical concepts as of Time, Death, etc.—in the poems of Grace, for instance, the concept of Death and its significance assumes a vital role; (4) there are other young writers who belong to the urban poor intellectuals, whose tragic awareness of the present is also tinged with a rebellious faith in the material and spiritual liberation of man—these poets are not all Marxists, but their attitude to life is one of active faith and hope.

In conclusion, one may say that young poets, short story writers, novelists and dramatists are all experimenting with contemporary life and attempting to interpret it in a new way. Their modes of expression are often bewildering to older critics and readers. But, it is important that this spirit of experiment and search must be understood and sustained. It is only then that readers and critics will be able to sift the genuine from the fake. If contemporary young writers are helped to sustain their genuine search for beauty and truth, our literature will be assured its rightful place in world-literature.

> "Mysterious, ineffable Power
> possesses the (Poet's) Being.
> Soul unchained soars into the
> Vaults of Heaven,
> The spectacle frightens the steed
> of Indra.
> Virility of Demons and nobility
> of Gods come to the Poet
> Cosmic Person eagerly communes
> with him.
> Within his heart shines a golden
> flame-disc, its divine rays
> shine forth.
> Gods sharpen their rusty weapons
> on the disc.
> Demons rush into the flame,
> destroyed like moths.
> Cosmos soon gets dissolved,
> absorbed into this Heart.

Words divine emerge and pervade
the ten boundaries of space . . .
This shall be! The Creator then
knows what and how to create.
This Power, Mother of Gods! blesses
the Poet.
No wonder he transcends
all Creation."
—Poet's Inspiration—Keshavasuta

"In the darkness of some unknown moment
I was born. Lord the Witness.
Thereafter, living was groping in darkness.
To this, Existence the Witness.
Hymns to Dawn in Rigveda, the numerous glosses,
and the inspiring teachings in Geeta,
And, the heart-throbs of many souls,
throbs which survived the terrible jaws of Time.
All these filled the sky-towering dome, Experience,
But even this could not support the weight
of my existence.
So, I live! All this Light shines on me.
My existence Darkness-filled.
Even as a leper, by the side of the traffic-laden
Highway, wretchedly struggling with his darkness.
When will this Darkness end? Shall I ever find
the Moment of Illumination?
For that Moment, this faith in living
and this dim awareness of Cosmos."
—My Story—Sateesh Kalasekar

Period : 1928-38

At last I am nearing the end of my literary journey consisting of ten waiting stations and I am now to describe this last halt. For, beyond the final destination (our own time) it is the great future in which no living man can enter though he can peep a little into it from his present position. To speak in plain terms this chapter is to deal with the 10th period of our history consisting of ten years from 1928 to 1938. Evidently this is the last period. But it is not the least one. On the contrary it is the most important period of the whole history of Modern Marathi Literature. For, the literary productions of this period have far excelled those of all the previous periods both in quantity and quality. This will be made clear by the comparative table of all the literary productions of all the 10 periods taken together. The table will be presently given. But let me refer as usual to the causes which have led to this wonderful growth of literature in this last period.

As stated in the previous chapter the Indian agitation against Simon Commission was very intense and reached even the masses of the country. This agitation became far more intensified and aggravated by the reactionary report of the Commission and by the still more reactionary and retrograde recommendations of the Commission. This phenomenon was so unique and astonishing that the British Conservative Government found itself at its wit's end and did not know what to do. But about this time there was a general election in England and the labour party got the majority and so they formed the Government and MacDonald risen from the actual labour ranks became the Prime Minister. This sudden change of Government in England was convenient for British people to effect some change in their Indian Policy. This was cleverly done by Lord Irwin the then Viceroy of India, declaring that the ultimate and inevitable destination of the Indian reforms was 'Dominion Status.' Absence of reference to this in the Simon Report was particularly resented by the Indian public. Further to pacify public opinion it was announced that the problem of Indian reform would be settled in a Round Table Conference to be held in London in which representatives of British India, Indian States (collectively called Indian India) and the British people would sit together and jointly deliberate about the exact form of the future Indian Government. But this first boasted Round Table Conference could not come to any agreement. Unfortunately for India, there came a financial crises in England and in this unexpected emergency the socalled National Government consisting of members from all parties was formed and its first act was to give up the Gold Standard which obliged the Bank of London to give actual gold for its notes. The general election gave support to the National Government but the party in real power was the Conservative party though MacDonald was still the ostensible head. Then came in quick succession the second and the third Round Table Conferences followed by Commissions and Committees for settling the details of Indian Reforms. At the second Round Table Conference Mahatma Gandhi was the only representative sent by the Congress. As the result of these conferences came the famous Government of India Act of 1935. The Congress made up its mind to contest elections and in 7 provinces (later on one more province was added) it got majority and consequently took office. This rapid recital of political events will show how astonishing and kaleidoscopic has been the character of these events. In fact, the whole period of 10 years from 1928 to 1938 has been replete with agitation, excitement and comparative satisfaction on the part of the people. But it may be doubted whether this recital is required in a literary history. This doubt will be set right when it is remembered that such abnormal times and periods lead to wonderful literary activity. For, men and women are moved and affected by such strange events and they naturally give expression to their ideas and feelings in language and these expressions form literature. With these preliminary remarks let me now go to give statistical account of the literary production of this period. As hinted before, I want to give here a comparative table, not of two periods as in previous chapters, but, a table of all the periods of our history. The table speak for itself.

As usual now I begin with the individual accounts of poets.

Durgaprasad Asaram Tivari

Durgaprasad Asaram Tivari is a Pancagaud Kanyakubja Brahmin. His grandfather came from Upper India to Burhanpur and his father Asaram came down further south and settled at Shendurni and took to agriculture for his maintenance. Asaram and his wife were both religious persons with a philosophic temperament. Both of them used to sing religious songs both in Hindi and Marathi. Young Tivari received his first impressions of songs and singing from his parents and soon developed a liking for them. Privately he learnt both English and Gujarati having studied Marathi and Hindi in his school. Tivari's mother died when he was only 8 or 9 years old. But by a kind of prevision she had predicted that Durgaprasad would be a great poet, which proved true. On the death of the mother the family had to suffer trouble and difficulty, the young Tivari had to cook and feed his father and then attend his school. The sole income of the family was the pension of Rs. 4-8-0 per month of his father. But even working under such difficulties the young man passed his second year Training College examination and immediately became a teacher in a government school at Paldhi a village near Shendurni his native place. He being a man of independent and patriotic spirit could not please his superiors and so did not rise in his service to the position he really deserved. Still he served the department for nearly 28 years and retired in 1935. Since that time he has been able to devote all his time and energy to his favourite subject of writing and publishing poetical works.

He wrote his first poem in 1909. In 1916 he published his first collection of poetical pieces under the name 'Kavya Kusumanjali' (Handful of flowers of poems). Then he published off and on his poems in book form. A large number of his poems may be classed as romantic. They were poems from 6 to 7 cantos and described heroic scenes from Rajput and Maratha History. Some of the stories were purely imaginary though they referred to olden times. The principal object of the Poet, besides the normal one of entertaining his readers, was to inspire a spirit of patriotism and of self-sacrifice for the country in the minds of his readers. This lesson he inculcated by the noble examples of his heroes and heroines. From this point of view his poem called 'Sangram Gite' (War songs) is, par excellence, a patriotic poem. Its popularity is very great as is seen from the large number of editions through which the book has passed. The book has also given him substantial amount of money as the deserved prize for his effort.

Tivari has published so far about 18 books small and great. His literary work has given him sufficient money and has enabled him to live in peace and comfort at Jalgaon in his own house about which the poet told me with pardonable pride that 'every brick of his house is the fruit of the sweat of his poetic brow.' His chief and popular books are the following :

1. Sangram Gite (War songs); 2. Mathura Kavya (A poem about Malharrav Holkar); 3. Kavya Kusumanjali (Handful of flowers of poems); 4. Kavya Ratnamala (Garland of gems of poems).

Anandrav Krsnaji Tekade

Anandrav Krsnaji Tekade is a Desasth Kanva Brahmin like Durgaprasad Asaram Tivari. Though his family lived at Mohapa, district Nagpur, Anandrav was born in 1890 at Dhapevadi only three miles from his village at his maternal uncle's house. His vernacular education was done at Dhapevadi and his English education at Nagpur. He studied upto the English 6th standard. About that time he had an attack of typhoid. He survived that severe sickness but became deaf and so his further education came to an end. He had from the beginning no liking for reading or study. Since his physical defect he could not study and hence he did neither learn Sanskrit nor Bengali. So all his knowledge was the result of hearing Kirtans, Puranas and lectures. Those who do not know him intimately do not believe such absence of reading or acquired learning on the part of Anandrav but he positively tells us that it is a fact. This again illustrates how a poet is born and is neither in need of education nor learning. Anandrav was brought up by his maternal uncle towards whom he felt filial love. He does not do any service or profession but has sufficient means to lead a decent life. Now let us turn to his literary activity.

Anandrav left school while he was in the English 6th standard as stated before. As he had nothing else to do he spent his time in seeing dramas staged in the locality. Then he felt that he could write a drama. This happened about the felt that he could write a drama. This happened about the year 1908 or 1909 when Anandrav was 18 or 19 years old.

Since that time he has been writing stray poetical pieces and poems. But his peculiarity lies in this that some lines suggest themselves and then there is a blank before his mind. So it takes months and some times years to complete the rest of the poem. But many of his poems are written at a dash and are completed without interruption or obstacle. For instance, he was pondering over writing a poem on the beautiful white flower called 'Cameli' but the actual performance came about years after. Similarly his fine poem 'Bhavagita' (song of sentiment) was completed after many years. This is really a wonderful peculiarity of the poet. It shows how Tekade's genius is eratic. His drama named 'Madhurmilan' (sweet union) was written in three months but belonging to three years; while his second drama 'Mathura' based on the story of Kamsavadh was written and finished in about three weeks! Anandrav cannot write on subjects suggested to him by others nor can he write in imitation of or on the model of other writers. By his literary activity he has not financially suffered though he has not made much money by it nor does he maintain himself on it.

One interesting incident out of many is worth telling in this short account of Tekade. During the hot season he annually comes to Poona and attends the Vasant Vyakhyanmala (series of spring lectures). Whenever he was present the secretary of the series used to request Tekade to recite a poem of his at the beginning and at the end of a lecture. About fourteen or fifteen years back he was present at the closing lecture of the series when Tatyasaheb Kelkar was president. As usual Tekade was asked to recite his famous poem 'Ha Hinda Des Maza' (This India is My Country). The audience consisted of about 6000 to 7000 people. No sooner did Tekade sing the first few lines of his song than did a small, smart bold boyscout come suddenly on the plat-form and loudly said that that song of Anandrav was the national song (troop song) and so he requested the President to ask the audience to rise and respect the Scout song. Tatyasaheb smiled at the bold request of the Small scout, but himself got up and requested the vast crowd to rise also. Accordingly they did. Then Tekade sang his song from its start. Now to turn to Tekade's literary and poetic work.

He has published so far three collections of his stray poems. The first collection was published in 1923 and contains about 175 poetical pieces. The second collection was published the very next year i.e. 1924. It contains about 105 pieces. The third collection was published in 1928 and contains about 95 pieces. The fourth collection is ready for publication but as yet the author has not been able to publish it, through some difficulty. He also intends to publish a collection of his short stories. As stated before Tekade wrote first two dramas and so they were published before 1923.

The dramas were the first fruits of his genius. Both of them are quite readable dramas depicting noble characters of heroes and heroines. But these dramas still lack the spark of genius which all his later poetical work shows.

From this point of view the three collections mark the maturity of Tekade's genius and poetical power. So it is very difficult to choose better or finer poems of his. Like Govindagraja's poem's Tekade's are all on a high level. Still out of his collections taken together the following may be selected as the best literary effort of Tekade.

1. Mazi Nirasa (my disappointment); 2. Usahkal (Dawn); 3. Anand (joy); 4. Murali (flute); 5. Candrasena; 6. Ram Ganes; 7. Tarile Maharastra; 8. Ha Hinda des Maza (This India is my country); 9. Nisan (flag); 10. Sevatce Magane (The last prayer); 11. Cameli (Cameli creeper); 12. Maza Maharastra (My Maharastra).

Madhav Trimbak Patvardhan alias Madhav Julian

He comes from a Kokanasth family naturalised in Baroda State. His father and mother were persons of peculiar temperaments. They did not pull on well with each other, both of them having conflicting natures. They had 3 sons of whom Madhav was the eldest. But the father, in spite of his excentricities, seems to have taken good care of his sons' education. At any rate all of them became highly educated and took to different professions. The middle son by name Haribhau was given in adoption to a landlord in Kokan and so assumed the name of Gokhale. Though he passed the High Court Pleader's examination he did not practise but looked to his estate and did, in his humble way, contribute to industrial development of the country by starting and managing a small soap factory. Quite recently he has begun to practise. The youngest is an M.B.B.S. He was very ambitious and wanted surgical work in a big place but as he did not find such work in India he ventured to go to Malaya States ann there he is now practising and doing well. Now to come to our poet. He was educated in Baroda College. He had taken Persian and English as his optional subjects both for his B A. and M.A. Examinations a very rare thing for a Deccani student. After passing his M A. Examination he came to Poona being attracted by the educational work of the Fergusson College and the D.E. Society. After the usual period of probation in which he showed his mastery over persian as also his talent as a Marathi poet he was taken up as a life-member. If he had continued a lifemembership of the D.E Society he would have been a valuable asset of the College in the subjects of Marathi and Persian and he himself would have been honoured and respected as a great professor of Marathi and Persian. But soon after Patvardhan's admission into the D E. Society, he came to see that there was a clique in the life-members' body which wanted to keep all power in its own hands. Patvardhan who was a radical reformer and a man of independent spirit did not tolerate the kind of treatment given to him and he began to expose the evil doings of the clique. So he was charged with some indiscreet conduct towards a girl student of the college (nothing really objectionable) and was made to put in his resignation. All this was done behind the back of the Governing Body. When the internal dissensions in the Society came to be known to the Governing Body and its Chairman Sir Mahadev Caubal, he saw the injustice done to Prof. Patvardhan. But it was too late to mend matters. Thus Fergusson College lost a great professor and Prof. Patvardhan lost his honourable position and had to be a rolling stone for some time. Knowing the intrinsic worth of the man, Rajaram College authorities and especially A. B. Latthe the then Diwan of Kolhapur took Prof. Patvardhan as a professor in that college. But curiously he was given principally English teaching work. Since then Professor Patvardhan is leading a quiet life devoting all his spare time and energy to his literary work critical and poetical. Some of his literary works are the following :

1. Virahatarang (waves of separation); 2. Chandoracana (construction of metres); 3. Sudharak (reformer); 4. Svapnaranjan (pleasure of dreams); 5. Pharsi-Marathi Kos (Persian-Marathi dictionary); 6. Umarkhayyam; 7. Draksakanya.

Sankar Kesav Kanetkar alias Girls

Sankar Kesav Kanetkar was born in 1893 at Phatyapur, district Satara. But his parents were living at Rahimatpur, in the same district. Naturally his earlier primary education was done and finished at Rahimatpur, while he learnt at Satara till his fifth English standard. His matriculation schooling was done in the New English School, Poona. Immediately he was taken up as a permanent teacher. While still working as a teacher he did all his college examinations and passed the B. A. examination in 1922 and his M. A. in 1930. So he had to struggle through his higher course with great patience. Being a very efficient teacher he was requested by the Rajasaheb of Phaltan to go there and serve the State as the head-master of the Mudhoji High School, Phaltan. Here he remained for four years. After his return to Poona he was made a professor of Marathi in the Fergusson College, where he is working still. Besides, he is at present an assistant superintendent of the New English School, Poona. Giris (his pet popular name) began to write poetry in 1911 when he was just 18 years of age, his first poem damed 'Brnga' being published in Haribhau Apte's Karamanuk. His first bigger poem named 'Abhagi Kamal' (Unfortunate Kamal) was published in 1924. The theme of the poem is a pathetic tale of the misfortune of a young widow. This pathetic and lyrical poem indicated that Girls was a young promising poet with his imagination just budding forth. 2 Ambarai is on a new subject of a farmer and his family; 3 Kancan Ganga is a poem of sentimental songs; 4 Phalbhar is a similar collection of songs; 5. Kavyakala is a collection of essays about art; 6. Natyachata (dramatic dialogues); 7 Kala (an independent book about art).

Yasvant Dinkar Pendharkar alias Yasvant

Yasvant Dinkar Pendharkar was born at Chaphal in 1899. He passed his University Final Examination in 1918 from the Sangli High School. After completion of his school education he accepted service as a clerk in the Education Department of Bombay Government. He is a valued member of the club. Now to turn to his poetic work. He is a prolific writer publishing his poems in quick succession. His literary works are the following :

1. Mitra-Prem-rahasya (A poem on the death of a friend); 2. Tutalela Tara (A poem on the death of Tilak); 3. Yasvanti (A collection of poems); 4. Indukala (A short poem addressed to a daughter of his friend. Later on this was included in Yasodhan); 5. Yasodhan (Wealth in the form of fame); 6. Bhavamanthan (Churning of sentimental songs); 7. Bandisala (School in a prison—A poetic story of an infantile criminal); 8. Jayamangal (A love poem); 9. Yasogandh (Smell of the utterances of the poet).

Besides the above independently published books Pendharkar has written short stories, criticisms and short essays. He had fondness for poetry. He was particularly influenced by Sadhudas of Sangli. All his poems are published under the name 'Yasvant'. Only one collection of poems named 'Tutalela Tara' was published under the name 'Tarakanath'. The above list will show how Yasvant wields a facile and fascinating pen. His literary production during a short period is very great. He has a fertile imagination and has made use of it in having new metres, new constructions, and new forms of literature. Yasvant began the practice of reciting poems as opposed to singing with musical instruments before the public. This novel practice was at first derided. It was thought that the poets themselves should not condescend to recite their poems. But Yasvant and his friends boldly went on with their practice and people began gradually to appreciate it, admire it, and derive real pleasure from hearing such recital. These recitations of poems have become now-a-days a regular part of social and school gatherings. Yasvant is a middle aged man. Still his imagination has neither waned nor shows signs of waning. So he may in time produce more and finer poetry. As it is, Yasvant occupies a high position in the literary world. He has caught the ear of the youths of Maharashtra. The subjects of his poems appeal to a varied class of people as he has tried to depict the experiences, the difficulties and sorrows of the lower strata of society. This is an entirely new and novel subject of poetry and so appeals to both the educated and the half-educated people.

The above mentioned three poets had already and independently made their name as poets. But they are also members of Ravikiran Mandal, to an account of which I must now turn. But it would not be appropriate and right if I do not here refer to another Mandal and its members. For it claims priority in time.

The founders of this Mandal were Messrs. Atre, Kanetkar, Sinde (Arvind) and Kelkar (Adnyatvasi). The Mandal was named Sarada Mandal and its object was to meet periodically and discuss matters about literature and art. But as the Mandal drifted from its original object and as there was no limit to nor any conditions to the admission of members Messrs. Atre and Kanetkar left the Mandal. So only two member-founders remain to be mentioned.

Bhaskar Nanaji Sinde

Bhaskar Nanaji Sinde is a Maratha by caste. He is an inhabitant of Satara, having a house of his own there. He was born at Satara in 1894, his father being a pleader there. Bhaskarrav became an undergraduate but on account of domestic difficulties could not continue his college course. He joined the Co-operative Department where he is still working. As to his literary work it is of a varied nature though it is almost all poetical. The peculiarity of his poetry is that it is mainly historical. He had the practice of writing verses on the Autumn of each passing year and of course such annual accounts were bound to be different from each other. These accounts of Bhaskarrav are a fine and fascinating reading. His other stray poems are published in Manoranjan, Citramayajagat and other Magazines. But unfortunately they have not been independently and separately published in a collected form and so they are lying buried and unnoticed in the columns of Magazines. But they are all worth-reading and it would be a boon to lovers of literature if either the writer himself or a publisher comes forward to publish the collection of poems of Arvind (pseudonym) under which he wrote all his poems.

Dinkar Gangadhar Kelkar

The last of the founders of Sarada Mandal is Dinkar Gangadhar Kelkar. He is an entirely Poona man—born, brought up and educated in Poona. He lives permanently in a house of his own and has a spectacles shop. He is a well-to-do man and has the hobby of collecting historical pictures and other relics. For a private individual his collection is wonderful and is worth a visit. Now as to Dinkarpant's literary work he was fond of writing poems from his early age. But he did not publish anything till his poetical genius was matured. Then he began to write under the pseudonym 'Adnyatnad' and 'Adnyatvasi.' His poems are published in a collected form under the name 'Adnyatvasici Kavita.' The poems are on varied subjects. But the speciality of Dinkarrav is that most of his poems are historical and are calculated to inculcate patriotism upon the young and the old. Kelkar is comparatively a young man still and so may come to write more poems. But there does not seem to be any prospect of it as he seems to be wholly absorbed in collecting historical pictures.

Let me now go to an account of the second Mandal that arose out of Sarada Mandal. The initiative was taken by Messrs. Patvardhan, Kanetkar and Pendharkar and four new members with the addition of the wife of one member were admitted to the Mandal. They used to meet every Sunday at the house of members by turn and there they discussed and talked subjects bearing on art and literature. The members of the Mandal were all persons of radical and reformed views on social matters. They had their definite ideals of conduct.

As the club met on Sunday it came to be joculourly called 'Sun-tea club' (club that met on Sundays for tea). As time passed these young men thought of publishing their literary productions. They began to hunt for a good and striking name. One of the members saw that there were 7 constant members, with the wife of one member in addition; so he suggested that the club be named 'Ravikiran Mandal' (Sun Rays Association) and the Symbol upon the publications of the club should be the constallation of 7 stars with Arundhati as the 8th by-star. This name and the symbol at once appealed to all the members and the name and the symbol were immediately adopted. Soon the Mandal actually began publishing results of their literary labours.

Its first publication named 'Kiran' (Ray) came out in 1923. It was severely criticised by no less a critic than Balkrsna Anant Bhide in the Vividhadnyanvistar. This criticism, though severe and calculated to damp the energies of the young poets, gave the unknown club a great publicity—a great advantage to a new club and its activities. Of course the club immediately published a rejoinder, defending its views and the new forms of poetry introduced by it. Without being depressed by hostile criticism, the club again came before the public with a new book called 'Usa' (Dawn.) This little book was very well received by the public and Mr. Bhide who denounced the first work came forward to praise and admire this book. Thus the young club came to realise the truth of the maxim "those who came to scoff remained to pray". By this incident the faith of the young poets in their own powers was enhanced and from that time their publications went on briskly and the club has published till now 26 books small and great. Besides these joint publications individual members have separately published some books both prose and poetical on their own account and in their own name. Let me now proceed to give brief information of the members and their literary work. But as I have already given the accounts of Messrs. Patvardhan, Kanetkar and Pendharkar, I shall now confine myself to the remaining five members.

Sankar Kasinath Garge alias Divakar

Sankar Kasinath Garge was a Yajurvedi Brahmin. Divakar was the surname of his first family, he having been given in adoption in Garge family and thus getting his second surname 'Garge'. He was born in 1889 at Poona. His Marathi and English education was done at the famous Nutan Marathi Vidyalaya. He passed his School Final Examination in 1907. Though he had a keen desire; like Gadkari, for higher education he could not pursue it on account of financial difficulties of the family. So he had to seek any job and anywhere he could find. Fortunately for him he got a clerk's post in the office of the Assistant Superintendent of Police. After the usual period of probation he was made permanent. After doing his official duties Divakar spent all his time in reading, in seeing dramatic performances and in visiting friends like Prof. Vasudevrav Patvardhan and Annasaheb Karkhanis. Divakar used to keep a diary recording events from day to day. Extracts from it will throw new light on many incidents of his life as also of contemporary persons and their doings. Any rich admirer of Divakar or an enterprising publisher should do this work, a man with a literary taste doing the work of selection of extracts. What a voracious reader Divakar was may be seen from his diary of 31 December 1910. 'This year I read quite well. The pages of all books read reached the total of 17,752 pages'. At first view the statement appears to be an exaggerated one. But if we distribute the total pages over the days of the year, the rate of reading appears quite feasible and within the power of an average man. Only one has to be regular in his habits and must devote some time every day to reading. Divakar's rate works out to be about 48 pages a day i.e. on an average three to four hour's reading.

Divakar's reading during the year 1910 consisted of the following authors and their works: Shakespeare, Mary Corelli, Conandoil, Mrs. Henry Wood, De Quincey, Tennyson, Wilcox and Molier. Besides these English authors he read some marathi dramas, novels and biographies. He was a great friend of Gadkari. Mr. Ekbote *altas* 'Sahakari Krsna' who was in the same office was equally his friend. It was at his suggestion that Divakar read Tolstoy's books. His remarks about the performances of dramas of his contemporaries are interesting and show his power of true appreciation of literature. About both Yasvantrav Tipnis' drama Kamala as also about Mama Varerkar' 'Kunja-Vihari' Divakar writes in his diary that the dramas made a poor impression. On the 7th of April 1911 he notes down that he completed his reading of the whole of Shakespeare.

It was after such preparation that Divakar began his literary career. He commenced writing, 'Rangel Rangarav' an adaptation from 'Yorkshire Tragedy.' He tried to adapt a famous book of a famous poet i.e. Goethe's 'Faust' and gave it an appropriate and significant name 'Pandit Vidyadhar' (Professor of Learning). Similarly he began to write novels by name 'Maha Sarpa' (Great serpent), 'Sareca Vilaksan' (Everything strange). By the way this was the very name adopted by Prof. Patvardhan for his unfinished novel. But the fate of both these projected novels has been the same i.e. they were not destined to see the light of day. He also began writing a drama named 'Sukh Ki Dukhkh' (Happiness or Sorrow). Why Divakar was not able to finish and publish these literary works of his is not known. Perhaps a careful and minute study of his diaries will throw light on this mystery. It was after these half-finished literary efforts that Divakar began to write his mature and permanent new type of literature i.e. 'Natya-Chata' (Dramatic dialogues and monologues). But by such excessive reading and writing within a short period of about two years Divakar so spoiled his eyes that he was declared to be unfit for service by the Police Department, and he had to resign his service in 1912. Then for some time he served the "Depressed Classes Mission" School of Vitthalrav Sinde. But finally he took up service in the Nutan Marathi Vidyalaya where he remained till his premature death in 1931 at the age of 43.

Now to turn to Divakar's literary work. Considering his vast reading, his literary preparation and the dramatic power shown in his actual work one feels that the actual output of his literature is very small. His sole book is one named 'Natya-Chata (Dramatic dialogues and monologues). It consists of a single volume of dramatic dialogues, monologues and short dramas numbering in all 60 pieces. His hard domestic life and his exacting official work in the Police Department probably left him very little leisure. His modest and diffident nature explains why Divakar was unable to write more than he actually did. An incident about his modesty is worth telling.

After Divakar wrote a number of dramatic pieces he went to Tatyasaheb Kelkar, the editor of the Kesari with a view to request him to publish a few of them and pay him some remuneration. Tatyasaheb was very busy then and told Divakar to come after three or four days. Divakar repeated his request very modestly and said that as the pieces were very short he could read a few of them in no time. Tatyasaheb consented to hear them. When Divakar read one or two pieces Tatyasaheb was so enamoured by the pieces and the novel style in which they were written that he listened to them for over an hour and agreed not only to print a few of them in the next issues of Kesari but to pay for them also. With a gladdened heart Divakar went to another literary luminary of Poona i. e. Haribhau Apte and made a similar request to him. Haribhau heard Divakar's performance with his little daughter and a lady friend of his by his side. When Divakar read his piece, named, 'Wordsworthce Phulpakharu (Words-worth's flower bird), the little daughter of Haribhau began to laugh through joy. Haribhau too was delighted to hear the fine and fascinating piece and immediately agreed to publish some of the pieces and pay for them. These interesting interviews of Divakar with two contemporary literary luminaries of Poona show how they valued his unique and new type of literature. In the separately published volume many of his pieces already published and paid for do not seem to be included. One would have certainly liked to read the piece which delighted the daughter and her father. Another literary work though of lesser value was the preparation of the Press Copy of the poems of Kesavsut for Haribhau. But Divakar did not like the delay which Haribhau made in its publication. By the publication of the novel literary pieces Divakar became known to his contemporaries and with many of them he formed a closer frienship. So in their company he passed his days happily and thereby he was enabled to bear with patience his domestic calamities i. e. the sad deaths of his natural mother, his adoped mother, his wife and lastly his son. The only tie that bound him to life was his daughter who survived him. But successive domestic calamities accompanied by the hard life he had to lead throughout his career, must have unconsciously and unknown to himself told upon his health and must have hastened his death though the immediate cause was the cold fever he had. As stated before the cruel hand of death carried him off to the great sorrow of his friends and the lovers of Marathi literature.

Divakar was an ideal man in every respect. He was a conscientious teacher doing his work with great zeal and efficiency. He was a kind friend and was ever ready to give his quota to good causes though he was not blessed with plenty of money. He was extremely regular in his conduct, moderate in his diet and neat and tidy in his living. His little lodging was a model for fine and delightful setting and arrangement. His collection of books was choice and well kept in his simple cupboards. He did not allow anybody to take away books from his little library. It was a misfortune of the country and its people that a fine gentleman and a finer writer like Divakar died so prematurely.

Vitthal Dattatraya Ghate

After the premature death of Divakar, Vitthal Dattatraya Ghate was selected to fill the vacancy. Ghate is a Maratha by caste. He is a son of the famous poet Dattopant Ghate whose poems are published under the name 'Dattaci Kavita.' After completing his education and passing his B.A., M.A. and B.T. examinations all in the first class he joined the education department and rapidly rose to be a Deputy Educational Inspector. Then he got an opportunity to go to England for securing Teacher's Diploma and after about nine months' stay there and after getting the diploma he returned home with his prospects in service greately improved. So soon after his return he was made the Educational Inspector of the Bombay and Southern Divisions of the Bombay Presidency, a post he is still holding. Mr. Ghate is a sociable and genial man of wide sympathies and liberal views. He is a competent officer doing his duty efficiently and consicientiously. He is too busy to devote time and energy to much literary work. Still he has to his credit some books. His special subject is History and he attained such fame in that subject that the Oxford University has requested him so write a book on it.

The following is a list of Ghate's books :

1. Natyarup Maharastra (Dramatised history of Maharastra); 2. Nana desatil nana loka (Many people of many lands); 3. Marathyancya Gosti; 4. Stray poems published in the Ravikiran Mandal seriesof books. All his books indicate

his learning, wide reading and varied experience got by travelling. They are all of considerable literary merit.

Gajanan Trimbak Madkholkar

The next member of the Mandal is Gajanan Trimbak Madkholkar. Gajanan was born and educated in Bombay upto the Matriculation examination, his father being a petty shop-keeper there. From his young age he had a passion for reading and had particularly studied Sanskrit literature. He read old poetry also. Thus he equipped himself for his literary work. He came to Poona and was given work on the staff of Kesari weekly. From there he went to Dnyanprakas as an assistant editor of the Daily. It was Madkholkar who introduced the weekly column in Dnyanprakas for literary criticism under the interesting and fascinating name 'Kavya-Sastra-Vinod (Poetry, Science and Humour). This became soon a very popular feature of Dnyanprakas Daily. It has been continued since then. From Poona Madkholkar went to Nagpur and became an assistant editor of Maharastra, a weekly newspaper of Nationalistic policy and ideal. He is still occupying that position. On account of the chief editor Ogale's chronic illness Madkholkar is now practically the chief editor. As to Madkholkar's literary activity, he is par excellence a literary critic and was required to do that kind of work in Dnyanprakas in its newly introduced columns of 'Kavya-Sastra-Vinod'. Moreover, he has constantly to write on current topics. He also writes now and then for Magazines and their special numbers. Besides these stray notes and articles his independent books in the different kinds of literature are the following :

1. Collection of poems; 2. Muktatma (a novel); 2. Bhangalele Deul (a novel); 4. Sap (a novel); 5. Gosti (Short stories); 6. Sukrace Candane (A short story); 7. Adhunik Kavipancak; 8. Visnu Krsna Ciplunkar; 9. Vilapika (An elegy); 10. Vangamay-vilas (literary amusement).

Dattatraya Laksman Gokhale

Sixth member of the club is Dattatraya Laksman Gokhale. He comes from a Kokanasth family of Haripur near Sangli. His father who was a well-to-do man of the place and had property there died in the first terrible attack of plague at Haripur in 1897-98 in which half the population of the town famous for old learning died and the town became a deserted village. So young Dattatraya was brought up by his mother. He was educated till his Matriculation at Sangli. Then he went to Poona and joined the Fergusson College. He had a brilliant University career passing his B.A. and M.A. examinations in the first class with English and Marathi as his optional subjects. Then he worked as a lecturer in the Fergusson College, Poona, and later on in the Willingdon College, Sangli. After serving 2 or 3 years in these institutions he joined Sangli State service and was made the Head Master of the Sangli High School. After some years he rose to be the Inspector of Schools in the State a position which he now holds. Mr. Gokhale is a very successful teacher. In order that he might be a better qualified teacher and be more useful to the State he was sent to Bombay for B. T. Degree. There also he won golden opinion both from his professors and fellow-students and passed the B.T. Examination, topping the list of successful candidates. Annasaheb (as he is familiarly called by his) friends) Gokhale is a sociable man with a fine temperament. His wife is a graduate and is working as a teacher in the Girls High School, Sangli.

Annasaheb is the least prolific of the members of the Ravikiran Mandal. He has some poetic talent but he has more critical powers. However, they have remained, till now at any rate, quite dormant and unused for want of time and through Annasaheb's easy-going nature.

Sridhar Balkrsna Ranade
and
Mrs. Manoramabai Ranade

The last but not the least member of the Ravikiran Mandal is Sridhar Balkrsna Ranade. His father was a leading pleader of Islampur, district Satara. Sridhar is the eldest son of Balkrsnapant. His early education was partly done at Islampur and partly at his maternal grand-father's place in Central Provinces. But for his higher education he came to Poona and joined the Fergusson College and passed his B. Sc. Examination. Then he joined the Agricultural College and passed his B. Ag. and M. Ag. Examinations. Then he took up Government Service in the Educational Department and was at first appointed a lecturer in Science. Later on he became a professor in the Islamia College where he is still working. Sridharpant is a quiet and taciturn man of few words. But he is very observant and is a man of feeling. He married the daughter of Balvantrav Hivargavkar of Ahmednagar. She was herself a graduate and later on passed her M. A. Examination. Like Ranade she was a poet too. As stated before both of them were members of the Ravikiran Mandal. Unfortunately Manoramabai died very prematurely to the great sorrow of her friends and relatives.

Now to speak about their literary activities. Sridharpant had fondness for Marathi literature though he had taken science as his special subject and though he had to specialise in it as a professor in a College. He published his first poem named 'Mani' (Female cat) in 1911 when he was 18 years of age. Thence-forward he has been publishing his poetical pieces under the name Sridhar in several magazines such as Manoranjan, Udyan and Lokamitra. Mis separate and independent poem is named 'Kalacya Dadhetun' (From the jaws of death). Sridharpant had such a severe sickness that he was almost on his death-bed. He miraculously escaped from the jaws of death, thereby getting as it were a second birth His severe suffering in his deadly sickness, his excited feelings while on his death-bed and lastly his ravings and dreamy thoughts about life present and future—all these are so vividly, so realistically and so feelingly described that one can not help sharing the feelings of the sufferer. This poem occupies a very high place in Marathi literature. Sridharpant is still comparatively young and his friends expect him to produce greater and finer poetic work from his high class genius.

Manoramabai was born in 1896 at Poona. All her education was done there. She passed her B. A. and M. A. Examinations from the Fergusson College, Poona. As stated before she was married to Sridharpant. They came to know each other while they were students in the Fergusson College. A mutual liking and attractian developed into love leading to wedlock. Manoramabai's stray poems were published in Manoranjan and Udyan under the names Gopikatanaya and Kumari Dvarakabai. Her poems show her high imagination. Her poetic composition was the fruit of maturity and enlightenment. Her thoughts and ideas were interesting and pleasant and her language was sweet and melodious. It is a misfortune of the country that she died so prematurely. It is heard that she has left a goodly amount of literary work behind her. The public expects that her husband would come forward and bring out a complete edition of her published and unpublished poems. It would be a fitting memorial to his dear wife. Manoramabai died in 1926 when she was just 30 years of age.

L. R. Despande

1. Dipavalici Bhet (1027); 2. Saprem Bhet (1927); 3. Sadha Bodh (1928); 4. Samarthya Milava (1928); 5. Ha Hindusthanca Dos (1928).

Manhoman

1. Uddhar (1933); 2. Sankhadhvani or Bomba-bomb and parodies (1933); Bimba (1934); 4. Sunit Ganga (1934).

V. G. Govekar

1. Atmanubhav—poem (1932); 2. Prasnottar Malika (1932); 3. Bodhamrt (1929); 4. Satik Bodh Nauka (1929).

V. G. Maydev

Mr. Maydev is one of the educated youngmen who were attracted by the noble and self-sacrificing work of Prof.

Annasaheb Karve in the cause of women's education. So, after completing his education at the Fergusson College Maydev joined Karve's University and works there as a Professor in the Women's College at Erandavana. But latterly after the sad and sudden death of Prof. Ciplunkar, Maydev has taken the begging bowl of the Institutions and spends his time in moving about and collecting subscriptions for the growing needs of the University. He finds that Bombay is the fruitful field for his uphill task.

His literary works are these:

1. Garibanci Gosta (1931); 2. Bhavataranga (1932); 3. Sisugita (1936); 4. Abhinav Gita; 5. Bhave Nirzar.

J. B. Josi

1. Pancaratna Gita (1931); 2. Timaji Makadace Caritra; 3. Ramaci Pade (1932); 4. Ram Mantraca Slok (1932);

P. V. Pathak

1. Rupavaril Abhanga (1932); 2. Krsnabodh (1931); 3. Sri Sant Damaji (1928); 4. Sri Sant Goroba (1928).

G. R. Sane

1. Bayakanci Navi Gani, Parts 1 and 2 (1931); 2. Bharatvarsaca Dharmik Itihas, Part 1 (1930); 3. Bharatiya Sangram (1928).

Y. R. Ksirsagar

1. Atmadnyani Pade, Parts I and II (1928); 2. Ekatari Bhajan; 3. Ramayan Puspagumpha (1928).

Sitarambova Srigondekar

1. Brahman Dharmace Slok (1930); 2. Cahapuran (1930).

D. A. Saraf

1. Sukarambha Samvad or Cigar and its Temptation (1931); 2. Dattakinkaraci Kavita (1931).

Sankarrav Kalburgekar

1. Rani Laksmibainca Povada (1931); 2. Sri Chatrapati Sivaji Maharajana Povada (1931).

N. D. Josi

1. Sri Datta Kavan (1931); 2. Datta Gita (1921).

V. V. Gokhale

1. Pancaratna Gita (1932); 2. Sacitra Pandhari Mahatmya (1932).

T. G. Gharpure

1. Subhedaraci Sun—poem (1934); 2. Lileca Samsar (1933).

Srikrsna Vaman Gadgil

Gadgil was born in 1898 at Deglur, district Nanded, Nizam's territory. He was educated upto the Inter Arts examination of the Madras University. After his education was over he joined the Account Department of Nizam's State and rose to be an assistant Accountant, a position he is still holding.

Now as to his literary activity it is considerable. He has written over 300 poetical pieces. He has written half a dozen articles under the pseudonym 'Vikrant.'

1. Phule Umalanyapurvi—poem (1936); Mazi Phule, Part 1 (1928).

K. B. Dhavale

1. Jaica Kunja (songs) 1936); 2. Malatict Mangalagaur (1932).

Pandit Atmaram

1. Prarthana Pustak (1930); 2. Rani Laksmibai (1929).

Mrs. Annapurnabai Desai

1. Strigitaratna Manjusa (1932).

A. R. Despande

1. Phulavat (1932).

D.G. Diksit alias Chandrakant

1. Gulab Gita (1934).

P.S. Gore

1. Bobade Bol (1932).

I now come to the class of dramatists of this period.

In this period there are 130 dramatists of whom about 80 writers have written only one drama. The remaining 50 writers have written more than one drama and done some other literary work. Two figures that stand out prominently in this period are Mama Varerkar and P.K. Atre. Of these Mamasaheb is older than Atre. Both of them are still active in their literary productions. But Atre seems to be a better favourite of the younger generation. Both of them have each written more than half a dozen dramas and still they are writing and in time may rival English Dramatists in this matter.

Bhargav Vitthal Varerkar alias Mama Varerkar

Varerkar has, like Acyutrav Kolatkar, had a chequered life and the literary genius of both matured rather late. Mamasaheb has had no University education but in fact he prides himself upon not having received it. So after completing his school education he took up Government service in the Postal Department. If he had continued in that service, perhaps his literary genius might have remained dormant and unused. But Varerkar took a prominent part in the general Postal Strike of the year 1913. His services were permanently dispensed with and Varerkar had to look out for another career. He tried his hand at writing dramas. His first attempt was a Sangit drama called, 'Kunjavihari.' It was moderately successful. His second drama had rather a long name, 'Haca Mulaca Bap', but it turned out a very successful light comedy on the stage. Like Deval's 'Sarada' which dealt with the social evil of child marriage Varerkar's comedy dealt with the social evil of exhorbitant dowry extracted by miserly parents of sons from fathers of daughters. About this evil there was practically unanimity of opinion among the sensible people orthodox or heterodox. But Varerkar's comedy being full of humorous and satirical scenes moved the audience to gusts of laughter now and then.

After this successful attempt Varerkar came to have confidence in his literary power and so he produced drama after drama in quick succession. Some of them were operas and not prose comedies. Some of these dramas tackled controversial social topics of radical nature. So they did not prove as successful as his first drama. In fact some of them proved total failures and dramatic companies had to stop staging them. Then Varerkar turned to novel writing. Here also the same thing happened. Some of his novels attained popularity at once but others fell flat. But there is no doubt that Varerkar is a versatile writer with a facile pen. He has also a spark of genius in him and has developed an attractive and humorous style of writing both in his dramas and novels. As every literary writer has occasions to compose poems and verses Mamasaheb has to be a bit of poet too. So he too may be called a poet though that is not his favourite line. He is a literary critic also. He is inordinately proud of the literary productions of Bombay writers and is very severe against Poona writers and particularly against what he calls the Kesari clique. In writing about it he loses all sense of moderation and goes to the length of abusing it. Inspite of these defects Varerkar is one of the great writers of the present generation. His temper is genial and his conversation is witty and lively. His literary vigour has not abated as yet and so he may produce some more literary work.

Some of his books are the following :

1. Sonyaca Kalas; 2. Svayamsevak; 3. Sattece Gulam; 4. Haca Mulaca Bap; 5. Turungacya Darat;

6. Kunjavihari; 7. Vidhava Kumari; 8. Godu Gokhale; 9. Dhavata Dhota; 10. Saungadi (Cinema-story); 11. Svairasancar—stories; 12. Aghat; 13. Venu Velankar; 14. Umalati Kali.

Prahlad Kesav Atre alias Kesavkumar

Pralhad Kesav Atre was born in 1898 at Sasvad, district Poona. He was educated in Poona Native Institution (Bhave's old school). He received his higher education in the Fergusson College Poona and passed his B.A. examination in 1927. In 1928 he found an opportunity to go to England for acquiring Teacher's diploma. After his return home he was made the permanent Principal of the Camp Education Society's High School, though before going to England he was working as the head of the School. Principal Atre is a versatile and prolific writer, writing dramas, cinema stories, poems, satires, school books, short stories and what not! From his very young age he had fondness for writing poetry on the objects that interested him and on any other thing that struck him. When he is in a mood to write he writes fast and without loss of time. He is full of fancy and imagination and with his varied experience both at home and abroad he has widened his mind. He is a radical reformer in social matters. He is equally keen and interested in politics. though as the head of a High School particularly in a part of Poona which is full of merchants of the non-Brahmin class and of different religions Atre has to be careful and cautious in his utterances. He has made ample money by his writings, a rare thing still in Maharashtra. His writings as stated above come under three classes—(1) dramas; (2) cinema stories and (3) poems. But so far he has chiefly confined himself to dramas. As a critic and appreciator of literature he has written much in different magazines.

His writings are the following :

1. Gurudaksina; 2. Virvancana; 3. Sastanganamaskar; 4. Bhramaca Bhopala; 5. Gharabaher; 6. Lagnaci Bedi; 7. Vande Bharatam; 8. Paraca Kavla; 8. Mi Ubha Ahe;

10. Dharmavir; 11. Beguman; 12. Premavir; 13. Brahmacari; 14. Brandici Batli; 15. Zenduci Phule; 16. Gitaganga; 17. Akarava Avatar; 18. Miscellaneous writings and articles.

Another prolific dramatist almost rivalling Messrs. Atre and Varerkar is M.N. Josi :

1. Sangit Giranivala (1929); 2. Sthanik Svarajya (1929); 3. Varhadaca Patil (1929); 4. Sangit Punarjanma (1932); 5. Sangit Vasikaran (1932); 6. Visvavaicitrya (1932); 7. Paisaca Paisa (1935); 8. Sangit Vinod.

D.G. Sarolkar

1. Rangel Rajkumar (1928); 2. Dehant Prayascitta (1928); 3. Subhamangal (1929); 4. Samrataca Sud (1930); 5. Bharatmateci Sresthata (1930); 6. Rajanca Raja (1931); 7. Padavidhar (1922).

S.A. Sukla

1. Sadhvi Mirabai (1930); 2. Saksatkar (1930); 3. Svargavar Svari (1931); 4. Satyagrahi (1933).

V.V. Vaidya

1. Sangit Gomateca Vijay (1929); 2. Sangit Svarthatyag (1929); 3. Svatantrya Vir (1930); 4. Gomantak Varnan (1930); 5. Kranti Yuga (1931).

G.K. Phatak

1. Jayajayakar (1927); 2. Desaca Dnyanadip (1928); 3. Pantanci Sun (1929); 4. Natyachata (farces) (1929); 5. Kurhad (Novel) (1929).

K.G. Pandit

K.G. Pandit was born in 1903 at Poona His primary and secondary education was done in the Wilson High School, and then he joined the Wilson College, Bombay. He successively and successfully passed his B.A. examination in

1924 and M.A. in 1926. Immediately he came to Poona and became a professor of English in the Fergusson College and soon became a life-member of the D.E. Society. Besides being a professor of English he is doing the work of the superintendent of the Navin Marathi Shala of the D.E. Society. He takes a keen interest in teaching the little boys and is successfully managing the School. He made many a useful change in the method of teaching and made the boys take greater and greater interest in games as also in hand-work and gardening.

Pandit's main work being to teach English in which he has specialised he could not devote much time to writing Marathi. But his innate love of his mother tongue inducted him to try his hand at writing in Marathi. First he translated Shalley's most humorous comedy School for Scandal. The humour in this is so subtle and so much dependent upon the idiom and meaning of English words and construction of sentences that it is very difficult to bring out the wonderful wit and humour of the original in Marathi. But Prof. Pandit has succeeded very well indeed. Another great Marathi writer has translated the same comedy into Marathi under a different name. It would be an interesting and useful study to compare the literary performances of the two senior and junior literary men. The name of Professor Pandit's comedy is Vartahar. It is his first drama. Yogayog and Sudharak are his other dramas. Pandit is a bit of a poet too and has written stray poetical pieces and particularly musical songs for children and boys by name Sulabh Sangit, Sugam Sangit and Sisu Gite. He is also a good hand at writing dialogues for recital at gatherings and prize distribution ceremonies.

Prof. Pandit is a radical social reformer of strong convictions. He has acted up to them, going in for intercaste marriage with the only daughter of the Bombay reformer Gajanan Bhaskar Vaidya.

Prof. Pandit is comparatively a young man and might have been expected to do more work in Marathi literature. But unfortunately he is suffering from chronic nervous disease and his doctor has asked him not to do any mental work involving strain.

1. Vartavihar (1931); 2. Yogayog (1932); 3. Pac Sulabh Samvad (1936); 4. Mulamulinca gadya-padya Samvad (1937).

V.L. Barve

Barve is an inhabitant of Chiplun, district Ratnagiri where his father was a prominent pleader. Barve received his primary and secondary education at Chiplun. For his higher education he went to Bombay and successively passed the several University examinations and became a graduate. Then he studied Law and passed his LL.B. examination. He immediately began practice at Chiplun and became at once a leading pleader of the place. He holds very radical views both in Politics and in social matters. He has a zealous and ardent nature and takes interest in many public questions. He is both a dramatist and a poet.

1. Lagna-mandap (1928); 2. Manik, etc. (1932); 3. Kalami Ambe (1934); 4. Kovali Pophale (1935).

A.V. Barve

1. Sangit Bhakta Pralhad (1928).

V.B. Ambekar

1. Kutal Kampu (School for scandals) (1921); 2. Bhav Chitre (1931).

V.G. Despande

1. Tyaga samrat (1934): 2. Umaji Naik (1934).

J.A. Naravane

1. Sangit Snehalata (1930); 2. Gunagaurav (1930); 3. Sangit Matrsandes (1929).

S.N. Bande

1. Bedi (1929); 2. Pancali (1933): 3. Buva (1934).

G.V. Gokhale

1. Sangit Pranapratistha (1928); 2. Sairandhri (1935); 3. Buvabaji (1937).

D.K. Bhangarde

1. Bhakta Kaj or Kamsavadh (1923); 2. Svarajya Toran (1932); 3. Siv Pundai (1934).

N.R. Dhole

1. Brahman Dves (1928); 2. Sangit Patitoddhar (1932).

Divakar Krsna

1. Sangit Tod Hi Mal (1934); 2. Kisorice Hrdaya (1934).

B.C. Gharpure

1. Svarajya Sadhan (1928); 2. Sivkalin Suddhikaran (1930).

Balvant Ramcandra Hivargavkar

Balvantrav Ramcandra Hivargavkar was a Desasth Brahmin from Ahmednagar. He was brought up and educated in his own place. After doing some odd jobs he took to business and took up the Agency of the famous American Insurance Company named 'Sun life' and canvassed throughout Maharastra and got a permanent income by way of commission. Then he became the manager of the Poona Branch of the Bombay Banking Company. When that Company failed Balvantrav lost his business and became dis-spirited and retired from active life. His son became an Engineer and is now Chief Officer at Ahmednagar. His daughter was married to poet Ranade.

1. Bhas Kavici Natake, Parts I, II and III (1931).

M.D. Vaidya

1. Sangit Dnyanesvar (1936); 2. Mahatma Dadhici (1932).

V.R. Subhekar

1. Hundyaca Hunda (1929); 2. Pratidnya Purti (1932).

S.R. Oka

1. Parakrami Pesava (1933); 2. Yadnya Mandap (1935).

P.S. Savant

1. Andhala Karbhar (1934); 2. Majurancya Samrajyat (1935).

S.N. Sahasrabuddhe

1. Khara Premasannyas (1931); 2. Sangit Rani Candravati (1932).

P.G. Sahasrabuddhe

1. Satyaca Vali (1933); 2. Vadhu Samsodhan (1936).

N.V. Kulkarni

1. Ksameci Ksama (1932); 2. Mangal Bhuvan (1934).

N.G. Kamatanurkar

He is a man from Sangli, his father being a State servant. After passing his Matriculation examination he came to Poona and passed his B. A. examination from the Fergusson College after a few years of leisurely study. Being the only son of his father who left all his property to him Kamatanurkar is not required to take to service or business. He has an educated wife. He is a great admirer of Gadkari. In his dramas he has imitated the style and manner of Gadkari.

1. Stripurus (1933); 2. Sajjan (1931); 3. Sri.

V. G. Desai

1. Prem Rahasya (1934).

Vasant Santaram Desai

Vasant Santaram Desai is a Sarasvat Brahmin. He was born in 1904 at Indore. Vasantrav is the youngest son of the more famous Professor Santaram Anant Desai of Indore. Vasantrav is highly educated. After passing his LL. B. Examination in 1925 he began to practise at Poona. He wrote a satirical and humorous book on Law, especially exposing the practices of bribery etc. It was thought that the book contained professional misconduct and contempt of Court. So he was prosecuted. But the High Court gave its judgment that the book was humorous only and so no criminal offence was committed by the young writer. This was a noteable triumph for a young pleader. Now he is working as a subjudge in the Judicial Department of the Government of Bombay.

Vasantrav has a linking for literature and has a literary, talent like that of his father. For within a short space of time he had done a lot of literary work. He studied modern Marathi literature and especially the dramatic one and wrote critical and appreciative articles on Messrs. Deval, Kolatkar, Khadilkar, Gadkari and even on lesser lights in the line. After such good preparation Desai wrote two dramas. The first one depicts the intrigue, ambition and villainy of the minister of a credulous King. The purpose of the play is to show, like Gadkari, the triumph of true love. The characters of the hero and the heroine are finely painted. The drama is a comedy ending in the unexpected happiness of the main characters concerned. As the first effort of the author the play is a creditable performance. The songs in the play are simple and melodious and give expression to noble sentiments. The drama is named Vidhilikhit (the writing on the wall).

The second drama is on the well-known story of the

wonderful devotion of Mirabai, the Queen of the young Rana Kumbh of Udepur. This is rather a trite subject. But the author has succeeded in giving an interesting picture of the life and selfless devotion of Mirabai. The characters of her husband and her mother-in-law are vividly painted. The dialogues are lively and interesting. The songs are fine and easy to sing. The end of the drama though tragic is striking. Use is made twice of miracles which cannot appeal to the present rationalistic age. Firstly Mirabai is made to drink actual poison and still she does not suffer from its normal fatal effect. Secondly, she disappears in the statue of God when Rana Kumbh coming to her room and seeing there Akabar Badsaha admiring his wife raises his sword to kill both of them. Barring the use of these miracles the rest of the drama is very interesting to young and old. The drama is named Amrtsiddhi. Both these dramas were staged by the pre-eminent Gandharva Natak Mandali. Vasantrav is still quite a young man and may write more dramas and may win fame as a great Marathi dramatist.

1. Amrt Siddhi (1933); 2. Vidhilikhit.

G. B. Despande

1. Sangit Lagnapurvi (1934).

K. Dhumat

1. Madira Pratap (1932) (Tolstoy's First Distiller).

C. G. Gadre

1. Krsna Karasthan (1936).

S. G. Ghaisas

1. Durdaivi Chatrapati alias Sambhaji (1933).

H. G. Ghodake

1. Premaca Bajar (1935).

K. A. Godbole

1. Sangit Pancangi Jugar (1931).

Mrs. Campu Gunaji

1. Ratnavali (1930).

S. V. Jog

1. Amaci Jat (1934).

Mrs. S. Kale

1. Dharmakalank (1933).

P. M. Kamatkar

1. Paisaca Paisa (1936).

B. M. Kanitkar

1. Vidya Mandirat (1929).

V. P. Karmarkar

1. Sacitra Sala (1935).

Vitthal Narayan Kothivale

Vitthal Narayan Kothivale's family lived at first at Vadekhede, district Satara. But Vitthal was born at Garoth in the Province of Malva, Central India. Vitthal is the maternal grand-son of Mahipatibova Tarabadkar, a famous saint, poet and Kirtankar of the pre-British period in Maharastra. Vitthalrav received his secondary education upto the Matriculation examination. But since then he took to writing Marathi dramas and made literature his profession and means of livelihood and leads a decent life, deriving income from the sale of his books as also from the copy-right of permitting dramatic companies to stage his plays. He is a very prolific writer rivalling Messrs. Varerkar and Atre though he is not able to secure their fame or popularity. Let us turn to Kothivale's literary labour.

He began writing when he was quite young. For it was in 1921 when he was only 16 that he wrote his first drama named 'Mahatmyaca Satyagrah' based on the Pauranik story of the kidnapping the cow of Rsi Vasistha. Public performance of this drama was made under the auspices of His Highness Madhavrav Sinde Maharaja of Gwalior by Patankar's dramatic company and was highly admired and appreciated by the enlightened Maharaja and the assembled audience. After this success and patronage from high quarters Kothivale got confidence. Then he produced his several dramas Pauranik, Historical and imaginary in quick succession and they proved moderately successful and gave the author due reward for his literary labours by way of pecuniary profits. Besides his tremendous dramatic activity Vitthalpant wrote various articles on contemporary dramatists and their works, as also on other subjects. Thus Kothivale has turned out to be a prolific writer of this period.

Some of his dramas are the following :

1. Mahatmyaca Satyagrah; 2. Dharma Sangram; 3. Ramakant; 4. Lagna Agodar; 5. Chedalela Chava; 6. Sonyaca Dhur; 7. Gramoddhar; 8. Bal Sangopan.

S. S. Ka·markar

1. Salini or Gramoddhar (1931).

P. D. Karve

1. Gurubaji—Farce (1937) (Tartuffe).

J. M. Kulkarni

1. Tarun Stri ani Purus (1934).

K. G. Kulkarni

1. Sangit Sampadika (1936).

V. R. Kulkarni

1. Garib Majur (1933).

Mrs. Manoramabai

1. Pranay Praciti (Gharjavai) (1936).

V. A. Lohe

1. Sangit Grhadevata (1934).

B. Y. Mhaisalkar

1. Prajeca Raja (1933).

S. L. Mankikar

1. Sangit Vakilanci Vakili (1927).

G. S. Nirgude

1. Setkari Vijay Natak (1930).

N. B. Paithankar

1. Pativrateca Vaikunth (1936).

B. N. Pande

1. Punarjanma (1929).

D. V. Pansare

1. Bap Natak (1932).

V. G. Phatak

1. Mathureca Raja (1935).

Miss Kasitai Potnis

1. Premal Raksas (1930).

B. K. Puranik

1. Subhedaraci Sun (1932).

P. V. Rahalkar

1. Nave Dole (1935).

R. G. Sinde

1. Sangit Satyabhas (on drink) (1930).

Now I come to the class of Novelists of this period.

In this period there are over 280 novelists. This is a very large number for a short period of 10 years. But causes of this phenomenon are not far to seek. It is a curious fact that while the unemployment among the educated classes reached its topmost level in this period the literary productions in all branches reached an equally high level. But though curious the phenomenon is easily explained. Because these educated young men have only a literary education and are not fit to get any employment in non-literary sphere, they try their hand at writing some thing in their mother tongue. Moreover, they know something of everything. So they can write something and they have the vast English literature at their command. They can, therefore, translate or adapt whatever strikes them as suitable or likely to catch attention of readers. Moreover, during this and the previous period there has been enormous growth of printing in the country. The written matter could be easily and cheaply printed. The great output of novel writers in this period is also due to the addition of a new form of literature which became very popular i. e. short story writing. With the rapid growth of education desire for reading interesting stories increased enormously. So magazines and weekly newspapers began to print short stories. Nay some magazines were solely devoted to this form of literature. So, as soon as a young man's stories are in print and come out in the columns of the newspapers or magazines he hastens to reprint them in a book form. These causes explain the enormous rise of novel and short story literature during the period of this chapter.

Of 280 writers referred to about 180 have written each one novel or a collection of one or more short stories. Some of them are really interesting. So I have made a reference to a few of them. But of such writers scattered throughout the Marathi speaking country it is very difficult to get information or to catch hold of their books.

About 80 writers have to their credit 2 to 5 novels or other books and these writers show some talent for writing literature and hence they deserve a place in this history.

About 20 in number take a high rank among novelists in Marathi. It is very difficult, as I was able to do in previous chapters with fewer numbers, to give pre-eminence or precedence-to a particular novelist. But here I classify them only as younger and older. Let us begin with the latter class.

Mr. Varerkar figures in this field also though he first made his name as a dramatist. In this respect he can be compared to Messrs. Khare and Godkari. But as I have already given an account of him a mere mention of his name here is quite sufficient.

Narayan Hari Apte

Narayan Hari Apte is a Kokanasth Brahmin from a respectable and Inamdar family naturalised in Satara district. After his secondary education was over Narayanrav took up the business of printing by starting a Press of his own and conducting a Magazine at Koregaon where he has built a nice and cosy cottage for himself. He does not prominently come before the public, living at his place and rarely coming to Bombay or Poona the centres for acquiring instant fame. But his books have been popular and have given him a good income. Recently his name has been brought forward very prominently before the public by a successful cinema film story based on his novel named 'Na patanari Gosta,' the film story being renamed 'kunku.'

Some of his books are the following :

1. Grhasaukhya; 2. Bhagyasri; 3. Divyadrsti; 4. Pahatepurvica Kalokh; 5. Vaibhavacya Kondanat; 6. Sukhaca Mulamantra; 7. Na Patanari Gosta (Kunku-Cinema Story); 8. Banarasi Bore.

N.S. Phadke

Phadke was educated in the Fergusson College. He passed his B. A. and M. A. examinations with Philosophy as his voluntary subject, securing prizes and scholarships in both examinations. After graduation he joined the staff of Sir Parashuram Bhau College in Poona, becoming its life-member a little later. But in the non-co-operation movement of 1919-20 he left the College, advising students too to do likewise. But after the failure of the movement he had to look out for a job. He moved from place to place. At last he was taken up by the authorities of Rajaram College as a Professor of philosophy. As a teacher he is very successful and is a favourite among students as he gives them full freedom and does not trouble them for study. He has made his name as a fine speaker too. But he has made a wider name and fame as a novel writer. His first novel called 'Alla ho Akabar' was an adaptation from Miss Correlie's novel and was published by Tatya Neminath Pangal. Then he began to write novels serially for several magazines. He also published some of them on his own account. When short stories came to be demanded he began to write them also. There is hardly a magazine for which he has not written. He is very exact in getting remuneration for his literary work. It is said he takes money in advance before sending his manuscripts to the publishers. He is now a middle-aged man. Still his imagination and power of writting have not waned. He is a versatile writer. He has written books on scientific subjects like Sexiology and on an entirely different one like the art of novel-making named 'Pratibhasadhan'. It was about this book that a storm of controversy arose about its being full of plagiarism though the author boasted in his preface that it was throughout his own original composition. But the critics proved beyond doubt that the ideas at any rate were taken from an American book little known in India.

His books are the following :

1. Biographies : Dadabhai Nauroji; 2. Terrence Masquini; 3. De Valera; 4. Essays : Manasopacar; 5. Manasonnati; 6. Sukhaca Samsar; 7. Santati-Niyaman; 8. Ajace Tarun

Stripurus va Tyajpudhil Prasna; 9. Pratibhasadhan; 10. Vangamay-Vihar; 11. Adhunik Gita; 12. Manasamandir; 13. Dramas: Yugantar; 14. Sanjivan; 15. Jadavaci Devi; 16. Totaya Natakkar; 17. Stories, Part I and II; 18. Novels: Alla ho Akabar; 19. Kulabyaci Dandi; 20. Jadugar; 21. Daulat; 22. Atakepar; 23. Niranjan; 24. Kalankasobha; 25. Uddhar; 26. Kasmiri Gulab; 27. Asa; 28. Pravasi; 29. Gujgosti; 30. Takancya Pheki.

D. A. Tulajapurkar

Another middle-aged writer is D. A. Tulajapurkar. He has written a single novel. But it is as big as 3 or 4 novels and is appropriately called "Maze Ramayan" (My Ramayan).

Mr. Tulajapurkar comes from Nizam's territory. He was a successful pleader in the State. But on account of his nationalistic views he was banished from there. Then he came to Bombay and began to practise there and made a good name in his profession. But having a literary turn of mind he devoted his leisure time in writing regularly in the Daily Sandes the famous and popular news-paper of Acyutrav Kolatkar. The popularity of Sandes may be partly traced to the fine contributions of Mr. Tulajapurkar though he wrote anonymously under the guise of the editor. But when he published his great novel in his own name he at once became a literary luminary and his novel was widely read and a second edition was soon printed. The famous letters named 'Vatsala Vahinici patre' are believed to have been written by him.

Satya Bodh Hudlikar

Satya Bodh Hudlikar is a self-made middle-aged man. He passed his B. A. and M. A. examinations from the Fergusson College with Science as his optional subject. Then he went to Germany studying there Geology in particular. He also made a deep study of German language and literature. On his return home he was fortunate to get the post of State geologist in Indore State. If he had not mixed himself in the intricate intrigues of the State and had confined himself to his own work his life would have been a very happy one and he could have devoted his leisure time and energy to literary work. But he had to leave State service on account of his having sided with the fallen faction. Since that time he has been conducting one school or another for little children on the kindergarten plan. At present he is a Superintendent of such a newly started school at Dadar. He is also a half-time professor of German in the Elphinstone College, Bombay. His literary activity is considerable. He is a versatile man full of energy and enthusiasm for any work that he may take up for the moment. But he is not steady and shifts from place to place and from job to job. Hence like a rolling stone he has gathered no moss. Consequently he is always in difficulties about money and has to take help from his friends now and then. But he is a jolly man. His conversation shows his wide knowledge of varied subjects.

1. Butaka Pandit (1931); 2. Tarun Vartarci dukhkhe (1929); 3. Gate Sukti va Subhasite (1932); 4. Pascim Aghadi-var Samsum (1932); 5. Kadhihi na Bhinara Mulaga (1932); 6. Sur Simpi (1933); 7. Baby (1924); 8. Dadace Lagna.

Jagannath Eknath Naravane

Jagannath Eknath Naravane comes from the virile land of Kokan, his native place being Naravan, district Ratnagiri. But his father went to Khandesh to seek his fortune and succeeded in becoming a manager of a ginning factory at Dhulia, district West Khandesh. Jagannath received his education in Poona where his maternal grandfather Bhausaheb Bapat a well to-do and well-known gentlemen of Poona was living. Young Naravane passed his School Final examination in 1912 when his father died suddenly of plague. So Jagannath's further education came to an end. He immediately joined the Military Finance Department, the great store house of service for educated young men of the middle class. After just finishing his minimum period of service Jagannathpant took two years' furlough preparatory to retirement and built a fine new house in the Deccan Gymkhana Colony where he lives and enjoys his well-earned rest. Now to refer to his literary activity. Being a contemporary of Kasinathpant Khadilkar a pleader and a leading citizen of Sangli and Prof. N. S. Phadke he wâs influenced by them and their example and turned his attention to writing in Marathi during his leisure time. His first book 'Daivace Khel' (playful doings of fate) was published in 1918 serially in Prabhat Magazine. It is a social realistic novel depicting the life of the middle class people of Maharastra. His second novel named 'Asanirasa' was published in 1923 and the very same year his third novel called 'Isvari Lila' was published. These three novels and two others i.e. 'Krsna Sarpa' and 'Bandhanacya Alikade' were published in the Suras Granth Mala series of Messrs. Kothari and Vora. After writing the above five novels in succession Naravane turned to writing dramas for boys and girls. In this line too he wrote and published in quick succession on his own account "Matrsandes" (1929), 'Snehalata' (1930) and 'Gunagaurav' (1931). These are short but interesting dramas covering about 40 pages. Then after some time he again wrote a social novel named 'Snehabandhan'. It was published in 1935 under the auspices and patronage of Vangmayopasak Mandal of Ahmednagar. This novel deals with a higher class of society and the characters chiefly consist of Mohammedan Sardars from Nizam's territories along with many Hindu characters. It is full of wonderful and striking doings of a celebrated out-law named Serkhan but who turns out to be Srikant a young Hindu Doctor without practice taking to robbery for money-making. He is the hero of the novel. The heroines are the two sisters Daliya and Pramila originally Mohammedans but who ultimately become converted to Hinduism. Pramila is a highly educated lady being a graduate. But she hates man on account of her belief that man dominates over women. But Srikant under the guise of Serkhan successfully proves how man is really superior to woman and possesses qualities like courage, daring and endurance—a fact ultimately admitted by proud Pramila. She begins to love Srikant but seeing him in love with her sister takes a self-denying vow of remaining a spinster for the sake of happiness of Srikant and her sister. Such is the tragic-comic end of the story. But the author promises to write a sequel to this novel in which he intends to depict the later life of these characters and particularly that of Pramila and her vow of celebacy. This present novel 'Snehabandhan' is finely written. The interest in the story is kept up till the end. Especially the mystery of the identity of Serkhan and Srikant is very well sustained being disclosed only at the end of the story. Naravane is soon going to publish a novel named 'Mayasabha.' Its subject is cinema and its defects. He thinks of writing a drama for ladies by name 'Hrdayaci Olakh.' Thus Naravane seems to become a prolific writer like Mama Varerkar.

V.G. Josi

1. Vyapari Vaibhav; 2. Mardani Saundarya; 3. Vagvilas (Tweyth night); 4. Amba nadi jalapralay varnan (1932); 5. Sangit Dhruvakhyan (1928); 6. Sangit Dharm Simhasan (1928); 7. Nisa (1929); 8. Rana Dundubhi (1930).

P.N. Misal

1. Sevati satyaca vijay (1928); 2. Yace nav mitraprem (1928); 3. Dattuca thorpana (1928); 4. Sadguni mulancya sangatit (1929); 5. Udar Bandhu (1929); 6. Sadvartanaci kasoti (1929); 7. Matrbhaktice phal (1929); 8. Adnyabhangace prayascitta (1930); 9. Keval apali kartabgari (1930); 10. Sanmitra darsan (1930); 11. Balak (1930); 12. Balbodh sudha (1931); 13. Gamaticya gosti (1931).

Damodar Narhar Sikhare

Damodar Narhar Sikhare comes from Miraj. He was born at Umraj, district Satara in 1905. He received his primary education at Dhond, district Poona, his school education at Baramati, district Poona and his college education at Sangli and Poona. He passed his B.A. Examination in 1927 and his M. A Examination in 1929. Then he worked as a teacher for three years. Since 1930 he has been on the editorial staff of Kesari. As such he has to write on a variety of topics. But Sikhare has found time to write a number of books :

1. Kranti Kiran (collection of short stories); 2. Sarva Srestha Hindi Darma (an essay for which Hindu Maha Sabha gave a prize); 3. Thorali Al (a novel); 4. Bhaici Krpa (a novel); 5. Divyabhav (collection of poems); 6. Manbindu (a drama); 7. Miscellaneous poems.

P.S. Desai and L.N. Josi

1. Agnivarsav (1928); 2. Zasivali Rani (1928); 3. Vivek Gutika (1928); 4. Priyapatniprem va dakkhanca Vagh; 5. Bandaca vanava (1931); 6. Grhadevi (1936).

G.V. Ciplunkar

1. Draupadici gosta (1931); 2. Garudaci gosta (1931); 3. Vir Abhimanyu (1931); 4. Saha Pandavanci gosta (1932); 5. Sati Sukanya (1932); 6. Bhimaci Katha (1933); 7. Sati Parvati (1935); 8. Bal Vir Candrahas (1937); 9. Kusalavanci Katha.

N.V. Kulkarni

1. Matrseva (1928); 2. Kautumbik gosti (1929); 3. Maisaheb (1930); 4. Samsarat (1930); 5. Majur (1931); 6 Sant Kanhopatra (1931); 7. Manik (1931); 8. Mazya gosti (1931).

Gopal Gangadhar Potdar

Gopal Gangadhar Potdar is a Rgvedi Desasth brahmin from Satara. He was born at Satara in 1896. His education was done in several Institutions of several places. His primary and secondary education was done in the Municipal primary School Satara and the New English School, Satara. Then he came to Poona and joined the Fergusson College and passed his B. A. examination in 1920. Then he went to Benares and took in 1921 the degree of L. T. of the Benares University. He passed his M.A. examination in

1928 from the now defunct Deccan College. After completing his education and after equipping himself fully to do teacher's work Potdar became the Headmaster of the High School of the Dhulia Education Society and worked there till 1930. Potdar is a thorough rationalist and a sincere follower of Agarkar and his teachings. Such an ardent reformer and a strong advocate of New Morality to boot was not expected to remain doing for long the humble work of a teacher carrying on the routine course of instruction to the young. So he gave up his job and joined the band of propagandists of Hindu Mahasabha as also of the Congress and travelled over Maharastra, Nizam's territories and Central Provinces and preached the doctrines and ideals of New Morality, delivering over 100 public lectures in these places. He also wrote articles on this and other allied subjects in the several Marathi magazines. This has been Potdar's propagandist work so far. Let me now turn to his literary work. It is very considerable and of varied nature. Potdar seems to possess a facile pen and has published so far about 10 books small and great on a variety of subjects and has on hand an equal number of books ready for publication Some of his books are the following :

1. Bhavabhet (a collection of poems); 2. Santiyuga (a novel); 3. Desaseva (a drama): 4. Kavya Kaumudi (Moon light of poems); 5. Chatrapati (epic poem); 6. Musaphar (a traveller); 7. Maharastra des (Maratha country); 8. Ratrani (Queen of the night); 9. Vilaksan Caurya (strange theft); 10. Parityakta-a novel (the deserted).

G.M. Virkar

1. Coravar Mor (1932); 2. Dada Ram Ram (1932); 3. Appasaheb (1932); 4. Bhuyaratil Rahasya (1932); 5. Panjabi Lala (1932); 6. Kalankit Kaumarya (1934); 7. Jivant Samadhi (1935); 8. Haran ki hatya (1935).

S.L. Thorat

1. Pandurangaci Katha (1931); 2. Sacitra Bal Isap Niti

(1931); 3. Nala Damayanti (1938); 4. Satyavan Savitri (1932); 5. Bal gosti (1932); 6. Bal Vir Maruti (1933); 7. Bal Arabian Nights, Parts I and II (1933).

S.N. Josi

1. Pancamrta (1927); 2. Phurasatitil 22 gosti (1929); 3. Urubhanga (1929); 4. Katha Samsar (1932).

N.P. Mahajan

1. Siteci Katha (1930); 2. Pauranik Katha (1930); 3. Devance Daha Avatar (1930); 4. Sri Krsna Caritra (1931); 5. Sri Ram Caritra (1931); 6. Rastriy guru sri Samarth Ramdas (1930).

V.G. Tahmankar

1. Harsa Caritra (1928); 2. Catur Isap (1931); 3. Tom Kaka (1932); 4. Mrtyunjay-farce (1934); 5. Maze Uchvas (1934); 6. Lapalele Khadak (1934).

There are about 70 novelists who have written two or more novels and short stories. Some of them are quite good and can be compared with the first class novelists. They are treated here promiscuously.

V.V. Abhyankar

1. Cinemala cala (1932); 2. Gubgubit taruni (1934); 3. Miss Indu (1935).

A.V. Apte

1. Bal Samvad (1929); 2. Bangali virancya katha (1932).

Mrs. Kamalabai Bambevale

1. Bandh Mukta (1931); 2. Kamalancya Kalya (1937).

J.V. Bapat

1. Cakravarti Napoleon (1932); 2. Bhagyoday (1932); 3. Eka gadhaace atmavrtta (1933).

P.S. Bavale

1. Gomatece Ramayan (1931); 2. Gomatecya Katha (1932).

V.K. Bhave

1. Khara Desabhakta (1930); 2. Pandavanca Adnyatavas (1931).

B.G. Bhide

1. Usadevi (1929); 2. Tejasvi satidharma (1933).

B.G. Bhide and P.S. Desai

1. Mongalai karasthan ani mardani saundarya (1930); 3. Javahirlal Nehru (1930).

V.V. Bokil

1. Phol Asa (1931); 2. Garanca Varsav (1936).

N.B. Chvan

1. Pahili Bhet (1933); 2. Mohan Pyari (1934); 3. Photo-sathi (1934).

N.S. Desai

1. Rasiyan Rajyakrantica Sanksipta Itihas (1931); 2. Ai (Gorkay's "Mother") (1932).

L.R. Despande

1. Aryabandhus Vinanti (1930).

S.V. Dhamankar

1. Khara Vir Purus (1927); 2. Svarajyaca Sudin (1929).

V. S. Ghate

1. Savitri Kathanak (1930); 2. Bhasmasur (1931).

V.S. Gurjar

1. Bhagya Laksmi (1935); 2. Devdas (1937); 3. Anjana (1935).

P.R. Jambhekar

1. Pratapi Pratapsimha (1930); 2. Vir Ratna Murarbaji (1930).

Mrs. Anandibai Jayvant

Mrs. Anandibai Jayvant was born at Baroda in (1894). She received her primary education at school, but she learnt English, Bengali and Gujarati at home. She had also a liking for painting. In this art the lady made very great progress passing not only the local J. J. School of Art examination but she also won diplomas from Landon Art School and from special classes elsewhere. Anandibai seems to be a voluminous writer and would surpass men writers in their own field. For she has already written half a dozen novels, over fifty short stories for old and young and miscellaneous articles on varied subjects. Anandibai read Dicken's famous novel David Copper field. This inspired her to write a Marathi novel on that model. So she wrote the novel named 'Kulakatha' and the wonder of the literary feat is that this novel consisting of 37 chapters was written in just 37 days. It is a very creditable performance indeed.

Some of her books are the following :

1. Kulakatha (1932); 2. Jagasi Bandakhori (1935); 3. Citodaca Candra (1936).

S.V. Joglekar

1. Hrday Harini (1931); 2. Heca Maze Patiraj (1933).

S.M. Josi

1. Dubari Pistul (1930); 2. Dasavatar (1932).

Y.G. Josi

1. Punarbhet, Parts 1, 2 & 3 (1936); 2. Akasatil Hire (1937); 3. Jivan Krtye (1937); 4. Tridos (1937); 5. Bolaka Cinema (1932); 6. Homakund, Part I, & II; 7. Maza Mulaga—a cinema story.

D.G. Kale

1. Jaganmateci Hak (1928); 2. Maranaci Bhiti Ki Bhitice Maran (1931).

B.M. Kancankoti

1. Rastrabhaktaca Atmayadnya (Lord Lytton's Rienzie) (1927) 2. Rajakumari (1932).

B.K. Kane

1. Jayakranti Devi Arthat Kalipujan (1931); 2. Premahuti (1931); 3. Tuphan—a novel (1932).

V.V. Karmarkar

1. Mulance Manoranjan Part I (1930); 2. Subodh Ram Caritra (1930).

B.R. Kate

1. Maujecya Suras Gosti (1931); 2. Santancya Katha (1932).

V.R. Khadilkar

1. Tyag (1929); 2. Ladhaipurvi (1931).

Y.K. Khadilkar

1. Samsar Sakat (1931); 2. Sadananda (1934).

V.S. Ksirsagar

1. Pracalit Mhanivaril Subodh Gosti, Parts I and II (1928).

M.N. Kulkarni

1. Matr Murti (1932); 2. Surangi Veni (1936).

M.M. Kulkarni

1. Sadgun Sudha (1931); 2. G.K. Devadhar's Life (1931); 3. Undarane Manjaras Marile (1932).

R.N. Lad

1. Marathyance Dasiputra (1927); 2. Sethaji Bhatajinca Dalbhat (1928).

H.R. Marathe

1. Grhaganga ki Devaganga (1929); 2. Hay ge Vilasini (1932).

N.G. Limaye

1. 21 Gosti (1931); 2. Sisukatha (1931); 3. Balgita (1931); 4. Niti Kunja.

G.R. Mate

1. Pati haca Paramesvar (1931); 2. Gulabi Pane (1932).

Y. P. Mehendale

1. Outa Ghatakece Rajya (1929); 2. Rajasattevar Halla (1931).

G.R. Mule

1. Sacitra Ramvijay Kathasar (1930); 2. Pandav Pratap (1930).

K. G. Naik

1. Tumacyatale Kahi (1933); 2. Sri Bhisma (1930).

Mrs. Santabai Nasikkar

1. Lagnaca Bazar (1929); 2. Haca ka Dharma? (1930); 3. Ramrajyasathi (1931).

P.V. Phatak

1. Sri Ramvijay (1932), 3. Kathasaramrt (1932).

Nilkanth Sankar Navare

Nilkanth Sankar Navare was born in 1896 at Satara. His father was a primary school teacher well-known in Poona district for his affectionate, obliging but witty nature.

Nilkanth was educated in the New English School, Poona and received his College education at the Fergusson College passing his B.A. examination with optional Marathi and Sanskrit subjects. He soon joined the Government Educational Service and was then sent to the Secondary Training College. Nilkanthpant turned out a very competent teacher making his name as a successful Sanskrit Teacher. So he was taken up as a lecturer in the Poona Training College.

In his school days he . . . very much Shakespeare's, Lamb's Tales. From that time he thought of writing such short and interesting stories in Marathi from Sanskrit dramas and other classical Sanskrit books. This literary attempt of Navare has proved a great success. He has written so far three such short story books—a book giving stories from seven famous Sanskrit dramas. The second book dealing with the theme of Raghuvams of Kalidas and the third book tells the story of the famous novel of Banabhatta named Kadambari. All these three books are a valuable contribution to Marathi literature and will be a constant source of pleasure to the young and the old. Moreover, these stories provide ennobling examples from Sanskrit literature. Navare is still a young man and may come to write many such books in Marathi.

1. Sanskrit Kavinci Natyakathanake (1928); 2. Kadambari Katha (1929); 3. Raghuvamsa Katha (1933).

H.T. Patodkar

1. Ramata Ram (1930); 2. Bahurang Balu (1930); 3. Thoranca Por (1930).

S. R. Patil

1. Gandhiji (1931); 2. Khara Sramajivi (1931).

K. R. Purohit

1. Sunya Jagat (resurrection) (1929); 2. Mazi Maitrin (1930); 3. Akas Puspa (1930); 4. Mai Kon? (1933).

Miss Gita Janardan Sane

1. Vathlela Vrksa (1936); 2. Nikhalaleh Hirkani (1936); 3. Latika (1937).

N. D. Sarpotdar

1. Unad Pendya (1931); 2 Sambhavit (1932); 3. Mudrika (poem) (1932); 4. Candrarav Move (1932).

S.B. Sastri

1. Cirjivan, parts I and II (1927-28); 2. Anala Jvala (1929); 3. Navi Ksitije (1936); 4. Chotyancya. Mothya Gosti (1928); 5. Ganapatrav Nazar Caritra (1930); 6. Bal Vir Lavankus (1931); 7. Rankaca Rav (1931).

Y.N. Sinde

1. Dharmaci Vilhevat (1929); 2. Surya Mavalala (1929).

Mrs. Anandibai Sirke

Mrs. Anandibai Sirke comes from a high class Maratha family and was born in 1892. Her father was a State servant in Baroda. Anandibai was educated in Baroda and learnt both Marathi and Gujarati languages. Later on she learnt privately English and Hindi and thus she fitted herself for doing both literary work as also social and public work such as becoming a member of a School Board, doing Honorary Magistrate's work. But Anandibai's more permanent work is that in literature.

In 1902 she read Haribhau Apte's social novel 'Pan Laksat Kon Gheto' and was inspired to do literary work of the same type. So after preparing herself by the study of old and new literature she took to writing and published her first short story in 1910. Then she off and on wrote such stories and published them in different magazines. So far two collections of her stories by name 'Katha Kunja' and 'Katha Vikas' have been published in a book form and they are highly praised by critics. These short stories of Mrs. Anandibai deal with domestic life of middle class families. They are realistic; only very few are adaptations from foreign stories. These stories show Anandibai's been observation and her sympathetic handling of human foibles. All her stories are with a purpose. They make interesting reading for young and old. Her style is simpler clear and flowing. She is still comparatively young and may come to write many more books. Nay, she has already prepared two more books which may be published in the near future. In her literary work Anandibai is encouraged and helped by her husband who occupies the high position of an administrative officer at Jalgaon.

1. Katha Kunj (1928); 2. Katha Vikas 1934).

V. S Sukhathankar

1. Tolstoy's Bodh Katha (1934); 2. Bharatiy Sahirancya Gosti (1935); 3. Tagorancya Nitikatha (1935).

K. N. Sutar

1. Mulanca Vivekananda (1929); 2. Bal Yesu Khrista (1929); 3. Bal Sadhu Eknath (1932); 4. Bal Gautam Buddha (1932); 5. Bal Dnyanesvar (1932).

G.G. Talavalkar

1. Maharsinca Prasad (1931); 2. Candrasekhar va Mohan (1931); 3. Saracacamatkar (1931).

Mrs. Bhagirthibai Vaidya

1. Ananda Padavar Cauda Caukadyance Rajya (1928); 2. Abhanga va Kathasar (1932).

G. M. Vaidya

1. Aitihasik Gosti (1932); 2. Nitikatha, Parts I and II

(1932); 3. Bal Nitikatha (1932).

M. G. Vora

1. Jagaca Bazar (1926); 2. Patanci Prabhat (1928); 3. Ratnagadaci Rambha (1932).

Now I come to the last class of novelists or storywriters to whose credit each there is a single publication. I also treat them promiscuously. No attempt is made in the crowded list of 180 writers to estimate the worth of their writings. I can refer only to a few of them.

Ananditanay

1. Indu Natu (1933).

B. N. Ambardekar

1. Bajabacya Gosti (1930).

N. L. Athavale

1. Ran Kolha (1932).

N. H. Avtade

1. Isya Mela Navara (1934).

M. R. Bhandarkar

1. Paralokaca Pravas (1932).

V. T. Bhate

1. Katha Sangrah (1931).

L. R. Bhide

1. Gujarathaca Nath (Munsi's Novel).

N. T. Bhide

1. Sangam (Tagor's Yogavog) (1935).

Mrs. Sarasvatibai Dabholkar

1. Hrdayace Kadh (1934).

D. M. Damale

1. Bakulici Phule (1936).

M.K. Damale

1. Atha Minite (1933).

Mrs. Malatibai Dandekar

She is the wife of Mr. Dandekar Educational Inspector in the Miraj Junior State.

1. Katha Malati (1935).

Visvanath Pandurang Dandekar

Visvanath Pandurang Dandekar was born at Mehasana, Baroda State in 1905. He was educated at Baroda and at places in Kathiawar. He is an M.A. and is a professor of Marathi in Baroda College. He began writing when he was only eleven years old. He earns something by his writings. He is fairly a good writer. His books are the following :

1. Kalyanci Mal; 2. Pherphataka; 3. Tekadivarun—Short essays; 4. Bharatiya Samrajyasathi—Translations; 5. Life of Sir Sayajirav; 6. Short articles on a variety of topics.

Y.N. Date

1. Bepatta Bapace Bete (1927).

C.G. Desai alias Bakulray

1. Vina (1934).

D.M. Despande alias Mukund Kumar

1. Anarkali ani Salim (1928).

Mrs. Kusumavati Despande

1. Dipa Kali (1935).

K S. Despande

1. Navin Majedar Gosti, in Parts (1933).

P.Y. Despanae

1. Sukalele Phul (1931); 2. Sadaphuli (1933).

V.G. Despande

1. Candrajyot (1928).

V.N. Despande

1. Sukh Svapna (1928).

S.K. Devbhakta alias Sarasvati Kumar

1. Simhasth va anakhi tin gosti (1933); 2. Lakhya Laktarya (about Gadkari) (1928).

G.G. Divakar

1. Ekaca Ratna (1934).

C.G. Diksit

1. Duheri Samsar (1935).

S.S. Dhole

1. Dhenukatha Sangrah (1931).

V. Daundkar

1. Motyaci Kudi (1935).

R.A. Ekabote

1. Mulanca Mitra (1933).

S.G. Ghaisas

1. Jayadrath (1931).

T.G. Gharpure

1. Natak Company (Satire) (1936).

S.R. Gokhale

1. Kamala Kant (1931).

V.V. Gokhale

1. Kirtan Sindhu, Parts, I, II & III (1932).

M.K. Josi

1. Kalica Narad (1933).

S.S. Junnarkar

1. Phulvat (1936).

B.K. Kale

1. Majedar Gosti, Part I & II (1933).

S.G. Kantak

1. Kanasace Dane (1936).

Datta Raghunath Kavathekar

Datta Raghunath Kavathekar is a Desastn Brahmin hailing from Wai, district Satara. After completing his secondary education Dattopant took service in the Military Accounts Department. In the early period of his service he had been to Arabia for three or four years. He has also travelled extensively in India.

He had a natural liking for literature. But he began writing after having gained sufficient experience of social life of his time. Though he has written some stray poetical pieces his speciality lies in writing social novels and short stories. His first novel is named 'Vikhurlele Prem'. He began writing it on 10th May 1934 and finished the novel on 31st May 1934, i.e. he wrote 21 chapters of the novel in the same number of days. This is really a great literary feat especially for a novice. But it shows the vigorous fancy of the author and his great command over Marathi language. This first attempt of the author proved a great success, the novel being admired by veteran critics like Messrs. Kelkar, Josi and Potdar.

Then he published two collections of short stories named 'Gulabacya Pakalya, (petals of rose) and 'Ujedatil Andhar' (Darkness in light). The two collections together contain about two dozens of short stories. They are all about educated men of the middle class of Hindu Society. These educated men are more or less all of reformed views and they seem to be fond of high living. They want their wives to be full of youth and beauty and particularly neat and tidy in their dress and demeanour. In fact they all have a predilection for new ideas of life and conduct. But they also seem to be prone to the temptation of those things and want to have intimate relations, some times criminal, with other men's wives. Of course courage, virtue and presence of mind of these wives save them from the clutches of these young men. Thus many a story may be called a love story but love of a married man to a married lady. But there is a healthy moral to these stories i. e. triumph of reason and virtue. Some stories tell the tale of the love of money, pomp and show on the part of the heroines and indicate how these lead to cruelty and unfaithfulness on their part involving underserved sorrow and calamity upon innocent persons. The skill of the author is seen in the fine delineation of mental feelings and sentiments of the characters. All his stories are very interesting. The characteristics of his fine literary painting are seen to greater advantage in his novels than in his short stories. For here he has a wider and ampler canvas to work on. So he can describe more fully and more minutely the inner working of the minds of his several characters.

1. Vikhurlele Prem (1935); 2. Gulabacya Pakalya (Petals of rose); 3. Ujedatil Andhar (Darkness in light).

Kasinath and Yasvant Narasimha Kelkar

Kasinath and Yasvant Narasimha Kelkar are the elder and younger sons of their far-famed father Narasimha Cintaman alias Tatyasaheb Kelkar. So it would be better to write about them here to-gether.

Kasinath, the elder one was born in 1900 at Poona. He

was educated in the New English School and the Fergusson College but unfortunately he had to give up his course due to the non-coo-pera tion movement, which his father advocated in public and had per foıce to see it carried out by his sons. So Kasinathpant took his degree in Tilak Mahavidyalay then newly started. In 1927 he passed the Advocate's examination. Though he passed the Law examination he did not take to legal profession; in this case he followed the example of his father. Literature was as it were in the family, so young Kasinathpant began to write in Kesari and made literature both his profession and pastime.

Besides writing articles on current topics he has written four important and substantial books on Hindu Sociology and Hindu System of Law. They are very valuable books. They show Kasinathpant's wide reading and his power of expression in Marathi. He is a promising young writer and is sure to come to the front in the near future. His works are the following :

1. Ramayanavaril Kahi Vicar; 2. Striyancya Hakkaci Sudharana; 3. Navya Smrtici Avasyakata; 4. Hindu Vyavahardharma Sastra.

Yasvant is the younger brother and was born at Poona in 1902. He was educated in Nutan Marathi Vidyalay and Sir Parashuram Bhau College. But like his brother, he had to leave his college course due to non-co-operation. Then he joined the newly started Tilak Mahavidyalay and passed its final exmination and got the degree of 'Vidyavisarad' (Expert in learning). Then he was taken up on the editorial staff of Kesari where he is at present. Before he took up this perma-nent job he got the rare opportunity of of working for three years in the research regarding the Pesva Daftar entrusted by Government to the famous Historian Govindrav Sardesai. He worked for some time as an assistant editor of 'Aikya' the weekly of Satara newly started by Vagbhat Narayan Despande under the guidance and pecuniary help of Ravsaheb Kale of Satara. Yasvantrav has a literary talent and is sure to shine in various fields like his father. For, already he has written poems, historical essays and critical articles on a variety of topics.

His writings are these :

1. Gita Dvidal; 2. Gita Gumpha; 3. Aitihasik Povade; 4. Vasaici Mohim; 5. Miscellaneous essays and articles.

A.A. Moramkar

1. Visaprayog (1929).

K.M. Nadkarni

1. Hrday Ninad (1935).

V.J. Nadkarni

1. Sri Pandav-Pratap Kathamr (1931).

J.S. Naik

1. Nandan Vanat (1934).

Y G. Naik

1. Nandadip (1935).

V.K. Nerurkar

1. Sri-Sarasvatica Prasad (1933).

G.B. Nirantar

1. Malati (1934).

S.R. Oka

1. Vikramacya Ujjayanit (1934).

Mrs. Indirabai Pendse

1. Samaj Drsye (1932); 2. Lalita.

M.N. Pitale

1. Paisa ki Prem? (1930).

N.S. Pohanerkar

1. Bagasahi Kunja (1931).

N.D. Savarkar

1. Maran Ki Lagna? (1933).

Mrs. Kamalabai Tilak

1. Hrday Sarada (1932).

V.R. Tipnis

1. Vinod Manjusa (1932).

Mrs. Usadevi

1. God Svapna (1936).

Now I come to the most unmerous class of writers i.e. prose writers of this period. This exceeds all others in all periods the total reaching to the tune of 526. Of this number the vast majority are one-book writers. They are no less than 395, while 130 writers write each more than one book. Of these again 20 writers write each more than half a dozen books. These are really great literary writers of this period. Let us begin with them treating them in a promiscuous way.

High above the biggest prose-writers of the last but not the least period of this history stands the grand and majestic figure of Dr. Sridhar Vyankates Ketkar. In vastness, variety and volume his literary productions excel even those of the greatest writer Tatyasaheb Kelkar. In artistic presentation of subjects, in methodical arrangement of material and in the flowing style of writing Kelkar may have excelled Dr. Ketkar whose style, like his external appearance, was rough and out-spoken though vigorous. But there is no doubt that as far as quantity goes Dr. Ketkar has put in double the output of that of Tatyasaheb. Before describing the giagantic literary work of Dr. Ketkar let me give a brief account of his life which is extraordinary and interesting.

Sridhar Vyankates Ketkar

Sridhar Vyankates Ketkar was born at Raipur in Central Provinces. His family hailed from the virile land of Kokan, living at first at Sujanwell district Ratnagiri and doing the business of scribes of Pothis (old type of indigenous books written on paper or on palm leaf). But poverty made the family leave its home and come to Central Provinces to seek its fortune. Sridhar's father was a postmaster at Raipur. But he died prematurely leaving his sons orphans. In consequence their mother took her sons to her husband's brother living at Amravati, Berars. So Sridharpant's secondary education was done there. He passed his Matriculation examination at the age of 16. His elder brother became an M. A. and took to the teacher's line, but he too died soon after. The death of his brother was followed by that of his mother and sister. Thus Ketkar became homeless and a lonely creature on the face of the earth. But this calamity was a blessing in disguise. For Ketkar felt that he had no domestic responsibility and he could wander all the world over. During his School days as also in later life Ketkar showed uncommon rage for reading all manner of books that came to his hand. Among boys and teachers he was regarded as a well-read young man with a fund of information on all subjects. So he was jestingly nick-named 'Encyclopaedist' (an unconscious and jocular prediction that turned out to be true). For his College education Sridharpant went to Bombay and joined the Wilson College. For his B. A. examination he took up History and Roman Law as his optional subjects. He remained in the College for five years from 1901 to 1906; but left it without securing any degree on account of his not having given sufficient time to study the prescribed courses. But his literary bias and activity showed themselves in his starting in 1906 a magazine called 'Maharastra Vagvilas' (Play of Marathi speech) with the help and cooperation of Balkrsna Santuram Gadkari who became a novelist later in life. But before the year was out Ketkar left the magazine to its fate and went to America for his further and higher education selling all his ancestral house and property against the advice of his uncle. He joined the Corneil University. The first thing that he did after coming to America was to secure the B.A. and M.A. degrees which he could not get in India.

Then he began the study of sociology. This being a very wide and extensive science he studied a number of subjects allied to and useful for the proper understanding of the grinciples and laws of sociology. After this he seriously applied his mind to secure the Ph.D. degree. For this he selected for his thesis the subject of History of Caste in India. During this period Ketkar received a Scholarship from His Highness Sir Sayajirav Gaikavad. He got the Ph. D. degree after the approval of his thesis by the examiners and he used the material collected for the thesis in publishing two books by name 'History of Caste in India' and 'Essay on Hinduism'. These books were highly spoken of both in America and England. Dr. Ketkar was offered a professorship of Sociology in an American University but for accepting it he had to become a regular citizen of America, a matter of some delay and difficulty. So he gave up the offer and went to England in 1911 where he remained for about a year. There he got an opportunity to meet and form acquaintance with learned men specially interested in India and her culture.

Dr. Ketkar lived in America for full five years during which time he made himself acquainted with the life and ideals of the American people. He also came into close contact with the naturalised Indians living permanently there. This varied experience remained stored in his mind and he made good use of it in his novels written much later in his literary career.

While he was in English he joined 'The Nobodies Club' (a curious but significant name) where he became acquainted with Miss Edith Kohun who knew a number of European languages and had taken a diploma in Marathi of the 'School of oriental studies'. Dr. Ketkar met Miss Kohun many a time and began to like her. But neither of them had any thought of marriage though there was a secret and unconscious attraction towards each other. This acquaintance was kept up by Dr.

Ketkar by regular correspondence with Miss Kohan after his return to India in 1912. Like every other young man he had to face the problem of what to do after his return home. But he got a job, though temporary, of professorship of Sociology in the Calcutta University. He taught the post-graduate students the subjects of Economics, Politics and Law for a year. But as he was also expected to do some under-graduate teaching which he thought below his dignity he left the Calcutta University at the end of the year. But the literary fruit of this one year's work was even in his publication of the books i.e. 'An Essay on Indian Economics' and 'Hindu Law'.

After leaving Calcutta Dr. Ketkar wandered throughout the length and breadth of India, visiting even Ceylon. While at Madras and the cities of Andhra Des he came into contact with patriotic people of Southern India who thought of the great need of having linguistic Provinces so as to facilitate and develop the peculiar culture and literature of each Province. Dr. Ketkar liked the idea and lectured on she subject with his characteristic enthusiasm giving his strong support to it. He was surprised and delighted to see another literary activity of the Telagu people i.e. the preparation and publication in Telagu of an Encyclopaedia. While in America Dr. Ketkar had acquired vast store of knowledge on a variety of subjects. He had personally seen how vast schemes were undertaken and carried out by the American people. He had witnessed the organising and cooperating spirit of the people by which they were enabled to accomplish apparently superhuman enterprises. Thus his mind was full of ambition to do something grand and giagantic and his unconscious training in America added to what he saw people of a comparatively backward Province like Andhra undertaking a great literary work made him form a definite and determined plan of preparing and publishing a Marathi Encyclopaedia. Immediately on returning to Nagpur he consulted the local leaders and other influential people of Maharastra and when he got an encouraging response from them he boldly put forward the vast scheme of forming a limited company and of collecting three lacs of Rupees for financing the preparation and publication of the Encyclopaedia. On the 8th of July 1916—a memorable day in the annals of Marathi literature and language—he launched his company and at once began canvassing for shareholders to the company and subscribers to the Encyclopaedia. He now felt the need of assistants, helpers and co-operators in this great and stupendous enterprise—persons not only knowing English but also European languages and literatures. He could secure without much difficulty young and educated men to do the literary work under his guidance and supervision. But he found it difficult to secure a European helper with the necessary qualifications. He saw that Miss Kohun would quite suit his purpose. So he at once wrote to her and offered to take her on the literary staff of the Encyclopaedia. She too readily accepted the offer and came to India and began work under Dr. Ketkar's liked each other while they were together in England. The daily meeting of young men and their working together was bound to lead to closer friendship developing into real love. Such was literally the case with Dr. Ketkar and he made up his mind to marry Miss Kohun. But he showed his characteristic patriotism and liking for Indian culture by first converting Miss Kohun to Hindu religion by an old Vedic ritual named 'Vratyastoma' and then marrying her according to Hindu ritual and giving her the name of 'Silavati' (one having character). This is the interesting story of Dr. Ketkar's marriage with Silavatibai. She proved a faithful wife doing all her domestic duties and looking to the comfort and happiness of her husband. The couple was fond of children but unfortunately their wedded life was not blessed with them and so they adopted a brahmin boy from Thana Orphanage and a girl 10 days old from a maternity home in Bombay. Both the children were brought up by the couple and Mrs. Silavati is proud of these, grown up children, now, they being her only solace in life after the sad and sudden death of Dr. Ketkar.

After this interesting recital of Dr. Ketkar's domestic life let me return to his literary work. As stated before Dr. Ketkar launched his great scheme and had to contend with initial difficulties due to the apathy and indifference of the educated public. He found that Poona was a better place for speedy progress of the work, therefore, he shifted from Nagpur to Poona. Many people laughed at the idea of an Encyclopaedia in the undeveloped Marathi language with its absence of technical terms for expression of scientific truths. But when Dr. Ketkar by his tenacity, perseverance and patience succeeded in bringing out volume after volume of his Encyclopaedia the state of mind of many a man was that described in the celebrated saying 'those who came to scoff remained to pray'. At last the vast work was accomplished by the end of 1926 thus taking up full 10 years. Let me now give an idea of the vastness of this great enterprise. First he published a bibliography of books in Marathi small and great. Then he successively published 23 volumes of the Marathi Encyclopaedia with its index. The first five volumes are the sole work of Dr. Ketkar and they give, taking India as a centre of civilization, an account of the world from its earliest beginnings to its present state, history of the civilization of the different peoples who inhabited and still inhabit this globe. In fact these five volumes give a brief outline of universal history. This is the peculiar feature of Dr. Ketkar's Encyclopaedia. All the Encyclopaedias published in other languages Indian or European are wanting in this feature. Like an ordinary dictionary they all begin alphabetically from A and go down to Z. This part in Dr. Ketkar's work begins from the sixth volume and ends with twenty third volume. Of course in this latter part he had to depend mainly upon his assistants, collaborators and specialists whom Dr. Ketkar had invited to write on their special subjects. But all the literary work done by these men was looked into and amended according to his views and opinions by Dr. Ketkar himself. What an exacting and exhaustive work for 10 years! Dr. Ketkar must have breathed a sigh of relief when at last he finished his great enterprize. But Dr. Ketkar knew no ease or rest. No sooner did he complete his first vast undertaking than he thought of having supplementary volumes named 'Mahayuddhottar Jag' (World after the Great War) and he had made ready a rough copy of them. Then he formed the plan of writing a history of Pracin Maharastra and actually published one volume and made ready the remaining volumes for publication. Mrs. Silavatibai intends to publish this work as the last desire of her dear husband. This is the tale of his bigger work. To a man of Dr. Ketkar's wonderful brain-power lighter work like novels, dramas and poetical pieces was a flea-bite and so during the period of the writing of the Encyclopaedia he published stray poems named 'Govind Pautra' (Grandson of Govind), six novels i.e. 1. Gondavanatil Priyamvada (Sweet speaking girl of Gondavan); 2. Paraganda (The absconded); 3. Asavadi (The hopeful); 4. Gavasasu (Mother-in-law of the village); 5. Brahman Kanya (A Brahmin Girl); 6. Vicaksana (Discussion) and one drama named Strisattaprabhav Natak (Power of the authority of women). Besides these literary works Dr. Ketkar started a magazine called 'Vidyasevak' (Servant of learning) and a daily named Pune Samacar (Poona news). But these were mush-room efforts doomed to failure. This continuous, tremendous and exhausting mental work and physical strain told even on the robust and strong constitution of Dr. Ketkar. For some years he had diabetes which ultimately carried him off in 1937 to the great sorrow of his family, his friends and the public of Maharastra nay that of the whole of India. Unlike many of his queer and strange views and opinions he wished that his body after his death should not be cremated but should be buried in the Hindu burial ground. And Silavatibai and his friends carried out the last wish of Dr. Ketkar and his remains now lie buried on the banks of the Mutha river.

Out of the host of literary helpers that Dr. Ketkar gathered about him during eleven to twelve years of what might be styled as his 'Encyclopaedia activity' Messrs. Date and Karve did the lion's share of the work. For this lion's share and for their subsequent independent literary work they deserve a place near that of Dr. Ketkar in my History and so let me give their account here.

Yasvant Ramkrsna Date

Date comes from the virile land of Kokan living at the

small village named Kinhal, taluka Dapoli, district Ratnagiri. He was probably born there in about 1889. But his secondary education was done in Dhulia High School from which he passed his Matriculation examination in 1909. Then he joined the Fergusson College Poona and passed his B.A. examination in 1913. After some time he went to Nagpur for his law study and took his LL. B. degree in 1916. From 1917 he was taken up on the editorial staff of the Maharastriya Dnyanakos of Dr. Ketkar where he remained till the end of 1927. He did a good deal of literary work in connection with the Encyclopaedia though his name does not appear in print. However his part in the publication of the Bibliography volume was predominent. After leaving Dr. Ketkar's work Messrs. Date and Karve formed the plan of preparing and publishing Marathi Sabdakos (Marathi work dictionary). Both of them being trained under the able guidance of Dr. Ketkar and having learnt at first hand the ways and means by which he accomplished his stupendous task they were quite confident to realise their plan though great and difficult. Accordingly they started work by opening an office in Poona and doing canvassing work of securing subscribers for their Kos. After the wonderful success of Dr. Ketkar the public too came to believe in the capacity of the Maharastriyans to accomplish great works, and so both the Princes and the public helped Messrs. Date and Karve liberally. Hence they were able to complete the Kos, to print it and deliver the copies to the subscribers in the prescribed time. All this was done within ten years from its commencement in 1928.

In composing their dictionary Messrs. Date and Karve had no occasion to display their literary capacity. However the work of writing prefaces to each volume describing the origin and growth of Marathi language and discussing other aspects of Marathi is decidedly a literary work and Date has succeeded very well in it. Now he has formed the plan of preparing Paribhasa Kos (Dictionary of technical terms) and he has in mind the project of preparing English-Marathi Dictionary.

Cintaman Ganes Karve

His family lived at Panchnadi district Ratnagiri but on account of poverty came to Avalas, taluka Haveli, district Poona. But Cintaman was born at Baroda in 1893. He spent his childhood in Mysore State. He became a permanent resident of Poona in 1903. Naturally all his education was done in the Institutions of the Deccan Education Society, Poona. After graduation in 1917 he took up temporary job in Bombay and kept up terms for LL. B. examination.

In 1919 he was taken up on the editorial staff of the Encyclopaedia a position he held till its completion in 1928. As stated already Karve joined Date in the scheme of the Sabda Kos and that joint-work was finished within the allocated time and to the satisfaction of the public. Now both of them have formed the plan of preparing a dictionary of technical terms and after accomplishing it they are thinking of writing English-Marathi Dictionary. Messrs. Date and Karve are jointly working for their literary ventures and so their activities are almost identical and are being pursued with one mind. Both of them are still young and they may in time win more and more laurels in the literary line.

Before I proceed to an account of individual writers from the class of the commoners I should like to refer to the literary work of a few enlightened princely personages of Maharastra. It is a matter of pride to a Maharastriyan that almost all the Princes of Maharastra are educated and enlightened and they have not only interested themselves in the development of Marathi literature but some of them have done a little literary work too.

Srimant Narayanrav Babasaheb Ghorpade

Eminent among such is Srimant Narayanrav Babasaheb Ghorpade whom I have already referred to in connection with the Ichalkaranji Fund for the encouragement and publication of Marathi literature. I now give a brief account of his life and particularly of the Marathi books that he has written.

Narayanrav was born in 1870. He was adopted by the late Chief of Ichalkaranji Srimant Govindrav in 1876. He was educated in Rajaram College, Kolhapur, Elphinstone College and Law College, Bombay. He received full powers of the Ruler in 1892. Since then he has introduced many reforms in his small State and quite recently that is in 1938 he has promised to give further concessions and rights to his subjects including the grant of a Legislative Assembly. In this respect his hands are tied down. For being a feudatory of the Kolhapur State he can not introduce any Law or make any change in administration without the consent of His Highness the Maharaja of Kolhapur. However within the limited powers that he possesses he is doing all he can for the benefit of his subjects.

Srimant Babasaheb has travelled over the whole of India and has seen the countries adjoining India like Ceylon, Burma and Malaya States. He had gone to England and to Europe more than once. He has written a fine book in English named 'My impressions of England and of English people'. He has not written much in Marathi though he is fond of speaking in Marathi and many of his speeches in Marathi have a literary character. He is now nearing 70 years of age and still he is reading and writing and is carrying on the administration of the State, which is becoming day by day a very difficult and troublesome task.

His Marathi books are these :

1. Parne (Translation of Miss Clarke's book named 'Leaves'); 2. Dayal Bag (An account of Dayal Bag, a famous self-sufficient model colony of Agra); 3. Daksinetil Setici sampattik sthiti (Economic condition of farming in the south); 4. Samrat va Samradnyi yancya Hindusthanatil pravasaca aitihasik Vrttant (Historical account of the travels in India of the Emperor and the Empress).

Books published so far in the Ichalkaranji Series are the following :

1. Akasace Dekhave—D.G. Kelkar; 2. Manavjati Jivansar or Atmyace Avinasitva—L.T. Parnaik; 3. Marathica Samsar—V.H. Nerurkar; 4. Jarman Bhasa Praves—S.B. Hudlikar; 5. Tarun Warterci Dukhkhe—S.B. Hudlikar; 6. Padatya Phalaca Sandes—M.V. Apte; 7. Alankar Manjusa—Miss Balutai Khare; 8. Pracin Hindi Silpasastra—K.V. Vaze; 9. Nirukta—V.K. Rajvade; 10. Strijatak Pradip.

Srimant Bhavanrav Srinivasrav alias Balasaheb Pant Pratinidhi

Another enlightened Prince is Srimant Bhavanrav Srinivasrav alias Balasaheb Pant Pratinidhi. He belongs to the junior branch of the Ruling Chief Nanasaheb Pant Pratinidhi. After the deposition of Nanasaheb for his gross and criminal mis-management of the State and after non-recognition of the claims of Bhausaheb the younger brother of Nanasaheb, British Government selected Srimant Balasaheb as the Ruler of the Aundh State.

Balasaheb was born about the year 1870. He received his secondary education at Satara and his University education in the Deccan College from which he passed his B.A. about the year 1895. From his boyhood he had a liking for the art of painting and by constant application to the cultivation of the art he has now become the renowned artist of Western India nay of the whole of India. He has made a fine collection of pictures and statues in his palace at Aundh for which he recently built a beautiful building outside the city on an elevated and commanding site. He has himself painted many historical and Pauranik pictures. To the great and giant critical edition of Mahabharat, that is being printed under the auspices of the Bhandarkar Oriental Institute, Srimant Balasaheb is supplying suitable illustrations painted under his guidance. He has edited, with illustrations of his own, books named 'Pictorial Verul, Pictorial Ajantha, Pictorial Ramayan and Pictorial life of Sivaji in three volumes.

Balasaheb is himself a great athlete and is very keen in young and old taking regular exercise. He has devised a special mode of Surya Namaskars (Prostrate salutations to the Sun). He believes that by regular practice of this form of exercise (Namaskars) not only is a man able to keep his body hole, healthy and disease-free but also such practice is calculated to heal many an ailment of the body. He has written a Book on this subject and published both English and Marathi editions of it.

Balasaheb was the first to introduce political reforms in his State, giving the Legislative Assembly, a right to discuss and bring resolutions on the Budget. He was the first to appoint a Minister from the elected members of the Assembly. Quite recently he has promised to give full responsibility to the representatives of the people, he acting as a constitutional Monarch of the State. This is a great step and Srimant Rajasaheb is to be congratulated upon his courage and his keen desire for the good of his people. He is against the present system of Education and wants to overhaul it and introduce vocational and industrial training in the High Schools. He is a great advocate of domestic industries on a small scale as suited to Indian conditions. He has introduced all these reforms in his State though small it is and their beneficial effects will be visible to everyone who will pay a visit to the state.

Srimant Balasaheb is a fine speaker. He has a loud voice and speaks fluently and with vigour. He is very fond of speaking in Marathi. He is equally eager to write in Marathi and contributes to special numbers of magazines. His style is clear and forcible. His Marathi books are referred to already.

Another annual practice of Srimant Balasaheb has made a fine and lasting addition to Marathi literature. Out of his great respect and filial affection for his father, Balasaheb celebrates his anniversary and on that occasion he himself performs a Kirtan as a principal item of the programme of the celebration. For this Kirtan he takes a lot of trouble selecting a suitable philosophical doctrine as the first part of the Kirtan and an interesting story as its second part. For expounding the doctrine and describing the incidents of the story he finds out appropriate verses and songs from the old and the new poets. Lastly, he publishes these Kirtans before hand and distributes them among the audience. Balasaheb has a good voice and a fine power of exposition so his Kirtans become very interesting. It is an intellectual treat to attend to them. By this time a goodly number of Kirtans are published and they form a valuable addition to Marathi literature.

His grandson is the hair-apparent. Srimant Appasaheb is both a graduate and a Bar-at-Law. He has learnt the art of flying. He is still young. But in time he may show his capacities and talents and like his grand father make a name for himself.

Srimant Raghunathrav Sankarrav alias Babasaheb Pant Saciv

The third Ruler whose account is worth-giving is the Raja of Bhor. Srimant Babasaheb was born in 1878. He was educated in the Deccan College though he did not become a graduate. He ascended the Gadi in 1922. His is a bigger State than that of Aundh and Ichalkaranji with a revenue of nearly seven lacs of Rupees. He too like his brother Princes granted political reforms to his subjects, giving the Legislative Assembly of non-official majority. Quite recently on the occasion of his 60th birthday he has proclaimed further rights and privileges to his people.

Now as to his literary activity he has projected a series of illustrated volumes in Marathi, describing in detail his experiences in his European tour as also in his travels in India. The first volume is published and is worthy of the Ruler-writer. It is written in simple and clear language.

Srimant Babasaheb has a grown-up son who is the heir-apparent to the Gadi. He is a graduate himself and a lawyer to boot. He has an educated wife and both of them are poets and have published collections of their poetical pieces-named Tridal and Nirzarini (1932). The poems are the joint production of the Prince and the Princess. More books of the kind may be expected as time goes on. The poems are very interesting and show the poetic talents of the princely writers.

Sampatrav Gayakvad

Sampatrav Gayakvad was the younger brother of His Highness Sir Sayajirav. He was highly educated. He had travelled far and wide. The Maharajasaheb made use of his administrative capacity by giving him responsible posts in the State Administration. Sampatrav was a keen Sikari (Hunter). Both his books are interesting reading. They are as follows :

1. Nepalce Varnan (Description of Nepal); Africetil Sikar (Hunting in Africa).

Datto Vaman Potdar

Datto Vaman Potdar comes from a Desasth Brahmin family hailing from Kolaba district. Dattu (the colloquial for Datto fuller name being Dattatraya) was born at Biravadi, taluka Mahad, district Kolaba in 1890. But his father Vamanrav, having passed his LL. B. Examination, settled in Poona and began his practice there. So the young Dattopant received practically all his education in Poona, passing his Matriculation in 1906 and his B. A. Examination in 1910 from the Fergusson College with History as his voluntary subject. Potdar was a mediocre student. But from his youth he came under good influences and made up his mind to lead a celibate life and devote all his time and energy to public work. Naturally he took up the work of a teacher and after passing the usual probationary period he became a life-member of the Siksan Prasarak Mandali Poona which first conducted the Nutan Marathi Vidyalaya and later on the New Poona College (now Sir Parashuram Bhau College). In the High School Potdar worked as a teacher and when the Society started Sir Parashuram Bhau College he became professor of Marathi and History in the College. He was also successively the head of the Marathi branch and English branch of the Schools of the Mandali. As of the soon as he completed his promised period of service Mandali he retired in 1936. Since that he is devoting all his time to his favourite subject i.e. research work in connection with Maratha History. He is one of the most active members in the Bharat Itihas Samsodhak Mandala. He has been for long its secretary. In his capacity as secretary and research worker he has written acticles, essays and criticisms and has taken part in the discussions of the research society. This subject with its accompanying writing and speaking is Potdar's first love. But his second love is Marathi language and literature and now-a-days he has developed a third love towards the idea of the Maharastra University. To the attainment of the last object Potdar is devoting his sole attention at present. He has formed a private society for this purpose and moves from place to place to collect funds and to popularise the idea of the University. Of course this is an uphill task like that of Prof. Karve. But unless a donor comes forward to bring into being the University there is very little prospect of the idea materialising in the near future. Though Potdar has written much all of it is imbedded either in the columns of newspapers or pages of Magazines. But so far his important work is a book dealing with modern Prose, during the British period. It has a queer name i.e. 'Arvacin gadyaca vilayiti avatar' (English incarnation of modern prose.) He has separately published in leaflets and pamphlets his 'Advice to Students'. This is done in imitation of and in continuation of the published 'Upadesas' of Haribhau Apte.

Sitaram Ramji Tavde

Sitaram Ramji Tavde comes from a Maratha family of Ratnagiri, his father being a Military Pensioner, getting Rs. 7 per month. Sitaram was born in 1895 in a small village in Malvan taluka, district Ratnagiri. But his father came to Bombay and became a drill teacher in a private school. So Tavde's education was all done in Bombay. But while he was still studying in St. Xavier's College Tavde lost his father and so had to shoulder the responsibility of maintaining the family by accepting service as a teacher. But Sitarampant was a young man with ambition and fondness for studies, and had acquired the habit of reading from his young days. He passed his B. A. Examination in 1918. In 1930 he went to America. There he had to do odd jobs for getting money but he did them and became an M. A. and M. Ed. (Master of Education) of the Columbia University of New York. In order to get knowledge about the different educational systems prevailing in several countries of Europe he travelled over the whole of Europe and returned home in 1923 well equipped for his life's work. And soon he got such an opportunity. At that time Bhaskarrav Vithoji Jadhav, the well known leader of the Maratha community was a Minister of Education. He at once appointed Tavde as the Principal of the Training College for Men, Poona. Thus Tavde got an apportunity to make full use of the acquired knowledge and experience of education in Europe and America. Principal Tavde put new life into the old Institution and introduced many reforms in the methods of education. He organised the celebration of what he called 'the children's day' in Poona. Thousands of small boys attended this function and gradually this day came to be observed in many a school.

Such an enthusiastic man could not neglect the art of writing and speaking and Tavde succeeded in both the arts. He conducted the school magazine and wrote articles on educational topics. His separately published books are these :

1. Centenary Volume of the Training College; 2. Sadhu Santanci Sikavan; 3 to 6 books for children.

P.V. Pathak

He is a prolific writer. He writes on all manner of subjects. Many of his books are prose summaries of Sanskrit and Prakrit works. He has also written poems on these subjects. The total number of books written by this voluminous writer are about 35, small and great. Names of some of them are given at page 534.

K B. Babar

1. Life of Svami Ramtirth (1929); 2. Vidyarthi Sitaram (1930); 3. Mazya Gosti (1930); 4. Satyace Pujari (1930); 5. Life of Vitthal Ramaji Sinde (1930); 6. Ratnagirica Jotiba ani Jejurica Khandoba (1930); 7. Karmaviranca Prasad. (1930); 8. Eka Namunedar Vidyarthi.

M K. Karkhanis

He is a Kayasth Prabhu gentleman occupying the position of the Princial of Dhulia Training College. He has written a number of books for boys. He is a prolific wtiter of moderate ability.

1. Marathi Vangmay (1927); 2. Khodkar Bhau va Mulanci Tarambala (1928); 3. Susila—drama; 4. Siksak ani Siksan (1928); 5. Krsna Kumari Natak (1928); 6. Sadhvi Mirabai ani Sitadevi. (1928); 7. Manoranjak first book (1928); 8. Stri Ratna Panna (1929); 9. Adhyapan (1929); 10. Mulakarita Kavita (1930).

Mahadevsastri Divekar

Mahadevsastri Divekar was born at Ugar, Sangli State in 1888. He was educated at various places such as Ugar, Sangli and Belgaum where he studied up to the Matriculation standard. He read Dnyanesvari with Visnubuva Jog. He learnt the art of singing and that of Kirtan. Then he studied Sanskrit grammar, Vedant and Dharmasastra at the feet of Narayansastri Marathe a well-known Sastri in Maharastra. After the completion of his English and Sanskrit learning Mahadevsastri joined Prof. Vijapurkar's Samarth Vidyalay. After it was stopped by Government order Mahadevsastri started a national school on his own account at Arjunvad. But such institutions were short-lived everywhere. The same was the fate of Mahadevsastri's school. About this time a Pradnyapath Sala for the purpose of teaching the old lore with a smattering knowledge of English was started at Wai. Mahadevsastri joined it and did very valuable work for it and collected about 8000 Rs. Mahadevsastri from his young age had imbibed the spirit of social service. Being will prepared by his previous education and being naturally a capable person he was able to do excellent propaganda work. He has seen how the present Hindu religion has fallen from its old high position and how evils have crept in during the middle age of Indian History. So he took up the cause of reform of Hindu religion and society and did valuable work for the removal of untouchability and for the unification of subcastes among the Hindus and the reconversion of Hindus forcibly converted to other faiths. Mahadevsastri was of course against child-marriage, prohibition of widow marriage and was in favour of other reforms advocated by social reformers. And Mahadevsastri being a Sastri himself and being well-versed in old lore was able to convince orthodox people about the advisabilityof introducing these reforms in the Hindu society. The last valuable work that Mahadevsastri did was the exposure of the growing evil of what came to be called 'Buvabaji'. The practice of becoming a formal disciple of a religious Guru and of taking from him a Mantra for daily recital is a very old one. But latterly the practice has degenerated into a social evil. For the modern Gurus of Buvas form Maths and there gather a band of disciples both male and female. Here young girls, married women and particularly unfortunate widows are persuaded to come and to become disciples of the Buva who is represented as having divine powers and fulfilling the desires of ladies. So, many women become disciples and then they are made to satisfy the sexual desires of the Buva and his favourite male disciples. In fact, these Maths have become brothels (a very strong word no doubt) for immoral purposes. So Mahadevsastri has done a great service to Hindu Society in mercilessly exposing this growing evil in society.

Mahadevsastri's literary output is very great. His books have attracted public attention and he has been able to make money by his writings. In fact, he maintains himself on his literary work and is leading a descent life at Miraj. His books are these :

1. Brahmanatil Pot-jatince Ekikaran (1927); 2. Vidyarthi Dharma; 3. Arya Samskrtica Utkarsapakarsa (1929); 4. Hindu Samaj Samarth Kasa Hoil? (1931); 5. Asprsyatece Uccatan (1932); 6. Dharmasastra Manthan, Parts I and II (1933); 7. Brahmadnyan va Buvabaji; 8. Gitapradip; 9. Hindu Dharmasiksan; 10. Govardhan Brahmananca Itihas.

L. N. Josi

1. Sant Dnyandev (1929); 2. Sant Tukaram (1929); 3. Siva Pratap (1930); 4. Sant Namdev (1930); 5. Grhini Siksan (1930); 6. Balaji Visvanath Pesava (1933); 7. Bajirav Ballal Pesava (1935).

Dattatraya Govind Sadekar

Dattatraya Govind Sadekar is a Sarasvat Brahmin from Sada a small village on the borders of the Portuguese territory. His father Govindrav was the only brahmin in that village. He was very poor and could make a bare living by cultivating his little farm. There was no school at Sada and so young Sadekar could receive no formal education till he became twelve years of age. But he had a keen desire for education, so he acted up to the saying "Where there is a will there is a way." He left his house and went to Gunji where a friend of his father lived. Here he stayed at that friend's house and learnt upto the fourth Marathi standard and his education came to a full stop at that stage. For, his father grew very old and Dattopant was obliged to return home and to seek some service for getting money for the maintenance of the family. So he came to Belgaum and was fortunate to get a job in the Press of one Abaji Ramcandra Savant. He did all manner of work in the Press gradually learning the art of printing and of conducting a Press. He was asked by Savant to go about as a hawker and to sell the publications of the Press. Young Sadekar did all this hard and difficult work very gladly. For, thereby he met many people and made acquaintance with them. It was a silent preparation of what was to be his life work later on. His perseverance and patience in canvassing for the sale of books and particularly his persuasive tongue were the cause of his great success. When he found how profitable such business was he made up his mind to start one on his own account. Mr. Savant gladly helped young Sadekar by giving him his publications on credit and on liberal commission. The success of his venture with its great pecuniary profits induced Sadekar to start a magazine of his own by name 'Lokamitra' (friend at the people). For some time he used to get it printed in Belgaum at the Samacar Press. But in order to secure regularity in publishing and also to get the profits of printing Sadekar started his own Press called Dhananjaya (Victory of money) at Khanapur about 12 miles from Belgaum. He conducted his magazine for about 40 years and is still conducting it, though he has become an old man now. But his enthusiasm and vigour will shame a younger man.

This example of Sadekar is an extra-ordinary one. That a man with only a smattering knowledge of Marathi should be able not only to conduct a literary magazine but also to become in time a literary writer is itself a wonderful feat. When Dattopant was asked by friends how he came to write so well he told them that he simply began to put down on paper and in simple but clear language the thoughts that came into his mind and that seemed to him to be useful and interesting to the public. This again illustrates the truth of the remarks that a poet (as also a literary writer) does not stand in need of formal education or previous preparation but an innate desire to tell his ideas and feelings to others, suggest to him the necessary and proper language. For thought and its expression in words are indissolubly bound together and do really arise in the mind simultaneously. A thought without its expression is in fact no thought. So also an expression without a thought is no real expression, but a mere unmeaning jumble of words. I fear however, that I am rather rambling. But the extraordinary tale of Sadekar's life may justify a little diagression like the above one. Some of his books are the following :

1. Sri Gokarn Math Samsthanci Mahiti (1928); 2. Grha

Devata (1928); 3. Kala Vaibhav (1928); 4. Kukkali Yethil Itihasprasiddha Dharma Gudh (1928); 5. Photo Kasa Kadhava (1928): 6. Balranjan (1928).

N. P. Mahajan

1. Candrarav Caritra (1932); 2. Hariscandraci Katha (1932); 3. Pandav Caritra (1932); 4. Panca Kanya i.e. Ahilya, Draupadi, Sita, Tara, Mandodari (1932); 5. Sambhajici Katha (1936).

V. S. Sukhatankar

1. Hasata Khelata Buddhivikas (1932); 2. Rajputrane Sangitalelya Gosti (1932); 3. Nitidharma (Gandhi's book—1932); 4. Sahyadricya Payathyasi (1931).

Sadasiv Krsna Phadke alias Babasaheb Phadke

Sadasiv Krsna Phadke was born in 1877. His early childhood was spent at Bassein near Bombay where his parents lived. He is the brother of the famous Statuary of Bombay who began to prepare first Ganapati statues at the time of the annual Ganes Caturthi festival (4th day of the first fortnight of the Hindu month of Bhadrapad). These statues were highly admired by the public. Then he began to prepare along with the main statue of God Ganapati other pitures and statues depicting Pauranik and social topics. He became in time such a fine and superior artist that his pictures won prizes in the last British Exhibition held in England. So fine art and literature which is the highest of the fine arts seem to run as it were in the Phadke family. Babasaheb was educated in the Maratha High School conducted by Rajaramsastri Bhagvat, a school which produced the first Indian Senior Wrangler Appasaheb Paranjpye, who was Phadke's junior in the School by a year only. After passing his Matriculation examination Babasaheb worked as a teacher in the Aryan Education Society's High School, Bombay when Divan Bahadur Singane (later a Government pleader) was in charge of the School. Babasaheb then studied for the pleader's examination and passed it and began to practise at Panvel, district Kolaba. Though he could not join College and study Philosophy as his voluntary subject he had a great liking for it from his youth and he made a deep study of it and of modern religious movements in India. This zeal for Philosophic study made Babasaheb devote his time, money and energy to the writing and publication of big books on the subject. He has incurred enormous expenses for printing and publishing this voluminous literature of his. He formed the ambitious plan of writing a series of books on the new religious movements and gave it the name of 'Navayugadharma' (Religions of Modern age). The first volume of this series is named 'Brahma Samaj and Deva Samaj'. It consists of nearly a thousand pages. It mainly gives a detailed description of the Brahma Samaj (new monotheistic sect) founded by Raja Ram Mohan Ray. The author gives an account of his life and his deep study of the world religions and particularly of Christianity and how and why he was led to start his own new religion giving it the name of Brahma Samaj. Then Babasaheb severely criticizes the new religion, its founder and its followers. This severe nay defamatory criticism of the religious movement in Bengal enraged the Bengalis and some enthusiasts threatened to bring a suit against Babasaheb Phadke. It was through the influence of Divan Bahadur Singane who was then a temporary High Court-Judge that the case was compromised and the danger of trouble and expense of Babasaheb was averted. This big book shows the deep study and wide reading of the author but at the same time it brings out his bias and prejudice against the new religious movement. Moreover, the style of writing is verbose and uninteresting. These are the characteristic defects of his subsequent books too. But all his books contain information about philosophy in general and about religions in particular. His biographical books are free from the above defects and are interesting reading, Phadke is a voluminous writer and his literary activity is still going on. All his religio-philosophic books are bublished as a part of Navayugadharma Mala (Garland of new religious sects) as stated before, the first book giving an account of Brahma Samaj. The first volume and the others of the series are as follows :

1. Brahma Samaj va Deva Samaj; 2. Srimat Dayanand Caritra (Life of Dayanand Sarasvati); 3. Śri Datta-bhakta-rahasya (Secret of Datta devotion); 4. Jivanmukta Svami Maharaj yance Caritra va Sikavan (Life of Jivanmukta Maharaj and his teachings); 5. Śri Jivanmukta va Adhunik Tattvadnya (Sri Jivanmukta and modern philosophers); 6. Mayavad ani ajatvad (doctrine of illusion and that of non-birth); 7. Manobodh ani Nava Manu (Advice to the mind and new age); 8. Visnu Krsnasastri Puranik yance Vivecak Caritra (Critical life of Visnu Krsnasastri Puranik).

Dr. Madhavrav V. Kibe and Sau. Kamalabai Kibe

Dr. Madhavrav Kibe comes from a hereditary Sardar family of Indore State. Madhavrav was born in 1877 at Indore. He was educated at Indore College and Allahabad University from where he passed creditably his M.A. examination. After his education was finished he was naturally taken up in Indore State service and there he held high posts of responsibility and honour, rising to that of Nayab Divan for some time. Then he retired from service and enjoys his well-earned rest. As his family library of books on a variety of subjects was large and contained choice books in different languages Madhavrav naturally took to reading whatever pleased his fancy and taste. So he acquired a wide knowledge of various subjects and a love of literature both ancient and modern. He was induced to write in English by his College Professor and to do so in Marathi by Prof. Vijapurkar. So he began writing stray articles and essays for the several Marathi magazines and newspapers such as Tilak's Kesari, Vijapurkar's Granthmala and Kelkar's Sahyadri. He wrote also for special numbers of several magazines.

Occasionally Sardarsaheb delivered public lectures in English, Marathi and Hindi. He takes an active part in Granthottejak Mandal of Indore In fact he is the President of the Mandal; so also he has been elected as Chairman or Vice-President in the several conferences of Marathi poets and writers held in the chief cities of Maharastra. Though Madhavrav Kibe has not published separately and independently any Marathi book still his occasionally writings will, if published form a decent and good volume.

Madhavrav Kibe's wife Kamalabai is an educated lady. She takes keen interest in Marathi literature and has occasionally written articles and essays though she is more inclined to speak in public than write for papers. She is an earnest worker in the women's cause. She is a bold and out-spoken speaker and makes an impression upon the assembled audience by her earnestness and vigour in speech.

P.S. Sane

1. Life of Benjamin Franklin (1929); 2. Life of Sisira Kumar Ghos (1929); 3. Life of Rajavade (1928); 4. Life of Ravindranath Tagore (1930); 5. Gandhi Jayanti (1931); 6 Khandes Stotra (1931)

Raghunath Dhondo Karve

He is the eldest son, by his first wife, of the world famous worker Annasaheb Karve. He was educated under the influence of his father, his mother having died while he was quite young. He passed his M.A. with Mathematics as his voluntary subject. He took up service in the Education Department of the Bombay Government and soon became a Professor of Mathematics.

Raghunathrav had a spirit of independence and had developed a proud character unlike that of his father. He was comparatively a man of retiring nature though he was very strong about some social problems. A man of such character could not pull on in Government Service. He was superceded in service, so he wrote a letter of protest to the D.P.I. Such boldness on the part of a mere servant was not tolerated by the department and he had to retire from service. He had a liking for French. While in Bombay he had studied it privately and had become proficient in it. What he learnt as a mere hobby, now came to his assistance and he took private service as the secretary in a French Firm. He made money by tuition also. Thus he became a permanent resident of Bombay and lived in his own reformed style. Unlike his father Raghunathrav leads a completely Europeanized life. He truly enjoys that fashionable life and shows relish for it. Unfortunately his wife soon became a permanent invalid and got lameness. Raghunathrav with his knowledge of French had studied the science of the sex relationship and especially the subject of birth control. By this study he came to believe that for India with its growing population and its proverbial poverty the only way of relief is the popularization of the science of birth-control and of the remedies available in Europe. So he started a monthly magazine called "Samaj Svasthya" and without fear wrote from month to month on the subjects regarded as sacrosanct and gave expression to ideas opposed to current morality. He was taken to the Court once or twice for writing obscene things but he boldly defended himself and continued his course of writing on the subject.

He is a clear and bold writer. His magazine has become popular among young men and even among the middle aged people. Though educated men are unwilling to speak publicly on these topics Karve's views are silently permeating the minds of people.

His books are as follows:

1. Santati Niyaman (1928); 2. Baher Khyalice Dusparinam (1932); 3. Adhunik Kamasastra (1932); 4. Gupta Rogapasun Bacav (1932); 5. Tvaceci Niga (1935).

S. D. Karandikar

1. Puspa Rani (1931); 2. Krantikarakanca Rajanaitic Itihas; 3. Rajanaitic Karasthan; 4. Desatyagaca Itihas. (Shoukat Ussman's book—Peshawar to Mosco) (1929); 5. Life of Pati-vrata Savitri (1929).

G. M. Ciplunkar

He was a Kokanasth Brahmin. His father was a Mamlatdar and after retirement he lived in Poona where he had a house of his own.

The young Ciplunkar was educated in Poona in the Fergusson College and came under the influence of Annasaheb Karve. After graduation he joined the staff of the newly started Karve's University. For higher education he went to America and got his M. A. degree from the Minisota University. There he was attracted to the subject of Sociology and studied the science of the relations between the sexes and caught the reactionary spirit against excessive liberty of woman taught by men like justice Lindse. Of course he was for the education of women. But he was against co-education as also against the higher education of women exactly on the lines of men's education. So he became enthusiastic of Karve's curriculum and of the new and separate courses of study as well as of the separate schools for girls and grown up ladies and widows. He took up the work of propaganda about these subjects and wrote articles and books on them. The Kanyasala a girls school in the City of Poona was the result of his enthusiasm and strenuous work.

Ciplunkar led a very simple life. He tried different kinds of diet some times trying to live on fruit alone or on milk or an uncooked food. Thus he was a faddist in this respect. But he applied himself strenuously to his duties in the college and the University. He died prematurely leaving wife and children and a posthumouse book.

1. Arogya Marga Pradip (1926); 2. Mulanca Sivaji; 3. Vira Vidula (1931); 4. Viraca Vilap (1931); 5. Vilayatetil Pracalit Strisiksan (1928).

B. R. Abhang

1. Sulabh Marathi Gandharva Vivah Vidhi; 2. Sulabh Marathi Satyanarayan Vidhi; 3. Sulabh Marathi Lagnavidhi;

4. Sulabh Marathi Rojaci Devapuja; 5. Sulabh Marathi Tera Divasace Vidhi.

K. S. Chapre

1. Sri Adi Siddhesvarsvami Caritra (1931); 2. Virsaiva Matabodh (1931); 3. Hangal Srikumar Mahasvami Caritra (1932); 4. Life of Lingayat Sant Madar Ketayya (1932).

M. V. Apte

1. Aici Kartavye (1928); 2. Padatya Phalaca Sandes (1930); 3. Farade ani Raman (1931); 4. Indriy Rasayan (1932).

K. V. Karandikar

1. Ekeri Draksanca Ghad (1928); 2. Vadileya Ciranjiv (1932).

Daji Nages Apte

Daji Nages Apte is a Kokanasth Brahmin from Khed, district Poona where his father was a leading pleader and lived to a good old age and made large property. Daji his eldest son was born at Khed in 1888. His education was all done in Poona and Bombay. He was in the college in the exciting times when the Nationalist movement was very strong in Maharastra. The minds of young students became embued with the new idea of patriotism and nationalism. In Bengal young men went to the extreme of forming secret societies for overthrowing the British power in India. The same thing happened in Maharastra though not on a large scale. Daji had fellow students like Savarkar, Kanhere and others. Even from College days Dajipant had a yearning for writing in Marathi. One of the nationalist aim was to develop the Vernaculars and by writing in them to reach and capture the minds of the masses. But his father seeing the dangerous propensities of his son sent him away from Poona to Allahabad and Nagpur. Daji passed his LL.B. examination from Allahabad University and began to practise at Baroda.

At this time Paranpe's Kal news-paper was very popular.

Dajisaheb began to write in that paper. He wrote an article 'Mrtyuca Darbar' for the paper. Though Sivrampant Paranjpe was a shrewd and cautions editor inadvertantly he allowed that article to appear in his paper for which and for other violent and seditious writings Paranjpe was prosecuted and punished with rigorous imprisonment. Though legally Government could not do anything against Apte his name went into the black-book of Government. Moreover, Dajisaheb was practising as a pleader at Baroda. But he was not a man for Law, his inclination being in the line of literature. He found a good opportunity at Baroda to devote his time and energy to literary work. In time, he became a recognised leading literary luminary of Baroda. So he was often elected as President and Chairman of literary.Conferences. He is a good speaker and in his younger days he had won prizes in elocution competitions. His latest book may be regarded as his master-piece. It is in three big volumes, being the life of Sir Sayajirav Gayakvad. He has written a lot of articles in newspapers and other magazines.

His works are the following:

1. Sudharana ani Pragati (1906); 2. Life of Mirabai; 3. Hindi Sumeri Samskrti (1928), 4. Narsimha Meheta (1933); 5 Nitisastra Prabhodh (1933); 6. Sulabh Nitisastra (1933); 7. Life of Sir Sayajirav Gayakvad in 3 volumes.

G. D. Kelkar

1. Gyasacya divyavar basavinyacya topya (1927); 2. Bambunce Harature (1927); 3. Blanketaca Karkhana; 4. Phinail va Phinail powder (1928).

H. N. Katve

1. Prasna Vicar (Astrological work)—(1932); 2. Rahu vicar (1932); 3. Tej (1932).

K. B. Kulkarni

1. Pesavyance Payapos (1928); 2. Mogara (poems)—1929), 3. Life of Aravind Ghosa (1935).

R. P. Kanitkar

1. Pandit Motilal Nehru (1930); 2. Vaman Malhar Josi (1930); 3. Ravindranath Tagore (1932).

V. G. Kale

He is a Kokanasth Brahmin from Poona. He comes from a very poor family of a priestly class esteemed low even in that class. So young Kale had to educate himself by self-effort and during his college career he had to do some work that come to his hand. Fortunately for him young Kale got the rare opportunity of being a reader of Ravsaheb Ranade. Ravsaheb was known to be a tremendous reader himself and he made his readers do similarly. But unlike the common run of readers or persons who came into contact with great men Vamanrav Kale made a very good use of that rare opportunity to read with, to converse with and discuss with such a great man on a variety of topics and especially on Economics in general and Indian economics in particular. At the feet of Ranade Vamanrav learnt the methods of investigation and collection of statistical information. This association with a great economist laid the foundation of Kale's future fame and name.

After passing his M. A. Examination in History and Economics Kale was taken as a probationer in the Fergusson College and in due course he became a life-member of the D. E. Society and professor of Economics in the Fergusson College and soon earned a good name as a successful teacher. At this very time the Arts courses were revised and for Intermediate Arts examinastion a new subject Indian Administration was prescribed as a compulsory subject. Prof. Kale took this opportunity and wrote a text book dealing with the prescribed course for Inter Arts. The book became at once popular and editions after editions of the book were published. By this book alone Kale made a lot of money. Later on other professors came into the field and Kale's income was some-what reduced. Then Vamanrav wrote a big text book on Indian Economics useful for both B. A. and M. A. studdents taking economics as their optional subject. This book too is very popular with students of all Indian Universities and hence there is a large sale of this book too.

Soon after Dr. Paranjpye became a Minister of Education, he used his influence with Government in favour of Kale and he was appointed a member of the Tariff Board for about 2 or 3 years on a salary of Rs. 2000/ per month. This gave him further opportunity to study the economic and industrial problems of India. So he soon came to be recognised as an all India specialist in Indian Economics.

After his term of service was over Prof. Kale retired from the Fergusson College though he still gives lectures to post-graduate students of the Fergusson College. Thus all Prof. Kale's literary work has been on the subject of Indian Economics and allied problems and he wrote mostly in English. But he wrote stray articles in Marathi for Marathi magazines and their special numbers. His indepedent Marathi works are the following.

1. Indian Economics 2. Hindusthanaci Reserve Bank (1935); 3. Vyapari Uladhali (1935); 4. Byanka ani tyance Vyavahar (1934); 5. Arthasastra; 6. Viksiptaravfarce; 7. Essays in various magazines.

L. T. Puranik

1. Manavi Jivan or Atmyace Avinasitva (1927); 2. pralhad Caritra (1930);

K. A. Keluskar

1. Gunajirav Dhondabarav Ghule (1934); 2. Govind Janardan Borkar or Gajanan Svami Jyotisi (1932); 3. Madhavrav Raghoji Rokade (1227).

Tambe Sastri

1. Srimat Ehagavadgiteci ojasvi Sikavan (1930); 2. Rastronnati Lekhamala Pancadasi (1928); 3. Valmiki Ramayan,

Parts I & II (1931); 4. Maze Ayusyaca Jamakharca (1931).

Svami Sivanand

1. Dampatya Rahasya Vidnyan (1930); 2. Brahmacarya hec Jivan ani Viryanas hac Mrtyu; 3. Manovanchit Santati.

Vaijanath Kasinath Rajvade

Vaijanath Kasinath Rajvade is a Kokanasth Brahmin hailing from Kokan. He is the elder brother of Visvanathpant Rajvade. Both the brothers made a name in their chosen profession. The elder brother was born in 1860 at Vasai, taluka Pen, district Kolaba. He received his primary education first at Pen and then at Poona. He did his High School course in the Poona High School. Then he joined the Wilson College, Bombay. But he passed his final B. A. Examination from the Deccan College. He was for three years a Daksina fellow in the Deccan College. After passing his M. A. Examination with English and Sanskrit as his optional subject Rajvade accepted professorship of English in Sindh College at Karachi. Here he remained for eight years and made a great reputation as an excellent teacher of English literature. In 1895 Prof. Kelkar of the Fergusson College died suddenly and prematurely. So to fill up his place Prof. Rajvade was prevailed upon to give up his lucrative post of professorship at Karachi and join the Deccan Education Society as a Life-member. Rajvade with a rare sense of self-sacrifice came to the College. He found here a wider scope for his work. He was able to teach English to thousands of students. He was highly respected and feared by students. Though he was professor of English in both colleges Rajvade had a great liking for Sanskrit language and literature. It was really his first love but he could not do much while he was absorbed in teaching English for which he had to read much. But after completing his pledge of twenty years' service in the College Vaijnathpant retired from service honoured by both his Colleagues and students. Since his retirement he is able to devote all his time and energy to his favourite work Sanskrit research, except for a short period of about four years when he was made Principal of Surat College. Like Ravsaheb Ranade Rajvade has a bad eye sight which was further spoiled by excessive reading, So now-a-days he has to take the assistance of a reader and a writer for all his reading and writing work. Rajvade is very regular in his habits and so even at this green old age he is able to do high class literary work. His principal literary work is about Sanskrit language and literature. His Marathi writing is only a bye-product and an occasional pastime. But he has made a valuable contribution to Marathi literature by translating into Marathi the obscure and difficult grammatical work in Sanskrit the 'Nirukta'. His book is published in the Icalkaranji series. A greater work Rajvade has done in ascertaining the correct meanings of words occurring in the Rgved. By comparative study of the several passages in which the same word occurs he has tried to ascertain the true meaning of words. This work of his is written in English and is an interesting reading though it is on an obscure subject.

His Marathi books are these:

1. Yaska's Nirukta; 2. Kesavasutancya Kavitance Pariksan; 3. Two essays about Kalidas' Sakuntal; 4. Brahmankalin Jatibhed; 5. Anglasarasvataca Itihas; 6. Kadambari (Philosophy of fiction) (1928); 7. Sankirna Nibandh, Parts I & II (1932).

R. A. Rairkar

1. Life of Prafullacandra Ray (1933); 2. Premace Tattvadnyan (1935); 3. Santati Niyaman (1935).

D. S. Kulkarni and B. G. Nene

1. Nisagita (1928); 2. Govindagraj (1929); 3. Tukaram (1933).

G. B. Ciplunkar

1. Maharani Laksmibai Zamsi (1927); 2. Nibandh Kasa Lihava (1928).

R. G. Bhide

1. Narayan Maharaj Caritra (1936); 2. Pandit Madan Mohan Malaviy (1932); 3. Subhas Candra Bose (1929).

S. S. Pandharkar

1. Rasayan Sastra (1930); 2. Samanyavastudharma (1928).

Mrs. Santabai Pardesi

She is a widow living in Dharangaon as a teacher. She was born in 1908.

1. Devi Ahilyabai; 2. Rajmata Jijabai; 3. Viramata Vidula; 4. Santa gita.

R. M. Bhamburkar

1. Samarth Ramdas (1933); 2. Life of Karn (1933); Life of Buddha (1934).

G. V. Patvardhan

1. Nana Yesu Surve Yance Caritra (1930); 2. Acardharma (1930); 3. Matesvari—Novel (1929).

Janardan Sakharam Karandikar

Janardan Sakharam Karandikar is a Kokanasth Brahmin. He was born at Kundgol, Jamkhindi State in 1875. His High School education was done at Jamkhindi High School from where he passed his Matriculation examination. Then he joined the Fergusson College and in due course passed his B. A. Examination. Then he went to Bombay and from the Government Law College passed his LL. B. Examination. But having no inclination for pleader's profession and having a literary turn of mind, he took to journalism as his permanent profession after doing for some years teacher's work at Mudhol, Dharwad and Talegaon. He was taken up on the editorial staff of Kesari in 1912 where he became permanent. After the retirement of Tatyasaheb Kelkar Karandikar became the Chief Editor, a position he still holds. In that capacity he has to write on all manner of subjects, long leaders, leaderettes, notes and what not. But besides his routine work in Kesari he found time to write articles in magazines and has to his credit the following works. Karandikar is a speaker as well. He has a trenchant style. He has been able to keep the high level of Kesari newspaper.

1. Jagatil Krantikarak Ladhaya (1908); 2. Kautiliya Arthasastra, Parts I & II (1926 & 1928).

B. N. Athavale

1. Rikamtekada Bandya ani Hausi Akka (1930); 2. Nava Karar (1929).

P. B Athavale

1. Jagatil Vidyaman Dharma (Traslation of World's living religions) (1935); 2. Pracin Sahitya (1934).

D. B. Barve

1. Grhasastra (1928); 2. Sarir Sangopan Sastra (1930).

Vasudev Krsna Bhave

Vasudev Krsna Bhave was born at Miraj in 1884. His father Krsnajipant was a renowned school-master serving in Satara district. Naturally Vasudevrav received his primary education under the direct influence of his father. His High School education was done mostly at Miraj but he passed his School Final examination from Satara High School in 1904. As his father was unable to give college education to his son, he had to service private or Government. So his career proved a chequered one for about a decade. With his hot blood he took part in the picketing movement. There was a severe fight between volunteers and a European officer. So he was fined

Rs. 135. After this incident Bhave took up the Svadesi movement. He learnt the art of weaving and tried to earn his living by manufacturing cloth. But as is well-known one cannot get living wage in the weaving line. So Bhave left it and returned to the teacher's profession. Here he found his true vocation. So he made up his mind at this late age to acquire higher liberal education and by dint of self-effort he studied privately for the Matriculation and passed it as an external student in 1912. Then he joined the Fergusson College and succeeded in passing his B. A. examination in 1917, though he had to work hard and had to meet with difficulties. Thus at the age of 33 he completed his higher education. But he had now found his real vocation. From his young age he had fondness for reading books and especially newspapers. So he was influenced to write for newspapers.

So after passing his B. A. examination he took to journalism as his profession and became an assistant editor of Lokasangrah a newly started nationalist paper. But it proved short-lived and soon came to an end. Bhave's literary talents were marked by Tatyasaheb Kelkar, the editor of Kesari and Bhave was taken up on the editorial staff of that paper. His literary work was highly appreciated by the authorities of the paper and gradually he came to occupy an important position in the editorial staff of the famous paper. In this capacity Bhave has to write on a variety of topics and on the spur of the moment. So he formed his own lucid and clear style, and became an expert in the art of successful journalistic writing. He has a facile pen and can write quickly. But he has fondness for writing on subjects of more permanent interest. Bhave is now recognised as a great Marathi writer. His works are the following :

1. Turkance Samrajya; 2. Brahmanetarvadace Svarup; 3. Khara Desbhakta (novel); 4. Pesavekalin Maharastra; 5. Pritivivah (drama); 6. Daksa Kanya Sati (1935).

Sripad Ramcandra Parasnis

Parasnis' family is a renowned family of Satara. Rav

Bahadur D. B. Parasnis who made a great name as a historian and a research worker was the uncle of young Parasnis. He was born at Vikhale, district Satara in 1901. His primary and secondary education was done at Satara. For his higher education he came to Poona and joined the Fergusson College from where he passed his B. A. and M.A. examinations (the latter was passed twice and in three subjects—English, Sanskrit and Marathi). Then he took to the profession of teaching by becoming a teacher in Ahmednagar Education Society's High School. There he showed his efficiency as a teacher and he was appointed the Head-master of the High School. But he did not remain there long. He came to Poona as a teacher in the New English School, Poona. From there he went to the Willingdon College Sangli as a Professor of Marathi. He was soon taken up as a life-member of the Deccan Education Society and sent to Satara to assume the responsible position of Superintendent of Satara New English School where he is still working.

As to his literary work it is not inconsiderable, taking into account the heavy responsibilities of a life-member of the Deccan Education Society and especially those of a big school of nearly 1000 students. He has carefully studied both modern and old Marathi literature, as is seen from the series of four books that he and Professor Mahadev Ramcandra Paranjpe of the Siksan Prasarak Mandali wrote for Messrs. MacMillan and Co. These books contain both Prose and Poetry selections from the writings of poets and writers. This series is a valuable addition to the text books for High Schools. In the selection as well as in the notes and brief notices of authors Parasnis has indicated his power of appreciation of Marathi literature. Besides this series which is a joint work and occasional essays and writings in Magazines he has independently published the following books :

1. Life of Sir Isaac Newton; 2. Biography of Gopal Krsna Gokhale (Bhai Paramanand prize was given for this); 3. Modern Marathi containing its brief grammar, essay writing and a short History of the Marathi language and

literature (jointly with Prof. Kulkarni of Elphinstone College); 4. Translation of Prof. Patvardhan's Wilson. Philological lectures on the Bhakti School in Maharastra; 5. Translation of Cintamanrav Vaidya's History of Sanskrit literature (A big book of seven hundred pages ready for publication).

Ramcandra Sripad Jog

Ramcandra Sripad Jog was born at Gadhinglas in Kolhapur State at his maternal grandfather's house. His father was a brilliant student of the New English School Poona and won Nana Sankarset Scholarship for proficiency in Sanskrit at the Matriculation examination. He equally distinguished himself in the College examinations showing particularly his fine command over the English language. He was a favourite pupil of Gopal Krsna Gokhale. On account of bad eyesight as also due to domestic difficulties he could not graduate and had to seek service. For some time he served in the Akkalkote State. Hence young Jog studied upto his sixth English standard in the Akkalkote High School. But about that time Sripadrav got the post of Head Clerk to the Chief Officer, Poona City Municipality where he rose to be an assistant to the Chief Officer. It was the improved financial condition of his father that enabled young Jog to receive higher education. He successfully and creditably passed his B A. in 1923, and his M.A. in 1925 from the Fergusson College. Immediately after his passing M.A. Ramcandrarav was appointed in 1926 professor of Marathi in Hansaraj Pragji College, Nasik. Here he worked for about six years. He was then taken up as a professor of Marathi in the Furgusson College and was soon made a life-member of the Deccan Education Society and then he was transferred to the Willingdon College Sangli as a professor of Marathi. Prof. Jog has made a good name as an able teacher of Marathi and is very popular with his students. He is a keen sportsman and takes very great interest among students, taking part in their sports and social gatherings. Now to turn to Jog's literary work. Prof. Jog did not make haste to write and publish his poems while he was still studying in the College.

He published two small collections of poems mostly ol ve poems by name 'Jyotsnagita (Song of Moonlight) and 'Nisagita' (Song of night) after passing his B. A. and M. A. examinations. Prof. Jog received the pen-name 'Nisigandh' by accident in this way. A certain poem praying the Nisigandh (flower smelling at night) flower to bestow its purity upon the author appeared in the Fergusson College magazine. The poem was a commonplace performance, but found its way to the college magazine because of the writer being a lady student. So Prof. Jog sent a rejoinder headed 'Sikavuni vimalata na yetase' (Purity does not come by instruction). This rejoinder appeared under the name 'Nisigandh'. Since then the above name stuck to Jog permanently. But Prof. Jog's permanent contribution to Marathi literature is his 'Abhinav Kavyaprakas (New light on Poetry). This name is a little altered echo of the famous Sanskrit work on Poetics by Mammata. The book is an exposition of Poetics in Marathi, a book which differs from others of its kind by giving a detailed discussion of the important topics and theory of Sanskrit Poetics in addition to the discussion of mere Alankaras (Figures of Speech). It also takes into account relevant views in English criticism and deals with modern forms of poetry though of course the bulk of the book is devoted to the exposition and criticism of important Sanskrit authors. This book of Prof. Jog is undoubtedly a valuable addition to Modern Marathi literature on its scientific side. It is deservedly recommended as a text book for the M.A. examination of the Bombay University.

Jog's fourth book is on its way to publication. Besides these separately published books he has written stray articles by way of criticism and of reviews of books. They are not still published in a book form. Prof. Jog has fine literary capacity and finer power of clear exposition of difficult and intricate topics. He is still comparatively young and may therefore come to make valuable addition to Modern Marathi literature.

Narhar Kasinath Gharpure

Narhar Kasinath Gharpure is through and through a Poona man imbibing as it were its spirit from his birth there in 1904. Practically all his education was done in Poona in its several schools. But unfortunately while still a school student of twelve years of age only he lost his father. So for getting his subsequent higher education he had to undergo a good deal of trouble. By strenuous effort however he completed his University education and passed his B. A. examination in 1924 with English and German as his optional subjects. After a few years he passed his M. A. examination with the same subjects. Then he served in a school in Bombay and while there he filled his LL. B. terms. Then he came to Poona and worked as a teacher in several Poona High Schools passing the Secondary Teacher's Certificate examination, during that period. In 1927 he passed his LL. B. examination and then for three years from 1929 to 1931 he practised in Civil and Criminal Courts of Poona.

But Gharpure probably came to see that to succeed as a lawyer was no easy job, compared with passing examinations. So he took up the Professorship of German in the Fergusson College. While working there Gharpure was fortunate to secure the scholarship of the Indian Institute in a German academy. So he went to Germany and joined the Cologn University and received the Degree of Ph. D. in 1933 for proficiency in German language and literature. After returning home he began to teach German in the New English School and the Fergusson College. Thus Narharpant had to lead a chequered career for a few years. But at last he was permanently settled in life with a fixed work of his liking when he was admitted as a life member of the Deccan Education Society. Since then he is working as a professor of German in the Fergusson College.

But Prof. Gharpure has a wonderful fund of energy and along with it great ambition. Hence he has become an active member of about a dozen societies and institutions in Poona, working either as President, or Vice-President, Chairman or Secretary.

Now to turn to his literary activities and their actual output. This output is enormous looking to the short time between the conclusion of his student life and his settled work as a Professor.

He had fondness for reading and writing Marathi articles and essays from his very young age. But unlike some impatient young writers he did not publish what he wrote in those early days. His first article was published in 1927 in the Nutan Marathi Vidyalay Magazine. Since then he is continually writing for the numerous Marathi magazines. His literary activity has not resulted in any pecuniary lose to him, though he has not made any money out of it. Besides these stray writings Gharpure translated a German novel into Marathi under the name Vedapisa. He has written a drama by name Grhapas which is still unpublished. At present he is engaged in writing a memorial volume on Mahadev Moresvar Kunte. This is just in the fitness of things, Gharpure being a maternal grandson of the Great Kunte.

His works are the following :

1. Publication of all the writings of Annasaheb Kirloskar, the father of Sangit drama in Marathi; 2 Vedapisa (adaptation of a German novel); 3. Stray articles and writings in papers and magazines; 4. Life of Mahadev Moresvar Kunte.

Gajanan Sripad Khair

Gajanan Sripad Khair is a Yajurvedi Sakhiya Brahmin, his family being a permanent inhabitant of Poona. Gajanan was born in Poona about the year 1900. His father was a postmaster but he died when Gajanan was only six months old. Thus he was left practically an orphan. For what could his poor mother do? She brought him up till Gajanan came of age fit for school instruction. She was an affectionate lady for whom Gajanan feels deep love and respect. On account of utter poverty of the family Gajanan had to learn under great difficulty and by self-effort. He had to be a Madhukari like Mahadev Moresvar Kunte. It is very difficult for a foreigner to know exactly what a Madhukari is and how he lives. Madhukari is a poor boy who begs from door to door and receives cooked food part of which he eats after going home and the remaining part he keeps for his night meal. He has to go about in hot sun, bear-headed and shoeless. Such is a brahmin Madhukari! But many a brahmin boy has lived and learnt under such conditions, and attained fame and fortune in after life. Messrs. Ketkar and Kanitkar, seeing the hard life of such orphans and with a view to improve their lot started an institution called Anath Vidyarthi Gṛha at Chinchwad near Poona where they could hire a building at a cheap rent for the accommodation of the orphans. They appealed to people who already gave Madhukari (the daily cooked food) to the orphans to pay instead monthly contribution in kind or money to the institution where these orphans live. They where made to live as cheaply as possible and to do even their cooking and other domestic work by turns. Gajanan was admitted into Anatl : Vidyarthi Grha when he was in the sixth English Standard. After completing his education he became a life-member of the institution and is now one of its prominent members.

Gajananrav passed his Matriculation examination in 1916, his B.A. in 1920 and his M.A. in 1923. Immediately he took up the work of the Anath Vidyarthi Grha. By this time the Grha had been shifted from Chinchwad to Poona, the latter proving a more suitable place. Dr. Khair has in all given 12 years' service to his institution.

In 1931 Gajananrav went to America and studied there for two years getting A M. degree (corresponding to M.A. of Indian Universities) of the Columbia University and Ph. D. degree of the New York University. Some pecuniary help was given to him by his Grha but he had to supplement it largely by doing odd jobs. He even cooked at the houses of Indians naturalised in America and thus got money for his education. All this hard and strenuous life of Dr. Khair bears out his innate love of learning. He not only learnt the subjects for his degree examinations but made a special study of the teaching methods and different courses of study taught to American boys so as to make them self-sufficient and capable citizens. From America he came to Europe and saw the educational systems of England, Germany, Russia and Switzerland and returned home in 1933. Then he wrote a big book in Marathi, giving an account of the system of education obtaining in each of the countries he visited. This is a very interesting book and gives very detailed information about the countries and their educational systems. After four years' stay and work in Poona Dr. Khair went to Japan in 1937 and remained there for six months. During this short stay he made a close study of Japanese education as he did that of European countries. On his way back he visited the beautiful island of Bali where there is still a Hindu King and where Hindu civilization at the time of its spread beyond the boundaries of India is still to be seen.

Dr. Khair's literary works are the following :

1. Jagatil Samajakranti va Hindusthan (Social revolution in the world and India); 2. Pascimatya Siksan Paddhati (Method of Western Education); 3. Japanci Jivankranti (Revolution in the Japanese life); 4. Japanci Siksana Paddhati (Method of education in Japan—to be published); 5. Bali Betatil Bharatiya Samskrit (Indian civilization in the Bali island).

Maheswar Anant Karandikar

Mahesvar Anant Karandikar is a Kokanasth Brahmin. He was born in 1909 at Chinchani, district Thana. He received his secondary education in Akola High School, Berar. His Higher education upto his M.A. was done in several Colleges i.e. Mission College, Indore; Sir Parashuram Bhau College, Poona and Wilson College, Bombay. He passed his B.A. and M.A. examinations in the first class with Marathi as his selected subject. Soon after he was appointed a professor of Marathi in the Lingaraj College, Belgaum.

Though still young he has earned a good name as an efficient teacher of Marathi.

Now to turn to his literary work. Like Prof. Jog of Willingdon College Prof. Karandikar began writing only after completing his College career and after being well settled in life. He seems to possess a facile pen and a fertile imagination, though he does not seem to have poetic power. For within a short time he has put considerable literary work. All his books are in prose. They are the following :

1. Kucambana Konaci ? (Whose difficulty ?); 2. Vangmaya Carceci Mulatattve (Principles of literary criticism); 3. Khanavalice Phayade (Advantages of a hotel) humorous essay. Karandikar has edited Vaman Pandit's poem 'Dvarakavijay (conquest of Dvarka) as also some Sanskrit texts for college students. His literary activity in Marathi is due to his innate love of Marathi literature. He was influenced and induced to write in Marathi by his teacher Mr. Cincalkar. He has not made money by his writings so far.

G.B. Borvankar

1. Maharastraca Gostirup Itihas (1928); 2. Musalmani Karkirda.

Y.M. Cakradev

1. Svadesi Sudha (1930); 2. Udbhijasastra Pravesika (1927).

Siddhesvarsastri Citrav

1. Bharatvarsiy Pracin Caritra Kosa (1932); 2. Rgvedace Marathi Bhasantar (1928).

K.B. Desmukh

1. Pracin va Arvacin Kshatriy yanca sacitra itihas, Parts I & II (1930).

D.G. Dhabbu

1. Samarthanca Maharastra (1921); 2. Yasoda or Janata Janardan (1931).

B.R. Dhurandhar

1. Gita Bodh (1931); 2. Life of Tukaram (1928).

Dhananjay Ramcandra Gadgil

Dhananjay Ramcandra Gadgil comes from the Province of Nagpur. His father Ramcandra Bhargav Gadgil was a leading pleader at Nagpur. Naturally Dhananjay was educated at Nagpur in the Patvardhan High School. For his higher education he was sent to England in 1918 and there he joined Queen's College Cambridge and specialised in Economics. Dhananjayrav came out of the University as a young man with a brilliant career and a keen desire to serve his country, having got M.A. and M. Litt. (Master of Literature) degrees of Cambridge. He returned to India in 1923 and was immediately taken up in the Finance Department of the Bombay Government. But having a liking for teaching and research work he gave up his lucrative job and became the Principal of the Surat College. While there he became connected by marriage with the daughter of the great liberal leader of Maharashtra Rav Bahadur Kale of Satara who had made up his mind to start an Economic Institute called 'The Gokhale Institute of Economics and Politics.' He made an endowment of a lac of rupees for the maintenance of the Institution. He appointed Dhananjayrav as the Director of the Institute. So he came over to Poona. He does Post-graduate teaching and devotes his main energy to the research work on Economic questions concerning India in general and Bombay Province in particular. So Gadgil's work being concerned with All-India problems is mainly done through the English language. Like that of Prof. Kale Gadgil's Marathi writing is only a bye-product. Still he is a clear writer and his books are quite readable and full of information. His works are these :

1. Hindusthanca Arthik Itihas; 2. Stray writings and articles in Magazines.

K. G. Gharpure

1. Maharastratil Sap (1928); 2. Pani ani Arogya (1928).

V. H. Gharpure

1. James Garfield (1930); 2. Natyasastra (1930).

G. M. Gule

1. Hindusthanca Rajya Karbhar (1927); 2. Marathyancya Gosti (1928).

P. P. Gokhale

1. Gokhale ani History (1933); 2. Jagrt Satara (1935).

V.V. Hardikar

1. Daksin Haidarabad (1931); 2. Haidarabad Samsthan Varnan (1931).

Mrs. Apurnabai Despande

Mrs. Apurnabai Despande was born in 1911. She was a bright girl and throughout her educational course of Prof. Karve's Women's University she won prizes and scholarships and passed the graduate's examination of the University. She had a natural liking for poetry and literature from early age. She has written simple poems and stray pieces for children. She has also written short stories and dramatic pieces. She is still young and may produce many more literary books.

V. N. Jaccal

1. Set Hiracand Nemcand Dosi (1936); 2. Sri Sadguru Subharay (1936).

B. B. Josi

1. Ksetra Nirmalesvar (1931); 2. Vajresvarica Itihas (1934).

B. R. Josi

1. Vividh Nibandh Sangrah (1927); 2. Ran Phule (1928).

D. S. Josi

1. Sulabh Sastriya Dnyan (1931); Hindustanca Itihas (1928).

P. G. Josi

1. Kokanaci Navi Bhatseti (1933); 2. Kalami Ambyaci Lagvad (1932).

Y. G. Josi

1. Sangit Srimukhat (1930); 2. Mangal Prabhat (1932).

Morsevar Gopal Kale

Moresvar Gopal Kale comes from a Kokanasth family of Roha, district Kolaba. But on account of poverty it removed to Kavad near Bhivandi, district Thana where Moresvar was born in 1894. After his vernacular education was over he joined Government Training College, Poona and passed the third year's examination in 1913. Then he secured service for two and half years as a teacher in a Government School. Then he took six month's leave in 1916-1917 and used it for travelling. He was influenced to traval by reading a book of Satyadev named 'Ameriketil garib Vidyarthi' (A Poor American Scholar) translated by Gunaji of Belgaum. For, that book gave him the secret of travelling by a poor man, that secret being nothing else but to use his legs mostly and to spend money only when it was absolutely necessary. So Moresvarpant used the six month's leave in travelling as far Himalayan tracts of India and in seeing Nepal. Kale had a robust constitution capable of bearing any strain. His dress in travelling was not like the usual loose dress of a Maharastriyan but it made a fine impression. With his long woolen coat, with his strong and tall stick, with his close fitting cap and his small and light kit hanging from his shoulder, Kale appeared a perfect pedestrian traveller. From that time he became known among his friends and acquaintances as 'Payi pravasi Kale (Pedestrian traveller Kale).

Soon after his first trip Kale left Government service and came to Poona. Here he was taken up as Teacher in Nutan Marathi Vidyalay. Here he worked for about 16 years. There was some hitch between him and the authorities of the School and his services, were dispensed with. Kale regarded the treatment given to him as illegal and unjust. Kale's Kokani spirit of litigation became awakened which made him to file a suit against the School for his pay etc. The suit is still going on. Of course Kale had to find out some other job to get money and he became an agent of Common wealth Insurance Company as also of Hind Benefit Society. All his pedestrian travelling was done while he was still a teacher in the school, his financial condition then being moderately satisfactory. So he could spend a little money and could use his long vacations for travelling. But since he left the school he could not find time to travel. It was only towards the end of 1938 that he travelled to Southern India and went as for as Rameshvar and to Malbar as far as Travancore. He returned to Poona quite recently (i. e. in the last week of January 1939) and of course he proposes to write soon an account of his trip. This would be his fourth travel book—the fist three published years before have become very popular. Especially his book on Kashmere has gone into third edition.

Kale has shown how a poor man can do and enjoy travelling and derive benefit from it without spending much money by doing most of travelling by walking from place to place and living in Sarayas and Dharmasalas (free resting houses) to save money on hotels. He was prepared to receive help either in kind or money from charitably disposed people. Kale's feat is wonderful and is sure to evoke admiration from one who knows his life. His books are the following:

1. Mazya Himalayatil Yatra (1933); 2. Maza Kasmirca Pravas (1930); 3. Amaci Mhaisurci Yatra.

Anandrav Cannappa Sedjale alias Ambikaprasad

Anandrav Cannappa Sedjale alias Ambikaprasad belongs to Lingayat community. He was born in 1908 in Sholapur and was educated there. He began his literary career in 1926 with the production of the short play named Tejasvi Tara'. He has a facile pen and within just a decade he has brought out about half a dozen plays and half a dozen novels and short stories. The list of his would-be plays and cinema tales is a large one indeed ! He is just, thirty years of age. So he promises to be a voluminous writer rivalling the literary giants of the last generation. He has also none journalistic work and is at present working as co-editor of Sudarsan a weekly paper of Sholapur.

His short play named 'Banavatanca Bazar' is a social play about untouchability advocating removal in an interesting manner and pointing out the vice and hypocrisy of the higher classes of Hindu society. It is quite a readable play.

Y. M. Kale

1. Nagpur Prantaca Itihas (1934); 2. Gonda Lokanca Itihas (1927).

Anant Kanekar

Anant Kanekar was born in Bombay in 1905. On account of the early death of his father he was brought up by his mother and maternal uncle. His school education was done in the Cikitsak Samuh High School, Bombay. He passed his B. A. in 1927 from St. Xaviers College and his LL.B. in 1929. He practised three years but had no heart in the profession. He worked as director and secretary of 'Manvantar,' a dramatic company of educated men and women started for staging new plays. But on account of internal quarrels the institution became short-lived. Anantrav is at present co-editor of a newspaper named 'Citra.'

He began writing poetry from his school days. But for writing it he wants to get a mood. As for prose writing he can do it whenever he desires to do so. He has so far written a large number of short stories and short essays. He had been to Europe and thereby has enlarged his experience. He has written an account of it serially in his paper. His works are the following:

1. Candarat va itar Kavita; 2. Tutlele Tare; 3. Jagatya Chaya; 4. Gharkul (drama); 5. Simpale ani Moti; 6. Pikali Pane.

Y. G. Kanetkar

1. Life of Sakharambapu (1935); 2. Life of Arvind Ghos (1931).

G. N. Kanitkar alias Balukaka Kanitkar

1. Daridra Narayanace Caritra (1931); 2. Svavalambi Gram Ghatana (1931); 3. Marathyancya Mulakhat (1936); 4. Setkaryanci Chavani (1936).

Srinivas Narayan Karnataki

Srinivas Narayan Karnataki was born in 1865 at Shahapur. His family belonged to the priestly class and as such in his early years young Srinivas was made to recite Vedas for four or five years. But his father, seeing the uselessness of that learning sent him to Shahapur School at first, then to Belgaum High School from where he passed his Matriculation examination in 1884. In his school career he was regarded as a bright boy though he was not very industrious and studious. Then he came to Bombay for his college education and studied there for two years. But on account of financial difficulty as also due to illness he had to give up his college career. He then took up service in the Customs Department. While serving here there was a theft of Rs. 2000 from the treasury for which Srinivasrav was rightly held to be responsible though the theft in reality was committed by the office peon. The superior officers as also the friends of Karnataki knew that he was innocent. So he was continued in service after he had made good the stolen amount which he did with the ready help of his friends. After three years the theft was discovered and the peon was found guilty. So Government returned the sum of Rs. 2000 to Srinivasrav. Such was the due reward for his honesty. After faithfully serving Government Srinivasrav retired in 1920 and since that time he is staying in Poona, a fairly old man.

Though he used to write both in Marathi and English while he was in service, he devoted all his time and energy after retirement to literary work for which he had prepared himself by his stray writings in newspapers and magazines.

His chief literary works being biographical he may be called a biographer of modern times. Till now he has Published four fairly big biographies of Dr. Bhandarkar, Justice Telang, D. Bhau Daji Lad and Sankar Pandurang Pandit. These are all carefully written lives after securing all available information about these leaders of Hindu society. Srinivasrav has developed a fine sober style befitting a serious subject like biography. All his books are very interesting and are full of information and anecdotes about the people about whom he has written. All these biographies have been very well received by the public and have became a valuable addition to the biographical section of Marathi literature.

1. Life of Dr. Bhandarkar (1927); 2. Life of Dr. Bhau Daji Lad (1931); 3. Life of Telang; 4. Life of Sankar Pandurang Pandit.

M. S. Kelkar

1. Mahatma Gandhi (1932); 2. Siv Chatrapati.

G. V. Kelkar

1. Tilakanci Bhasa Saili (1931); 2. Vakilana Samansa (1928).

G. D. Khanolkar

1. Lala Lajapatray (1931); 2. Visnu Govind Vijapurkar (1928) 3. Prem ani Vidvatta va Itar Katha (1932); 4. Life of Sripad Krsna Kolatkar (1927); 5. Modern Literary Men (1927); 6. Essays.

Miss Balubai Khare

1. Alankar Manjusa (1931); 2. Striyancya hakatici Sudharana (1930).

S. D. Kshirsagar

1. Gomantak Suddhica Itihas (1931); 2. Dharmavir Kumar Hakikatray (1932).

Raghunath Sastri Kokje

1. Dharma Svarup Nirnay (1933); 2. Nava Acar Dharma (1936).

B. S. Kohotkar

1. Khadyapadarthance Prthakkaran (1930); 2. Calcutta (1933).

M. P. Kolhe

1. Pancayat Kamkaj (1932); 2. Pancayat Pradip (1932).

M. M. Kulkarni

1. Purva ani Pascim ani Yuropatil Pravasaci Tipane (1932); 2. Cakravarti Napoleon (1934).

B. N. Kumbhar

1. Amaca alpa Pravas (1932); 2. Khedegav va Siksan (1932).

A. R. Lagu

1. Life of Gopalrav Govind Patvardhan (1930); 2. Life of Purusottamrav Daji Patvardhan (1936).

J. S. Medhekar

1. Kitak Paricay (1930); 2. Sastriy Sulabh Gosti (1931).

Balibhai Mehta

1. Khadi Mimamsa (1930); 2. Vaibhavsali Hindusthan (1930).

G. V. Modak

1. Yuropace Adharastambha (1934); 2. Lahan Mulanca Maharastra (1934).

M. G. Modak

1. Sikshan Sastra va Adhyapan kala (1931).

B. K. More

1. Nhavi Jatica Itihas (1928); 2. Nhavi Samajacya Unnatica Rajmarga (1928).

G. P. Murdesvar

1. Kaivalyasagar (1931); 2. Dnyan Sagar (1931).

V. R. Nerurkar

1. Marathica Samsar (1928); 2. Akabarace Vedasadhan (1930); 3. Utkantha (1936); 4. Nirzar (poems) (1936); 5. To Ksan (1924); 6. Dudhari Suri (1928).

Dvarkanath Narayan Raje

Dvarkanath Narayan Raje deserves a mention not because he was a great literary writer but simply for the singleness of purpose with which he studied his favourite subject. He wrote books on his favourite subject in simple and clear language with many examples of horoscopes of famous men.

Dvarkanath Raje was Kayasth Prabhu by caste. He was born at Panvel, district Kolaba in 1883. For his secondary education he went to Kolhapur. After successfully completing his course he took service in the Postal Department and spent his life in the faithful discharge of his duty. It was at this time that he was led to the study of Astrology. He quietly and in his leisure hours fully studied this subject and read both European and Indian books. He also studied the horoscopes of his friends and of famous men in India and outside. After such full equipment he wrote his three works :

1. Jataknidhi; 2. Jatakrahasya; 3. Jataknidan.

G. B. Nirantar

1. Rasiyaca Gandhi (1933): 2. Hindu Dharmavaril Kalanka (1935).

G. P. Ogale

1. America Part I & II (1932); 2. Edison (1932).

K. L. Ogale

1. Vedakalanirnay (1928); 2. Kavikulaguru Kalidas (1934).

Narayan Mahadev Patvardhan

Narayan Mahadev Patvardhan comes from a Kokanasth Sastri family. He was born at Poona in 1891. He was educated partly at Janjira and partly in Poona receiving his higher education at the Fergusson College, Poona and passing the B. A. and M. A. examinations of the Bombay University. Patvardhan was a mediocre student in the College. But he was a attracted by Prof. Karve's educational work for the women of India and so he joined the body of the life-Workers of the Indian Women's University.

Patvardhan showed his practical zeal for women's education by educating his wife at home and then sending her to England for further studies. She is now working as a Superintendent in Baroda State while Patvardhan is conducting the Society's Girl's School at Sholapur.

He has written a number of books mostly for the use of boys and girls of school age. He has specialised in the various branches of Geography and has written stories imparting geographical and other information to the young in an interesting manner.

His story named 'Amaci Divali' is a fine piece of literature. Similarly his other books are quite readable and instructive to the young. So Patvardhan hopes to become in time a writer for the young, like Vasudevrav Apte of the previous generation. His book are the following :

1. Amaci Divali; 2. Jagatil Mauj; 3. Jagatil Mule; 4. Samrajyatil Apale Sambandhi; 5. Jagatil Pramukh Pike; 6. Amacya Induce Siksan.

B. B. Pavar

1. Life of Sambhaji Maharaj (1928); 2. Life of Sahu Maharaj (1930).

L. Pendse

1. Setkari (1933); 2. Gunhegar (1934); 3. Sahitya va Samajajivan (1935).

Mahadev Laksman Khambete

Mahadev Laksman Khambete is a Kokanasth Brahmin hailing from the virile land of Kokan. Mahadev was born at Anjarle (Murdi) district Ratnagiri in 1868. He passed his matriculation examination from Ratnagiri High School in 1889 and his district pleader's examination in 1893. He immediately settled at Jalgaon and made his mark in the profession. So he had a very lucrative practice. But Khambete was a versatile man. After having made money by his legal profession he turned to another lucrative business i. e. that of a jeweller. Here too he made his name as an expert jeweller and made large profits in this business. While he was in his business he applied his mind to the science of jewellery and wrote the following three books. It is these books that give him place in this history. But before referring to his books let me complete his life sketch. Mahadevrav was a very liberal—minded men. He made money but he gave it freely to all good causes that appealed to him. His charities have been numerous. They were given with fine discrimination. He gave donations to the schools of the district where he was brought up. Next, he gave money to an institution started in the district where he practised and made money. Lastly he liberally all causes calculated to do the good to the country at large. His books are the following :

1. Mauktik Prakas (1927); 2. Ratnapradip, Part I (1931); 3. Ratnapradip, Part II (1936).

G. P. Pethe

1. Life of Henry Ford (1930); 2. Life of Edison (1931).

R. G. Pradhan

1. Desa Seva (1930); 2. Plato va tyace rajakiy vicar (1930).

K. N. Pujari

1. Ksetra Ganagayur Varnan (1930).

R. G. Rane

1. Life of Pratapsimha Maharaj (1929); 2. Life of Catursing Bhosale (1933).

K. S. Risbud

1. Gita Paricay (1928); 2. Ukhane (1930).

G. R. Sangoram

1. Mahatmajince Vaiceroyas Patra (1930); 2. Mithaci Mohim (1930).

Sripad Ramcandra Tikekar

Sripad Ramcandra Tikekar is the son of the famous reporter of Kesari and the great Marathi writer Dhanurdhari. Sripad was born at Sholapur in 1907. He received his school education at Sholapur and his College education at the Willingdon and Fergusson Colleges. But he left his course in the middle in pursuance of the non-co-operation movement which captivated the minds of the young men. Then Tikekar took to literature and especially to his father's work of a reporter. But he became more enterprising than his father by going to the North Western Frontier of India and beyond and wrote accounts of his travels. His principal literary works have been connected with his travels and his work as a reporter.

His first work is named 'Simhala Saha.' This is a historical book giving the past and the present history of Afganisthan. It is a readable book but there are too many quotations from original sources which disturb and distract the attention of a reader. What the general reader wants is a plain and simple account of the things which he has seen and experienced. The style of the book is clear, simple and quite intelligible.

His second book is given an alliterative name 'Musalmani Mulukhatil Musaphari.' This is a travel book of about 200 pages. Tikekar went as a correspondent of the Kesari newspaper to Afganisthan, Iraq, Mesopotamia, and Baluchisthan. He went via Peshawar and returned via Quetta. He got interviews with big and influential people in the countries he visited. For, in modern times the correspondent of a paper is an important person. This is quite an interesting book. It gives interesting accounts of the several countries, their present condition and the manners and customs of the people there. The style is simple and clear.

Tikekar's third book is probably the first of its kind in Marathi. It is named 'Batamidar' (correspondent). This is book of about 300 pages. It is both interesting and informing. The writer gives at first a brief account of the art of journalism and then he gives detailed information about several kinds of reporters and the qualifications, mental and physical, required for success in their special work. He has given five actual examples from newspapers of good and bad reporting. This is a fine book indeed.

1. Batmidar (1934); 2. Musalmani Mulukhatil Musaphari (1931); 3. Simhala Saha (Description of Afganisthan) (1930).

Rev. D. S. Savarkar

1. Life of Parakrami Sandesta Irmaya (1924); 2. Life of Mahavir Kaupen (1924); 3. Antar Suddhi ani Matrpadaci yogyata (1928); 4. Candra Lila (1928); 5. Vyavaharik (1928); 6. Yesuvisayi Suras Gosti (1927); 7. Taranopaya (1931); 8. Paul Sadhuce Caritra (1931); 9. Sanka Nivrtti (1932); 10. Din Mala or Mary Slaton (1929).

Bhaskar Krsna Ujagare

Bhaskar Krsna Ujagare was born in 1887 in Bhamburda, a suburb of Poona. His father was a Marathi school teacher in a missionary school. Bhaskar was left an orphan by the sudden death of his parents during one of the plague epidemics of Poona. Bhaskar was educated at Ahmednagar Mission School and there he came to know the Rev. Tilak, the poet, from whom and from Bharde, a teacher in the Mission School Bhaskarrav derived his fondness for literature. From this time he began to write verses. Some of his verses are very fine and they are incorporated in Marathi prayer book. Bhaskarrav's eyes became spoiled and he went to Miraj Hospital where the eye specialist cured Bhaskarrav's eyes. This he regarded as a grace of Christ and made a vow to devote his time for the improvement of Indian Christian people. He wrote on a variety of subjects in various papers and roused public opinion. He did his best to interest his people in Marathi language and literature. He was the organising genius of the Indian Christian literary conferences held at Nasik, Bombay and Nipani between 1927 to 1933.

Ujagare published Rev. Tilak's poems in two volumes and he had prepared the materials of the third volume. So also he wrote a brief history of Marathi literature developed by Indian Christians. He later on lived at Saswad and formed there a society for discussing religious subjects common to all religions. His writings and public work show that he was not a bigoted Christian but liberal in spirit. He died suddenly while being operated upon for tonsils in 1935.

1. Narayan Vaman Tilak (1928); 2. Taranopay (1928); 3. Eka Karagrhavasi grhasthace atmavrtta (1928).

Dattatraya Visnu Parkhe

Another prose-writer from the school teachers' class is Dattatraya Visnu Parkhe. He was born at Miraj in 1891.

He was naturally educated at Miraj and for higher education he had to go out first to Kolhapur and then to Poona, and passed his B.A. and M.A. examinations from the Fergusson College. Being a State subject he was taken up as a teacher in Miraj High School. After the retirement of the Headmaster of that school Parkhe was made the head of the High School, a position he is still occupying. Besides this work of the High School Parkhe has to do in addition the work of the Inspector of State Schools.

Soon after becoming a teacher Parkhe took to literary work and began to write on a variety of topics in Manoranjan of Bombay. Subsequently he wrote two independent books named I 'How to conduct oneself in life' and 2 Tukaram. Both the books are highly spoken of by Marathi critics. I have myself written an appreciative preface to his first publication.

Dattatraya Sitaram Pangu

Dattatraya Sitaram Pangu comes from a very respectable and Tainatdar family from Kolhapur State. Dattatraya's father was a famous pleader of Kolhapur. It was a big family.

Dattatraya was born at Kolhapur in 1898. Naturally his primary and secondary education was done at Kolhapur; while for his higher education Dattatrayapant went to the now defunct Deccan College at Poona and passed his B. A. and M.A. examinations with Marathi as his special subject. Immediately in 1926 he was appointed a professor of Marathi in the Rajaram College, Kolhapur, a position which at present he is occupying. He soon became a member of the Marathi Board of the University. As every professor with a literary liking begins writing in Marathi in these days so Pangu also began writing stray articles on Marathi literature for magazines. He took to the study of Mahanubhav writers. In quick succession he edited and published 'Vatsalaharan' and 'Rukminiharan' of Samraj. Another old Marathi poem of poet Nages with the title Sitasvayamvar was edited and published by Pangu. Then he wrote a short biography of Cakradhar, the founder of Mahanubhav Panth and also wrote a critical life of Samraj whose poem Pangu had already published.

Sakharam Govind Virkud

A writer at present in Kolhapur State service like Pangu comes from the Janjira State and belongs to the non-brahmin community of that State. His name is Sakharam Govind Virkud. He was born at Janjira in 1894 and he received his early education at Janjira Murud. But for higher education he went to Bombay and joined the Wilson College and from there passed his B.A. examination in about 1924. Having a literary liking from his early age and some poetic talent he started a literary magazine called Maharastra Sahitya with the collaboration of Govindrav Tipnis who was then a professor of Marathi in the Elphinstone College. On account of the well established position of Prof. Tipnis in the literary circle and on account of his important contributions the magazine soon came to be recognized as a promising and interesting magazine. But Virkud's literary and political ambitions came in the way of the steady progress of the monthly. For, he first began to publish independent literary works such as Tipnis' summary of Kautilya's Arthasastra. Prof. Bhate's 'Prem ki Laukik' (Love or respectability) and other smaller books in quick succession. This was a great strain upon the finances of the monthly. Moreover as a non-brahmin Virkud contested an election of the Bombay Council. He lost heavily in this election, so the whole concern went into liquidation and all the ambitious projects of Virkud fell to the ground. Fortunately for him he was taken up as a Marathi teacher in Rajaram High School, Kolhapur, a position he still holds.

Virkud besides writing stray poetical pieces on historical subjects has published poems in Povada form on Viraratna Baji Prabhu and Tarabai, He is a poet of moderate poetic talent.

Dattatraya Balvant Mudgal

Dattatraya Balvant Mudgal is a Desasth Brahmin hailing from Mudgal a village in Nizam's territory. He was at Shirur, Ahmednagar district in 1901. He was an under-graduate and then took to service. He began writing in Marathi from 1921. He wrote on a variety of topics in prose and poetry and published his writings in the important newspapers and magazines of Maharastra. He also wrote a social novel named 'Sarvasva.' His attempt was to depict the village life of the lower strata of society in their own language, an aim in which he has moderately succeeded.

Mudgal had two very exceptional experiences, his dangerous experience of being half-drowned in Kalyan floods and his strange forgetfulness in which he ate the dry dates given by a Mantrik (magician) for removing the blindness of his brother. Such exciting and never to be forgotten experiences are sure to make a man communicate his feelings in literature.

V. A. Modak

V A Modak is a Kokanasth Brahmin. After passing his B A. from the Fergusson College he joined the staff of the Hindu Widows' Home and later on he was taken up as a life-worker after he passed his B. T. examination. He is now conducting the Satara Kanyasala of Karve's Society. His special subject is Geography. He has written the following books on the subject. They are good readable books both for children and for young men and women.

1. 'Bhugolavaril Kahi Vicitra Prani (Some strange animals on the earth); 2. 'Bhugolavaril Sahasi Pravasi' (Anventurous travellers of the earth), Part I & II; 3. 'Bhugolavaril Vanaspatice Prades (Vegetable parts of the earth); 4. Bharatiy Bandhavance Bhuprades (Provinces of brother Indians).

Sitaram Sakharam Sarpatil

Sitaram Sakharam Sarpatil is a Maratha gentlemen from

a respectable family from Kurundwad State, Southern Maratha country. He received his Marathi education at Kurundwad and then he passed the third year training examination of Kolhapur State. After passing it he became a teacher and is at present working as a lecturer in the Kolhapur Training College.

He has upto now written more than a dozen books on a variety of subjects. His poetical efforts are seen in his poetical versions of Bhagavadgita and Meghadut, two classical works in Sanskrit but entirely different from each other. To write either in prose or poetry versions of the Bhaganadgita is a favourite topic of all our Marathi poets. Marathi versions of Meghdut are not so numerous. Still half a dozen attempts are to be met with. Sarpatil's poetical pieces are worth reading and indicate a moderate degree of poetical talent in the writer. But they cannot come up to the level of the excellent poems of Krsnasastri Ciplunkar and Laksmansastri Lele.

Sarpatil's other books are written in prose and are mostly intended for school-boys. As such they are worth reading. The language is simple and flowing.

Sarpatil has written a book on the several teaching methods in vogue in Europe and America. As an introduction to the subject it is a good book and gives a clear but brief exposition of each method of teaching.

V. S. Vakaskar

V. S. Vakaskar is a Kayasth Prabhu by caste. He was born at Dhari in Kathiawar in 1884. All his education was done at Baroda. But on account of poverty and sudden death of his father while the boy Vakaskar was in the Matriculation class, he had to leave school. But his great self-sacrificing spirit, his love towards his father and his great courage and patience at a very tender age are seen in his giving his very flesh for being put into the bleeding wound of his father.

After the sad and sudden death of his father in spite of what he did for him to save his life, the young Vakaskar had to take to service and naturally he joined one of the Departments of Baroda State. There he served in several capacities and now holds a position of honour in State service.

Vakaskar had a liking for literature from his young age. He is a prolific writer. But his taste is towards history and historical writings and historical research. In fact, he followed in the footsteps of the great historian Govind Sakharam Sardesai.

Vakaskar has translated more than half a dozen books from English into Marathi such as, 'The Three Musketeers; 'Life of Sivaji' by Yadunath Sarkar; 'Lives of the Marathi Rajas of Tanjore.' His independent works are about the Gaikavad family and about lives of lesser known personages of history. Besides these books he has written many critical essays on historical subjects. He is a very careful research scholar. But he is very severe and cutting in his criticisms. All his books are quite readable and are a valuable addition to Marathi historical literature.

All the following eight persons are constant writers of the Srstidnyan magazine.

Gopal Ramcandra Paranjpe

Gopal Ramcandra Paranjpe comes from a Kokanasth family from Poona. However he was born at Karwar in 1891. Naturally all his education was done in the several institutions of the Deccan Education Society, Poona. For further higher studies in science and particularly Physics of which he became very fond he went to Germany and studied science in the Heidelberg and Berlin Universities from 1911 and 1914. But unfortunately for him the Great War broke out in Europe and he had to hurry back to India without getting Ph.D. degree though he was fully prepared for it and though he eminently deserved to get it. After his return to his country he went to Bangalore and did some fine research work there. In 1920 he was appointed a Professor of Physics in the newly started Royal Institute of Science at Bombay. He became the Principal of the Institute, an honour which an Indian had not got till then. At present he is the Principal and being comparatively young he may be able to do very useful work in that capacity.

Soon after he was appointed as a teacher he made his name as the most capable and popular teacher of science. He was very adept in treating the most difficult problems of higher Physics. He was particularly fond of delivering public addresses with lantern slides on the most wonderful discoveries in higher Physics. He had made a special study of problems like the X-rays and other newly discovered rays, the origin and splitting of atoms, radio activity, the wonderful film industry and manufacture of films. His power of clear exposition of the most difficult problems which even to educated men appear so perplexing is rare indeed. He is endowed by nature with a powerful but sonorous ringing voice. To hear his lectures is really an intellectual treat. Very few professors in Maharastra possess this wonderful gift of Paranjpe.

Now to come to Gopalrav's literary activity. He has a liking for literature, writing from his very young age. He wrote short articles in Karamanuk. He was the principal person in starting in 1928 with the help and co-operation of his young and enthusiastic friends, the first scientific magazine in Marathi by name Srstidnyan (Scientific knowledge). He has been a regular contributor to the magazine. Technical terminology of the several sciences is a subject to which he has given great attention. He was and is the president of the Committee appointed at Baroda to settle the technical terms for English words. His big book on this subject is nearly complete. This book would be a great literary work on the part of Paranjpe. For such a work involves an amount of thought and consideration and power of comparison between the terms in the several languages and their significance. Prof.

Paranjpe will have accomplished a great feat. He has spent so far over Rs. 2000 for this scientific hobby of his. But it is a hobby which benefits the Marathi language and literature.

Dinkar Dhondo Karve

Dinkar Dhondo Karve is the second son of Annasaheb Karve. He was born in 1899 at Poona. After completing his education in Poona, he went to Bangalore for further studies and passed his M. Sc. Then he went to Germany and studied Chemistry at Leipzic and Berlin and won the Ph. D. degree. Thus fully equipped he became a life-member of the Deccan Education Society, thus following the foot-steps of his father in a spirit of self-sacrifice. He married an equally educated lady, Iravatibai, daughter of Mr. Karmarkar. Mr. Karmarkar is an enterprizing engineer and merchant who went to Burma and prospered there. Iravati is also an M. A., Ph. D., her subjects being Philosophy and Sociology. She is also working as a professor of Philosophy in the Fergusson College. Both husband and wife are working in the same institution in the same capacity, a very rare thing still in India.

Dinkarrav's chief contribution to Marathi literature is his constant and regular writing to Srstidnyan, a monthly scientific magazine devoted to short essays on scientific subjects, giving short lives of great scientists, and finally mentioning every month scientific facts, more interesting than fiction. Besides these serial and stray scientific writings Dinkarrav has independently written the following books:

1. Sulabh Sastriya Dnyan (Easy course of lessons in science); 2. Sastriya Nibandhmala (Scientific essays); 3. Salopayogi Rasayan Sastra (Text-book on Chemistry).

Kamalakant Vaman Kelkar

Kamalakant Vaman Kelkar was born in 1902 at Dhupdal, near Gokak, district Belgaum. He was educated in the

Poona High School and received his College education at the Fergusson College and passed his M. Sc. with Geology as his special subject. Then he became a professor of Geology in the Fergusson College and later on he was made a life-member of the Deccan Education Society, Poona. He has written so far about four essays in English on the geological stones of Maharastra. His Marathi writings are the following :

1. Three humorous articles; 2. Seven scientific essays.

S. A. Parandekar

Prof. Parandekar is a son of Dr. Atmaram Gopal Parandekar who practised as a private doctor at Kolhapur. Young Parandekar was born in 1906 at Kagal in the house of his maternal uncle, Khajagi Karabhari of Kagal State. On account of the sudden and premature death of his father young Parandekar was left an orphan and his mother had to bring him up and arrange for his education. He received his secondary education at Kolhapur and passed his Matriculation in 1922. For his University education Parandekar successively went to several colleges in the Presidency having a provision for teaching science but ultimately passed in 1927 his B. Sc. from the Royal Institute of Science in the first class. He won the Akabarnvis Scholarship. With this pecuniary help and under the fine guidance of Prof. Ajrekar, young Parandekar got M. Sc. degree by writing and publishing a thesis on Botany in 1929. Immediately he was appointed a professor of Biology in the Rajaram College, Kolhapur, a position he is still holding.

Prof. Parandekar has written many an article on his research work in English magazines, Indian and Foreign. He was induced to write in Marathi by the constant reading of Srstidnyan, the Marathi scientific magazine (an indirect advantage of the publication of the magazine over and above the direct one of imparting western scientific knowledge to the general public). Accordingly he has written in Srstidnyan magazine so far about a dozen articles on several aspects and subjects in the science of Biology. The only independent book that he has published is Sulabh Vanaspati Vidnyan (Easy course on the Science of Botany).

P.R. Avati

P. R. Avati is a descendent of Naro Govind Avati who rose to a high position in the reign of Bajirav the Second. Young Avati was born in 1887 at Malunje (Budruk), district Ahmednagar. He received his secondary education in Ahmednagar Education Society's School. For his college education he joined the Fergusson College, Poona and passed his B. A. examination with Biology as his special subject. Then for further study of science he went to England and secured many a degree from English universities. On his return home he was appointed as a professor of Biology in the then newly started Royal Institute of Science where he is still working as a senior professor of Biology.

In the early days of Srstidnyan magazine Avati wrote constantly on a variety of topics concerning Biology. But latterly he writes in it only off and on.

Visnu Narayan Gokhale

Visnu Narayan Gokhale was born in 1890 at Poona. He received his University education in the Poona colleges and got the degrees of B. Sc. and B. Ag. Then for further studies in science he went to England where he secured the degree of Ph. D. and diploma of D.I.C. After returning from England Visnupant was taken up in Government service in the Education and Agricultural Departments. So at first he worked as a Professor in the Poona Agricultural College and now he is working in the Agricultural Research Branch being the head of the Dry Research Station at Sholapur. He first wrote in Marathi in 1927 and since that time he has been writing almost continuously either for the Marathi Scientific magazine or in the form of independent books. Besides his articles in the Srstidnyan, the following are his independent books :

1. Pasu, Paksi va Itar Prani (Beasts, birds and other animals); 2. Vanaspati-jivan (Plant life); 3. Srsti-niriksan, Parts I, II & III (Observation of nature); 4. Vilayatetil Ajab Gosti (Wonderful things in England); 5. Srstitil Camatkar Parts I & II (Wonderful phenomena in Nature).

K.S. Mhaskar

Dr. K. S. Mhaskar was born in 1879 at Nasik. He received his secondary education first at Thana and then in the Poona New English School. For his Arts course Mhaskar attended the Fergusson and Elphinstone Colleges and obtained B.A. and M.A. degrees. Then he joined the Grant Medical College and obtained several degrees in the several subjects of medical science. Then he went to England and there too he won many degrees and diplomas Mhaskar is probably the first brilliant scholar who showed his proficiency both in Arts and Medicine. His varied studies and versatility may be compared with those of an older and highly respected gentleman, Dr. Gopalrav Tambe of Indore. On account of his brilliant career Dr. Mhaskar was taken up in the Indian Imperial Service and was given the plague research work in the Parel laboratory. Practically all his service was done there though he was entrusted with different kinds of research work as necessity arose. While at Parel he has continuously done research work and has written articles on Hook-worm, Malaria, Dysentry etc.

But two of his researches came to the knowledge of even the common people who have admired the patience and sincerety of conviction of the doctor.

Dr. Mhaskar has tried to find out whether, as alleged very confidently by many a man, there is any real and reliable medicine or Mantra (spell) by which a person smitten with a serpent-bite can be or has been cured. About this matter he made immense enquiries and did a lot of experimental work by studying the serpents in the laboratory. He is firmly convinced by all this observations, experiments and enquiries made from medical men and magicians that there is no truth in the alleged cures from serpent-bite. He has thrown a challenge to the mantra-reciters for many a year but it has not been accepted so far.

In addition to the research work on serpent-bite, Dr. Mhaskar's Ayurvedik research work, his critical study of old medical works and his testing the efficiency of Indian drugs have appealed to the public mind and as stated before educated people have admired his wonderful and patient work in this line.

Dr. Mhaskar's domestic life has been very unfortunate. His only daughter died soon after her marriage. He also lost his wife. Two domestic calamities of this kind would have become unbearable to an ordinary man. But Dr. Mhaskar is patiently bearing the misfortune all these years and devoting all his time, money and energy to the progress of the Maternity Home which he started and is conducting with his money. Such self-sacrifice and such devotion to the single cause of niedical relief to women is rare among us.

Dr. Mhaskar was so much absorbed in his research work that he could not find time to write in Marathi, still he has written stray articles on the subjects of his research in Marathi. He writes on and off in the Srstidnyan magazine. A more serious work of his is the translation with explanatory notes of the old Sanskrit medical books. He has also re-edited Messrs. Kirtikar and Basu's books on the medical plants of India.

Late-Comer Writers

My readers will be surprized to see quite a separate section substituted in the place of the usual one of Christian, Israel and European writers. But I was obliged to do this by the fact that those writers dwindled in this period to a negligible number. But the far more important reason is that information about living writers who are scattered throughout the Marathi-speaking country and whom I had addressed letters requesting them to send information about themselves, came too late to be put in its proper place. Further, information about dead authors already published in less known magazines did not become available till the very last movement. So I made up my mind to give promiscuously an account of these late-comers.

These writers naturally form a motley crowd. They consist of poets, dramatists, novelists, prose-writers, story-writers, journalists and what not! But I am not sorry for what has happened and I hope my readers too will not feel grieved but on the contrary that will be glad to read this closing portion of the chapter. An appropriate simile suggests itself to me as regards this last section of the chapter. The whole of my History may be regarded as a literary feast consisting of ten courses and as in a European dinner the last course consists either of sweet pudding or ice-cream, so my last section will serve as literary pudding or ice-cream and I hope it will be eaten with relish and taste by the diners; or to vary the simile I may say that the last section is like an Indian dish called 'Kadbole' made out of the flour of 18 kinds of grain. With this explanation for a change in the chapter I proceed to give an account of these late-comer writers arranged partly on the principle of chronology and partly on that of seniority.

Anant Vaman Barve (1856-1923)

Anant Vaman Barve belongs to what I may call the second batch of Modern Marathi dramatists, the first one being that of Messrs. Trilokekar, Kirloskar, Dongare and Deval. So an account of his dramatic activities ought to have found a place earlier in my history. But till now I could get no detailed information of his life-work and literary legacy. For, I could not find it in books, where it was naturally expected, such as Sankarrav Muzumdars magazine 'Ranga-bhumi' or his more permanent book on the lives of the dramatists of his time or in similar books dealing with dramatists and dramaturgy. The truth must be confessed that Anantrav's very humble position, his simple and un-impressive appearance, and his constant association with second class and third class actors and workers in the dramatic line led to the neglect of his literary efforts and of his admirable self-sacrificing attempt to establish a Natyasamaj (Association of dramatic companies). He successfully held Natyasammelans for a number of years in Poona and elsewhere and tried to enlist the active sympathy and support of the public for the improvement and progress of dramatic companies, the class of actors and lastly of histrionic art in Maharastra. The gatherings and conferences held by Anantrav were quite successful but did not leave any permanent impression upon the educated people and they ceased to be held as soon as the guiding hand of Anantrav disappeared. In fact, I must confess that Barve met at the hands of the Poona public the proverbial treatment that 'a prophet is never honoured in his land'. But it is a fortunate thing that the merit and value of the great literary legacy left behind by Barve is recognised and appreciated by some educated young men of Nagpur. At the beginning of the year 1929 through the efforts of Dr. Barve (Anantrav's son), Mr. Gadkari, Mr. Madkholkar and Miss Jayavant, a very successful dramatic gathering was held under the auspices of 'Abhinav Natya Mandir (New temple of dramaturgy) started some time back and continued since then through the enthusiasm of Dr. Barve and his friends. This society has appointed a committee of Messrs. Banahatti, Bhole and Nene to make researches in Barve's literary remains and to prepare press copies of writings worthy of publication.

As a preliminary to this literary piece of work Messrs. Banahatti, Bhole and Nene have published a brief biography of Barve. This pamphlet was recently sent to me by Dr. Barve. I could, therefore, write a detailed account of Anantrav Barve.

Anant Vaman Barve was born in 1856 probably at Manmad, district Nasik. For, his father Vamanrav, coming from a very well-to-do and respectable family, had to take to railway service on account of the reduced condition of the family about the time of the birth of Anant. Vamanrav seems to have been soon transferred to Berar. So Anant was sent to Poona where his grand parents were living. They performed with great pomp the thread ceremony of young Anant. After the ceremony he was sent to his father's station Nandgaon where young Anant stayed continuously for about five or six years and so was able to complete his vernacular education upto sixth standard. For further education he was sent to his maternal uncle's to Poona where he studied regularly and zealously upto the Matriculation standard. This was the period in which the first makers of modern India like Messrs. Desmukh, Sarvajanik Kaka, Ranade, Ciplunkar, Tilak and Agarkar lived and produced by their stirring writing in papers and speeches on the platform a tremendous impression upon the minds of the public and especially upon those of young men. So it was quite natural that young Anantrav should be inspired by their writings. This was made obvious by his resolve not to seek Government service but to devote his main time and energy to the public good against the wishes of his parents. But he knew also his responsibility as a married man to make money by the sweat of his brow. So he took up the service of a teacher in a private school at Ghodnadi, district Poona. But as soon as the Aryabhusan Press and Kesari weekly were started by Messrs. Tilak and Agarkar in 1880 Anantrav returned to Poona and became a corrector and reviser of proofs in the press. By this service he came into close and intimate contact with those inspiring personalities. By then his ideas and ideals were once for all moulded and confirmed. This became manifest by his starting a magazine called Rajahamsa (Royal Swan) in 1882 on the express model of Nibandh Mala which was closed by that time. Barve conducted his magazine for five or six years during which period he wrote two dramas—his first drama being a farce named Patrakartyanci Sabha (Meeting of newspaper editors) and another named 'Bharat-Bhet' dealing with the pathetic meeting of Bharat with Ram after his banishment to the forest. Both these early attempts of Anantrav were only moderately successful but they show his leanings towards dramatic literature. These were strengthened by Visnusastri's essay on drama. The need of getting money led him to write dramas and give permission for their performance to dramatic companies. Being absorbed in this work Anantrav had to stop his Rajahamsa. From that time his literary activity went on ceaselessly till his death.

Between 1891—1896 Barve wrote five dramas i.e. 'Sukarambha', 'Gopicand', 'Rana Pratapsimha', 'Dhruv caritra', and 'Matrsiksaprabhav'. Some of these dramas were staged by Maharastriyan companies and became moderately successful. In 1896 Barve started a press called Vidyabhusan (Ornament of learning) and a weekly newspaper named 'Lokaseva' (service of the public). He made both concerns successful and so these eight or ten years were years of his comparative prosperity. His younger brother Gangadharpant came to Nasik to help Anantrav in his work. But he quarreled with Anantrav about the ownership of the press conducted in his own name alone. Anantrav generously gave away the whole concern to Gangadharpant without taking his own share in it and returned to Poona. From 1896 to 1908 Barve wrote 'Lokamatavijay' 'Victory of public opinion), 'Sudam', 'Pralhad', 'Saradamandan', (Venisamhar', 'Uttar Ramcarita' and 'Samajutica Ghotala'. 'Lokamatavijay is an allegorical drama on the model of Sanskrit 'Prabodh Candroday'. It deals in an interesting way with the discontent growing among the people of India due to the reactionary policy of British bureaucracy. 'Samajutica Ghotala' is an adaptation of Goldsmith's 'She stoops to conquer'. Out of his eight or nine dramas this is the only drama adapted from an English drama; all the rest of Barve's dramas are based on Pauranik stories. Besides these actual dramas that Barve wrote he was busy with schemes for the purpose of the improvement of dramatic art. So in 1904 he started a magazine by name Natyakala (Histrionic art) but it proved short lived and came to an end after five or six years in about 1910. It was in 1905 that through the strenuous effort of Barve the first Natya Sammelan with the establishment of a permanent Association of Bharat Natya Samaj (Association of Indian Dramaturgy) was held under the presidentship of Dadasaheb Khaparde, a leading public figure of Berar. His second activity was the starting of an Actor's Studio'.

He had the misfortune to lose his wife and his second son in 1916. But even under such clouds of calamity Anantrav's literary activity did not cease. His adaptation of 'Antony and Cleopatra' by name 'Srngarmanjari' was staged and became very popular. It would be an interesting study to compare this adaptation with that of Prof. Vasudevrav Kelkar. 'Pisaca Vivah,' 'Annasahebanci Dhandal,' and 'Saitan' are all adaptations from English dramas. But it is no use merely naming drama after drama which Anantrav wrote till his death. Let me now show to my readers the vastness of his literary legacy which is now being systematically investigated, as stated before, by Messrs. Banahatti, Bhole and Nene.

Barve wrote in all about 50 dramas small and great including operas and prose dramas. Out of this number about half are published and the other half await publication. His other literary writings contain biographies, histories, critical articles, and essays on all manner of subjects and reach the stupendous and astonishing total of about 75 books. What a wonderful legacy ! Of course Barve's writings do not come in the first class of Marathi literature. But they certainly occupy the second best place and are calculated to contribute towards the amusement and enlightenment of the literate public of Maharastra.

Narayan Murlidhar Gupte alias 'Bee'

Narayan Murlidhar Gupte is a poetic luminary of modern times illuminating the literary firmament along with Messrs. Govindagraj, Thombare and Rendalkar. As all his poems were published at intervals in magazines under the English pseudonym 'Bee' and never in his name even once, as he lived away from the centres of Maharastra and as he was of an extremely retiring disposition and indifferent to frame or name, his real name is not known even to those who take interest in Marathi literature. He is an old man now enjoying his well earned rest of many years from Government service.

Narayan Murlidhar Gupte is a Kayasth Prabhu by caste. He was born at Buldhana, a district town of Berar in 1872. All his education was done in Berar and after finishing it he at once took service under Central Provinces Government from which, after the completion of the period of his service, he retired on his well earned pension. His original home was Pen, a taluka town in Kolaba district. His family belonged to the class of hereditary Kulkarnis (village accountants) and its members did that work in seven or eight villages, the chief of them being Vasi : and so there the family is known by the name 'Vaskar' (inhabitants of Vasi). When about 1851 the province of Berar went to the Indian Government for administration Narayanrav's father came to Berar and became a permanent resident there.

Narayanrav's life has been a quiet and happy one. The only calamity he suffered was the death of his wife in 1933. Now to turn to his literary work.

'Bee' is exclusively a poet and nothing else. No doubt he seems to have written a few stray articles under another pseudonym in magazines. But being a cautious and conscientious Government servant he ceased from writing even such articles, though they were quite unobjectionable, after 1908, which marked the beginning of political agitation leading to disturbances. Thus it turns out that Bee's sole literary work is his poetry.

Bee did not begin to write poems before his poetic genius was fully matured. His first poem named 'Pranayapatrika (a love letter) was published in 1891 in Haribhau Apte's Karamanuk. It was highly admired by Haribhau. Since then he wrote stray poetic pieces and published them in the several magazines of Maharastra. They are like those of his contemporaries on all manner of subjects in which the poet's fancy found attraction. But all told they do not cover more than 121 pages of print and are about 38 in number. But like those of Messrs. Godkari and Tekade they are all superb and indicate the highest watermark of poetic genius. Principal Atre has written a long appreciative note about the poet, pointing out the high qualities of Bee's poetry and refuting the ill-considered objections against it by critics. A mere reference to the fine note of Atre will suffice here. For, it contains everything that a reader desires to know to be able to enjoy the poems of Bee.

Dhondadev V. Gadre Alias Kavyavihari

Dhondadev V. Gadre is a younger follower of the poet Kesavsut. He was born in 1894 at Haripur, a village near Sangli. He was educated at Sangli State High School from which he passed his matriculation. Srimant Babasaheb Patvardhan, Chief of Miraj (Junior) State, seeing that young Gadre was his subject and was a promising student, gave him pecuniary help and thus enabled him to get higher literary education Dhondopant passed his B. A. examination from the Fergusson College in 1917 and then his LL. B. examination in 1919. Immediately after he was taken up in State service. He is now a judge of the State doing his judicial work with zeal and efficiency. When the Willingdon College became a first grade College teaching the B. A. course in Marathi Gadre was appointed a half time professor of Marathi there as he was known to be a good Marathi scholar and a poet to boot. He did that work for three years. During these years Gadre was able to give more attention to the study of the old poets, and to modern Marathi writers. He thus became better equipped to do literary work. Now to turn to his literary activity.

Gadre had a liking for writing poetry. The beautiful surroundings like the confluence of the two rivers Krsna and Varana by the side of his native place, the fine old temple of Mahadev on the river bank with its fine sand, the finest and biggest grove of tamarind trees near the village and lastly, the fertile country round about his native place, must have unconsciously influenced Gadre's innate imagination. Further, the example and company of the great dramatist Govindrav Deval must equally have influenced young Gadre to take to literary activity as a hobby of his life. He assumed the name of Kavyavihari (Wanderer in poetry). He published his first poem named 'Phulanci vinanti' (Prayer of flowers) in 1912. Since then he wrote off and on his stray pieces and published them in magazines. But he is a slow writer. Kavyavihari does not require much time to actually write a poem but his dry-as-dust legal business interferes somewhat with his literary work. Some of his poems have been written in a single day, while he has written some poems years after the ideas came into his mind. So it seems his imagination is a little erratic. Besides poetry Kavyavihari has written one or two stories and some criticisms of books. But his main literary activity is concerned with poetry. His books published so far are these :

1. Kavyavihar (Pleasant wandering in poetry); 2. Sphurti-lahari (Waves of genius). The noteworthy feature of Gadre's poetry is that it indicates his keen desire for reform, his boldness in attacking cruel customs of old and his feeling for nature. His poetry is calculated to rouse the sprit of man-hood and exploit among young minds.

Madhav Kesav Katdare

Madhav Kesav Katdare is probably the youngest poet of this last period of our history. Compared with him D. V. Gadre is a little older in time and 'Bee' belongs to the early period of modern literature. So these three poets whose account are included in the late-comer writers' section represent three short periods of ten years each and their poetry indicates this difference of age.

Madhav Kesav Katdare came from southern Kokan, his native place seems to be Hedavi where his early life was spent, and where his early education was done in the school of a Tatya Pantoji (an untrained teacher conducting a small private school), during the three years from 1900 to 1903. From 1903 to 1907 his father Kesavrav engaged a tutor for the education of Madhav and his younger brother. While in his village young Madhav used to organise a Mela (singing party of boys) on the Gokul Astami day (Birthday of Krsna) and wrote a few songs for the singing party. He was a boy of hobbies. His first hobby was painting but his grand-father was dead againts it. So he gave it up and took to poetry as a hobby in which he could indulge without any hindrance from his grand-father. For writing poetry seemed to his grand-father like the writing of school exercises and so he did not object to it. In 1907 Madhav was sent to Ratnagiri for his High School education. Here for the first time he had to read books on Maratha History and Indian History. But he did not like the despising and condemnatory tone in which the writers of those books spoke about Indians in general and Marathas in particular. By his reading Haribhau Apte's historical novels and similar tales from the writings of his follow students, by hearing tales from Kirtankars (persons delivering mythologico-philosophical discourses with the accompaniment of music) and lastly by visiting castles and other historical places Katdare imbibed a feeling of patriotism and a resolve to write historical and patriotic poems. These tendencies were confirmed by his reading Sir Walter Scott's historical poems and novels. By the reading of these books Katdare came to know what a vast store of historical knowledge Scott possessed. So he began to collect historical books. During his high School days Madhavrav met two Mohammedan students who took Marathi as their second language on condition that Madhav should help them in getting mastery over the subject. Madhav's association with sober and thoughtful students of a rival religion literalised his mind. On account of the poverty of the family—a usual thing in the case of many young and promising students, Katdare had to seek service and he got a job in Bombay in 1912. Since then he has been a permanent resident of Bombay devoting his leisure, his energy and his money to his favourite hobby of historical poetry and of collection of historical literature.

Now to turn to the poetic work of Katdare. As stated before he had a hobby of writting poems from his boyhood. He published his first collection of poems under the name

'Dhruvavaril Phule' (Flowers on the Polar Star). He sent his books to as many poets as he could write to. But only Ananttanay wrote to him. Since then he met many other poets and particularly Gadkari. But he formed friendship with Ananttanay though their views differed from each other as regards the nature of a historical poem. This difference is seen if one reads their two poems on the same subject i. e. a poem on Bapu Gokhale (the general of Bajirav II) and that on the transfer of Bajirav's sovereignty to the East India Company.

Katdare's first historical poem on Baji Prabhu was published in 1910. Then he wrote a poem on the death of Hasan-Husein. From that time he has been continually publishing poems. They are as follows :

4. Sivaraj stava (Praise of King Sivaji); 5. Bayabai Apte (Daughter of the last Pesava Bajirav II); 6. Panipatcya Maidanavar (On the plains of Panipat); 7. Vajir Saha Ali Khan.

Bhaskar Dhondo Karve

Bhaskar Dhondo Karve is the youngest son of Annasaheb Karve. He was born in 1903 at Hingne (Budruk), taluka Haveli, district Poona. All his education from A. B. C. to B.Sc. was done in the several institutions of the Deccan Education Society. After passing his B. Sc. examination Bhaskarrav served as a teacher in the Mahilasram, Hingne. Then he went to Bombay for getting a teacher's qualification and passed the B. T. degree from the Secondary Training College. For being more efficient as a teacher and for getting wider experience and knowledge of educational systems obtaining in Europe he went to England and joined the Leeds University and after a year's stay and study he got the M. Ed. (Master of education) degree of that University and returned home. Bhaskarrav had a successful career throughout his University life both in India and England. After completing his education and after equipping himself for a teacher's work Bhaskarrav followed the notable and self-sacrificing example of his father and became a life-member of the Anath-balikasram, the first institution that Annasaheb Karve had started for the education of women in general and of widows in particular. He soon became the Secretary of the said society. Then he was made the principal of the Training College for women conducted by Karve's society, a post which he is still holding. Bhaskarrav has made a good name as an efficient teacher.

Now to turn to his literary work. As he is interested in the art of teaching he has written books mainly on that subject. They are a valuable contribution to modern Marathi literature on its scientific side. The following are his publications :

1. 'Mi Kasa Zalo ?' (How I was born ?); 2. 'Siksana-visayak nave vicar' (New thoughts about education : a collection of essays by several writers); 3. 'Adhyapan va Manas Sastra' (Teaching and Psychology); 4. 'Bhasavyavasaya' (Four books for primary schools with the help of Mrs Kaveribai Karve, wife of Bhaskarrav).

Visnu Sakharam Khandekar

Visnu Sakharam Khandekar belongs to the class of novelists and story writers of this period. He was born in 1898 at Sangli. He is the second son of Atmaram Balvant Khandekar but having been adopted by Sakharampant Visnu assumed his present name. His Marathi and English education was done at Sangli. For his higher education he went to Poona and joined the Fergusson College. But on account of his adoption while in college he had to go to his adopted father's house, leaving his college course. He then took up the teacher's profession and became the head-master of the Anglo vernacular School, Shirode, district Ratnagiri.

Now to turn to his literary activity. He had an instinctive inclination to write some thing from his early age. It was encouraged by the example of Govindrav Deval, the great dramatist of the previous generation, who often came to Visnu's father, and also by reading Haribhau Apte's novels and Kolatkar's dramas. Visnupant does not require a mood to write. He has a facile pen and can write fast. Though he is in poor health, his literary activity, since its commencement, has gone on uninterruptedly. It is on account of these peculiarities of the writer that he has been able to produce such a vast amount of varied literature within the time of his not very long literary career.

All his books small and great are about 25 in number. Visnupant has a fertile imagination. Though he is a middle-aged man now his genious does not seem to have abated as yet. So he may publish many more novels and stories. His unpublished writings are in number more than his published writings. So in time he may rival, nay excel, the giant writers of the older generation. Visnupant's novels and stories are all very high class literature like those of Haribhau Apte and so it is very difficult to point out his master pieces nor is it possible to refer to all his books. So I make a reference to a few from each class of his writings.

Novels : 1. Hrdayaci Hak (Call of the heart); 2. Kancan Mrga (Golden deer); 3. Don Mane (Two minds); Stories: 4. Nava Candrika (New moonlight); 5. Unpaus (Sunshine and rain); 6. Vidyutpravah (Current of electricity); Stories for talkies : 7. Chaya (Shadow); 8. Jvala (Flame); Plays : 9. Rankace Rajya (Rule of the poor); Lives: 10. Agarkar; 11. Gadkari; Essays: 12. Candanyat (In the moon-light).

Damodar Savalaram Yande

Damodar Savalaram Yande is not a literary man himself. But his claim to a brief account in this history of literature is justified by the fact that for over forty years he is connected with the publication of books. He has owned printing presses; he has been a proprietor of newspapers and magazines; he has published hundreds of books small and great on all manners of subjects; lastly he has encouraged young and promising writers by accepting their books for publication and giving them pecuniary reward and remuneration. Thus he has indirectly contributed a good deal to the spread and growth of Marathi literature.

Yande belongs to a high class Maratha family. He was born in 1861 and is still living though latterly he is not keeping good health. But he has now reached the green old age of 78 years. After completion of his education he took to business. At that time the Induprakas Press and Induprakas newspaper were being run at a loss and it was feared that they would soon die. Induprakas was the oldest Marathi newspaper of Bomay and Madhavrav Ranade was anxious that such a paper should not die. So at his advice young Yande took up both concerns and by his efficiency of management and organising power he soon made the concerns paying. The circulation of Induprakas rose rapidly and it again became an influential paper in Bombay and in Maharastra. As a Maratha Yande was able to approach His Highness Sir Sayajirav Gaikvad, Maharaja of Baroda and explain to him an idea of starting a paper in Baroda. So with his patronage and under his auspices Yande started a newspaper in Baroda called Sayaji Vatsal (Child of Sayaji) and later the more famous paper 'Sayaji Vijaya' (Victory of Sayaji). This also became a very popular and influential paper. This paper passed through vicissitudes of birth, rebirth and final extinction; in so far as after its starting it continued for some years; then it ceased to be published for some time; then again it was restarted and continued for some years and then finally it disappeared from the stage.

But Yande as a businessman made huge profits. He later on sold his Induprakas concern. His last activities are the foundation of Granthprasarak Mandal (Society for the spread of books) and the publication of a big monthly magazine called 'Dnyan Mandir' (Temple of Knowledge).

It is very rarely that brothers possess equal intelligence, attain equal educational and professional qualifications, follow the same profession, acquire equal fortune, hold similar political ideas and ideals, and suffer for them and lastly make an equal name and fame in society. But even with such striking similarity a closer observation of them is sure to detect many a point of contrast in their life and life, work. Such is the case with Bhopatkar brothers and Savarkar brothers and so it is better to give the accounts of both in immediate succession. Let me begin with the elder writers.

Bhaskar Balvant Bhopatkar

Bhaskar Balvant Bhopatkar, the elder of the two brothers, was born in 1874 at Thana. His education was partly done at Thana and partly in Poona. He passed his B. A. examination in 1897 and his LL. B. examination in 1901. He immediately began to practise in civil and criminal courts of Poona and soon acquired a fat practice. Naturally he came to be recognised as a leading lawyer of the Poona bar. He had from his youth imbibed the nationalist spirit and ideals preached by Balvantrav Tilak in his Kesari. But though in the political sphere he held rather radical and extremist views, he was comparatively an orthodox man in social and religious matters. For the proper propaganda of his views he started a weekly newspaper called 'Bhala' (Lance) in 1905 and preached his peculiar views on all current topics—political, economic, social and religious. He was a cautious and shrewd man like Sivrampant Paranjpe but in a momentary inadvertance and carelessness he published an article under the heading 'Narakatil Darbar' (court in hell). This article with additions of many extracts from other articles published in Bhala in 1906 were looked upon as treasonable and calculated to lead the minds of the young to discontent and disaffection and even hatred of British Government in India. So Bhaskarrav was called up before the magistrate, was found guilty and was awarded rigorous imprisonment for six months with a fine of Rs. 1000. Bhaskarrav was made to grind daily a large quantity of grain. With his fat body and with acquired habits of ease and comfort he found prison life quite unbearable and secretly made up his mind not to write or admit any article even remotely bordering on sedition or treason after his release from jail. This resolve was similar to that of Sivram Mahadev Paranjpe of Kal newspaper. But Paranjpe, immediately on his release from jail, stopped his newspaper permanently and devoted all his attention to the management of his Manohar Press. . . . Then he again revived it and continued it for another decade and ultimately stopped it permanently. Bhaskarrav's chief public activity was his newspaper. He very rarely delivered public fectures nor did he go out of Poona. Since his practical withdrawal from public agitation since 1906—1907 he concentrated his attention on his profession and built up a very lucrative practice. He made a further addition to his large income by conducting a law class from 1921. With the advance of age he has shown more decided tendency towards defence of existing social and religious customs. As such he is against almost all the reforms advocated by Mahatma Gandhi or by the social reformers. Thus he is against the active propaganda against untouchability and he violently deprecates attempts at the removal of caste differences which are, according to him, useful to keep the purity and characteristic qualities of different races in Hindu society. He firmly believes in the three restrictions implied in and required for the preservation of castes which he humorously describes by this well-chosen alliterative name 'loti-roti-beti bandha' (restriction of taking water or food or wives by persons of one caste from those of another caste). Thus he ridiculed the plan of having a common simple dinner consisting of 'zunka-bhakar' (Indian bread made of jowar and a cooked paste of gram flour made tasteful by the addition of salt and spices). This food is the daily diet of the lower classes and the idea of the reformers is that higher caste people should sit with the lower class people and partake of their daily food so that a feeling of equality would gradually grow in the minds of all people and the sense of inferiority would disappear from the minds of the lower-class people. All such attempts made by Bombay reformers were ridiculed as puerile by Bhaskarrav in his Bhala. In retaliation Bhaskarrav proposed to Poona brahmins that they should organise dinner parties with excellent dishes on the orthodox fashion and declared that he would gladly attend such dinners; so the Bombay reformers gave Bhaskarrav the nick name of Bojanbhau Bhopatkar (an alliterative name meaning Bhopatkar who is fond of dinners). Of course from a serious point of view these taunts and counter-taunts were really puerile. But Bhaskarrav seemed to enjoy them. So his weekly paper Bhala in its last days was full of such puerile matter. But uncultured people enjoyed the humorous and satirical writings of Bhopatkar and his paper had a short-lived popularity. But as stated before he stopped it in 1935 to the relief of serious and sober people.

Bhaskarrav's life is very interesting and hence I have dilated a little in describing his peculiarities and his views. Bhala and his writings therein are the sole output of Bhaskarrav.

Laksman Balvant Bhopatkar

Let me now turn to the life of Laksmanrav, the younger brother. Laksman was born in Poona in 1880. So it seems he was younger by 6 years than his elder brother. Lakshmanrav's education was all done in Poona. He passed B. A. in 1901, M.A. in 1904 and LL. B. in 1907. Thus Laksmanrav passed all his examinations without a failure. This indicates that Laksmanrav was one of the good students of his time. Since the starting of Bhala in 1905, Laksmanrav was a coeditor of the paper. Subsequently he was a coeditor of Lokasangrah and of Lokamanya. For salt satyagrah Bhopatkar had to go to jail for six months and later on he had to suffer in 1932 a similar punishment but only for 2 months. It was during this imprisonment that Bhopatkar showed wonderful courage, presence of mind and physical strength in killing single-handed and in his closed prison cabin, a serpent that attacked him at the night time. This must have given exciting experience to Laksmanrav. As to his public activities they are so varied and in so many fields that it is not possible to refer to them. Moreover they are not relevant to this history. So let me give a brief account of his literary activities. As stated before he was successively connected as editor with three papers and so he must have written innumerable columns of literary matter. But all of them are now buried and concealed in the files of the several newspapers. But unlike his elder brother

Laksmanrav has written fine and interesting literary books of pure imagination as also on the scientific subject of physical culture and exercise for men and ladies. He has written the following books : 1. Mazi Vyayam Paddhati (My system of physical exercise); 2. Dandapatta (The art of handling a stick and defending one-self); 3. Kusti (Wrestling); 4. Striyankarita Vyayam (Physical exercises for women).

All these four books bear on the subject of physical culture of the body and show how by means of proper and suitable exercises both strength and health of the body can be secured. These books of Bhopatkar impart very useful knowledge to every one and thus form a valuable addition to Marathi literature.

His remaining two books are more or less imaginative and are calculated to afford interesting and ennobling reading to young and old. 5. Navaratnaca Har (Garland of nine gems). This is a fine collection of 9 stories. Most of them deal with the heroes and heroines of history and narrate exciting events in their life. They are written in fine and fascinating language and are calculated to rouse a spirit of patriotism and a love of one's country in the reader's mind. 9. Mrtyucya Mandivar (In the lap of death). This is a romantic novel full of stirring and heart-rending scenes in which the hero has to suffer for his patriotic and self-sacrificing conduct. Ultimately for so called crimes against Government he is given capital punishment and priod to his execution he is kept in prison. But the hero patiently and without the least fear or sorrow is prepared to meet death. What an admirable picture is this ! Such persons are rare in any country and so their conduct is sure to evoke a sigh of sympathy from every one who comes to know their life story. While the hero was still free and a fine young man, a young and beautiful daughter of a rich gentleman fell in love with him and the hero reciprocated her love. In fact, they vowed to marry each other and in their heart of hearts had become husband and wife. But the punishment of death given to the hero settled, according to the fond belief of the father, the matter once for all, there being no possibility of the lady renewing her love for her almost lost lover. But the lady had firmly resolved to turn into a fact what had been already done though mentally. So she wrote, unknown to anybody, an application to the Governor of the Province that she should be allowed to marry the prisoner on the day of his execution; that she did not want to make any fuss about the matter; that the Governor should give permission for such a marriage and that for its being performed according to Hindu religious rights only 2 or 3 persons and about 2 to 3 hours would be required. Her extraordinary request appealed to the Governor's sympathetic heart and he sent an order to the jailor to admit the party to visit the jail and to permit them to perform the religious ceremony of marriage with the prisoner, he being given freedom for that period of time. So early morning on the last day of his life, the hero was surprised to see his beloved with a small party ready with materials for the marriage ritual. He was wonder-struck with the super-human courage and love of his beloved. But he tried to dissuade her from her mad course of conduct; but finding her unchangeable resolve he too consented to get himself married. So in the prison and on the lap of death as it were they were married and then after a few hours the hero was executed! What a fine story Laksmanrav has woven out of simple incidents. The novel is so fascinating and interesting that one cannot go to its end when one begins to read it.

To compare now the lives of two brothers, one finds that Laksmanrav has a more earnest and serious nature. His versatility, his self-sacrifice, his constant endeavour to do public good, his courage and patience in suffering (he recently lost his olny grown-up son) calamity are sure to create a feeling of admiration for the writer.

There is great similarity, like that of Bhopatkar brothers, in the lives and life-work of the two Savarkar brothers. Of the two brothers Vinayak and Narayan, the former is the elder and hence it is proper that an account of him should precede that of the latter.

Vinayak Damodar Savarkar

Vinayak Damodar Savarkar was born in 1883 at Bhagur near Devlali district Nasik. He seems to have been a precocious boy. For, it is said that he wrote a poem and published it in Jagathitecchu weekly of Poona when he was only 10 years of age. His early education was done at Nasik. He passed his Matriculation examination in 1901. Then he joined the Fergusson College. Poona was at that time a great centre of political agitation though Calcutta was a greater one. In Bengal the agitation did not remain a constitutional one but assumed a dangerous form. The Bengali youths formed secret societies each member taking a vow to kill at least one European. This dangerous form of agitation with the formation of secret societies captured the minds of Maharastriyan youths and it was the sentimental college students that were first affected. Vinayakrav became the leader of the like-minded students in the Fergusson college and formed a secret society. They used to meet at dead of night on the top of the college hill where there was the old temple of. For their future work they practised the art of shooting, fighting with lathis and weapons and lastly tried to learn bomb making. Though they were thus secretly preparing themselves for their life work they were outwardly regular and well-behaved students. They showed excellent progress in their studies and satisfied their professors.

Vinayakrav passed his B.A. from the Fergusson College in 1906. Then he went to Bombay for his LL. B. examination. While there he worked as the editor of Vihari newspaper. He also founded Abhinav Bharat Samaj. But that very year he found an opportunity to go to England with the scholarships of Syamaji Krsnavarma, an extremist nationalist who had established an India House in Paris from where he spread his views by pamphlets and books. He helped young Indians to receive education in Europe. But Savarkar's formation of secret societies and his participating in the murder of Jackson, the popular Collector of Nasik, by Kanhere and his associates had come to the knowledge of

Government and as the evidence against Vinayakrav was not strong enough to stand the test before the scrutiny of the bar and the bench, so Government did not bring any action against him. But it was morally convinced that he was a party to the plot of murdering Jackson. So his name was at the top most page of the 'black list'. Vinayakrav's acceptance of Syamji's Scholarship was itself a good evidence of his being an extremist and a terrorist. However, he went to England, lived there undisturbed and passed his legal examination and became a barrister. Since then Vinayakrav came to be referred to as Barrister Vinayakrav or Barrister Savarkar. After becoming a barrister he went to Paris and lived with Syamaji Krsnavarma and came back to London in 1910. But he was ordered to go to India. He knew that be would he tried there and put into jail. So when his steamer was nearing the harbour of Marseilles he leapt from his cabin porthole into the sea and swam, struggling against the waves, and reached the shore which was French territory and beyond British jurisdiction. What an extraordinary daring and courage is this ! This wonderful feat of Savarkar is an evidence that the work of the secret society was no outward show and that the physical and mental self-training received therein was a thorough one. But Savarkar did not escape from the clutches of Government though his daring feat caused a little delay. For Indian Government had to write for extradition of Savarkar to Home Government, which had to request French Government to give letters of extradition; the latter had to hold a preliminary inquiry to satisfy itself that the charges against the person were bonafide and then only it could give letters of extradition. What a difficult and delaying procedure is this ! But the formalities were gone through and Savarkar was brought to India, tried and sentenced to capital punishment (computed into that of transportation for life) and accordingly he was sent to the Andaman Islands. Thus before Savarkar was able to do any real and substantial good to the country with his brilliant career and his preparation for civic duties, his political life came to an end till the present times when he was allowed full freedom of activity. For, Vinayakrav was kept in the Andaman

Islands for about 14 years from 1911 to 1924. He was allowed to come to India in 1924 on condition that he was to live in Ratnagiri town and not to leave its limits and that he was neither to write nor speak on political problems. So he could do only social work and he did very good work in that line. He took up first the question of untouchability and by his persuasive eloquence and conversation he brought round at least the sensible high class people to his views. He visited the houses of the untouchables, taught them habits of cleanliness, asked them to give up eating the flesh of dead carcasses and similar disgusting ways of living. One of the ways by which he brought the higher classes and the untouchables together was to hold common dinners. His second and more successful way was to hold Kirtans. Lastly he made an effort to allow the untouchables to enter the temples. But this last reform was too bitter a pill for the orthodox to take. So he induced Kirad, a very wealthy well-to-do and charitably disposed local contractor from the fishermen's caste to build a new temple on the hill near an old temple. This new temple was of course open to all classes of Hindus. These were the activities which Vinayakrav could take to, according to the conditions laid upon him. Another very useful and interesting activity to which he could devote his time and energy was writing. To this activity with which this history is concerned I must now turn. But before I proceed to do it let me refer to Savarkar's wonderful hold over the minds of young and old. The secret of his hold lies in his exceptional eloquence. He is a Savyasaci speaker (speaker in two languages). In the first place, he has a powerful, sonorous voice which is neither harsh nor hoarse. Moreover, he has mastered all the arts of an orator. He speaks slowly with a smile on his face. His speech usually begins in a low tone but rises with the importance of the events and topics to which he refers. In fact, he makes use of the cadence of singing in his speeches. Besides these external graces of the art of speaking, Savarkar's deep and full knowledge of the subjects of his speeches and his wonderful command over both English and Marathi languages, his resolve not to mix up foreign words in speaking in his own mother tongue and, lastly, the easy riverlike fluency of speech produce a tremendous effect upon the assembled audience and it remains spell-bound during the course of his speech.

Lastly to turn now to his literary writings. As referred to already Vinayakrav was a precocious boy having an inborn talent for a fascinating exposition of his ideas and feelings in fine choice language which he had mastered from his early age by reading carefully Marathi literature old and new. So like his speeches his books too give light and delight to his readers. His books are the following: 1. Life of Joseph Mazini; 2. Svatantrya Yuddha: 1857; 3. Sikhanca Itihas; 4. Hindupad Padsahi; 5. My long banishment.

Dr. Narayanrav has a great similarity to Vinayakrav in his life and life-work though in a lower key.

Narayan Damodar Savarkar

Narayan Damodar Savarkar is the younger brother of Vinayakrav. He was born in 1886 at Bhagur. His early education was done there. His education seems to have come to an end with the completion of his secondary education. Probably he did not possess intelligence sufficient for and capable of acquiring University education or foreign education like that of Vinayakrav. So he took to public agitation and propaganda of extremist views in the Vande-mataram paper for which he was tried and put into jail in 1909 but was soon released. Again he was found at the place where a bomb explosion occurred while His Excellency Lord Minto was going in a procession so also it was discovered that he was in the know of and a party to the plot of murdering collector Jackson. So he was tried, found guilty and put into jail. After the period of his imprisonment he was released in 1911. Then he went to Calcutta, joined the medical school and obtained, in due course, the degree of L. C. P. & S. He also studied Homeopathy and got the degree of L.M.S. Further he learnt dentistry and became an expert in it. Since then he became known among the public as Dr. Savarkar. He came to Bombay and began his practice

there but more as a dentist than as a practitioner. Soon he contested a municipal election in Bombay and became a member of the Bombay Corporation. Now to turn to his literary activity. It is not very great nor striking. Dr. Savarkar was more disposed to speak and do active public work. However, he was for some time an editor of 'Sraddhanand' newspaper and in that capacity he may have written some thing. The only independent book that he wrote is—
1 Jaica Mandap (A bower of a creeper called Jai).

Krsnaji Laksman Soman alias Kirat

Krsnaji Laksman Soman belonged to the small class of writers who are far more known, from the beginning of their literary career, by their pseudonym than by their actual name. Kirat (his pseudonym) has never liked to be in the limelight of fame or name, being a man of retiring disposition. But by his superior literary work 'Kirat' has attained a name similar to that of 'Bee.' Though known to the public by his name Kirat, he is addressed as Bhausaheb Soman by his relatives and friends. Krsnaji was born in 1865 at Khanapur and a very sad though memorable event is recorded in Krsnaji's life i. e. that a boat was overturned in the river flood near Khanapur on the very day of his birth.

He was educated at Khanapur, Belgaum and Poona. On account of the poverty of the family as also due to his constitutional infirmity. Bhausaheb could not complete his collegiate education and had to seek service somewhere. He got an appointment in a Department of the Bombay Government from where he retired after the period of his service was over and since then he has been enjoying his well-earned rest and pension for a period longer than that of his service. In this respect Bhausaheb Soman can well compare with Divan Bahadur K. R. Godbole. Bhausaheb is a simple man with equally simple habits. In appearance he looks rather grave and forbidding.

But as soon as one talks to him for sometime one is convinced of his kindly and genial nature and his wide reading with a fund of information on a variety of subjects. Though he was a Government servant, he was a thorough nationalist at heart and in his private talk he was glad to express his views fearlessly. He used to write though anonymously on current political topics. He was equally interested in dramaturgy and dramatic literature. Though he read and occasionally wrote on all manner of subjects, his favourite subject of deep and enthusiastic study was history. His deep study is evidenced by the series of articles he wrote under the title 'Dhanurdharis Kirataci Salami' (Fighting salute of a hunter to a bow-bearer). It was published under the assumed but significant name 'Kirat' (Hunter) and this name since then stuck permanently to Soman.

The second series of Kirat's historical articles was published in Kavyetihas magazine. It dealt with the social condition of Maharastra in Sambhaji's times. This topic is quite different from the routine account given by historians of those times. His third important historical writing is his learned and critical preface to his translation of Bhasa's dramas. But this is only one side of his varied literary activity His published writings have filled 10 to 12 thousand pages of print. What a huge literary output by a man who, all his life, lived away from the chief centres of Marathi literature!

His two dramas which are certainly his masterpieces in that line are named 'Mazi Bahin' (My sister) and 'Panipatca Durdaivi Mohara' (Unfortunate hero of Panipat). Both these dramas were staged for some time and had become deservedly popular. But the dramatic companies began to stage the dramas of younger and more pushful writers and hence Kirat's dramas fell into the background. Still he is writing dramas and some of his dramas await publication. Kirat began his literary career when he was only 14 years of age and it has continued till now. This means that he has been a writer for the last sixty years This is indeed a wonderful feat excelling that of long lived, far famed writers like H. G. Wells and Bernard Shaw.

Some of Kirat's published books are the following :

1. Sakunica phasa; 2. Bhasakavici Natake; 3. Mukta Dhara (A novel); 4. Panhalgadca Killedar (A novel); 5. Mazi Bahin (a drama); 6. Dronasankop (Rage of Drona); 7. Malati-Madhav (An adaptation); 8. William Tell (An adaptation); 9. Dhanurbhang (A drama).

Nates Appaji Dravid and Mrs. Mathurabai Dravid

Nates Appaji Dravid belongs to the Dravids of Southern India. A large number of them came up during Maratha rule to Maharastra, to greater Maharastra as far as Central India, became permanent inhabitants there and got merged among the Maharastriyan brahmin castes. They were well-known for their Vedic learning and accurate recital of Vedas. So many families were patronised by Rajas of Satara and the Pesvas of Poona. For instance, the family of Prof. Krsnaji Nilkanth Dravid of the Fergusson and Willingdon Colleges was granted lands and a house at Yavatesvar, a fine and salubrious hill with an old Mahadev temple near Satara with an annual cash tainat (hereditary grant of money) for its learning. Natesrav's family was settled in Berar where he was born about 1873. Immediately after passing his M. A. examination in 1895 he was appointed a professor of the newly started Maharastra College (probably known as Bhave's College).

But unfortunately the College was permanently closed after a year's existence. Then Dravid was taken up as a professor in the Fergusson College. If he had continued there he would have been a valuable asset to the Fergusson College, he would have made a name for himself as an efficient teacher of his subject and he would have found ample leisure for doing literary work and indulging in his passion for reading. Having a rather retiring disposition he was not so very fit as a political and social worker moving among people and doing public lecturing and propagandist work. But Gopalrav Gokhala was thinking about this time to start what he called 'The Servants of India Society'. He was looking out for young enthusiastic men fit to become life-workers of the proposed Society after undergoing training for five years. The Society was started in 1905 with three members, Messrs. Devadhar, Dravid and Patvardhan, and Gokhale as the first member. Natesrav, filled with enthusiasm for doing public service; was attracted by Gokhale's persuasive tongue and he agreed to become one of the first members of the proposed 'Servants of India Society'.

It was about this time that Gopalrav Gokhale bought the whole concern of Aryabhusan and Dnyanprakas Press and the oddest Marathi weekly paper Dnyanprakas from Haripant Gokhale. They were not paying concerns then. The weekly paper was also not popular and was being run at a loss. But Gokhale felt that for spreading liberal views both in politics and social reform a newspaper and a press were essential for proposed Society. Natesrav who had a liking for writing in Marathi was made the editor of Dnyanprakas. Natesrav gladly and enthusiastically took to this work. While in the Fergusson College he had formed friendship with life-members of the Deccan Education Society and particularly with Messrs. Limaye and Bhate. With their help and with his own fine writing Natesrav improved Dnyanprakas. Soon it was turned into a daily paper. When people saw that there was improvement in the literary style of the paper, in the presentation of news and in leaders and notes the circulation and popularity of the paper gradually increased and it became a self-supporting concern though as yet not a paying one. Since the management came into able and efficient hand of the young associates of Gokhale the Press became at once a paying concern Natesrav continued to be the editor of Dnyanprakas from 1906 to 1911. In 1911 Gokhale made up his mind to open a branch of the Society at Nagpur and Natesrav was sent there as its head and organiser.

There Natesrav felt the need of an English paper and so he started an English weekly named Hitvad. He put a motto for the paper which is characteristic of Natesrav's ideals and views. It is this : 'They are slaves who dare not be in the right with two or three.' Since then he devoted his energy to the development of the paper as also that of the new branch.

When the idea of village improvement came to the front he took to that new work with enthusiasm. It is this work, a little away from Nagpur, that now absorbs Natesrav's attention.

Natesrav had deep convictions about the need of social reform in Hindu Society. So he was in favour of almost all reforms advocated by men like Messrs. Ranade and Agarkar. When he became a widower he acted up to his convictions by marrying a widow. Fortunately his choice fell on an educated widow from a respectable family. Her name was Mathurabai Kelkar. She was the daughter of Govindrav Kelkar who was a subjudge in the judicial department of the Bombay Government and who after retirement lived in Poona. Mathurabai received her education privately. But she learnt English and was particularly good in Sanskrit. She is now Head-mistress of a Girl's School at Amravati. Now to turn to the literary activity of both the husband and wife.

As stated already, since his transfer to Nagpur Natesrav had mainly to write in English. But for six years he wrote constantly in Marathi on a variety of topics current and academic. He writes in a clear and interesting way. Occasionally he contributed articles to magazines. But his main contribution to Marathi literature lies in what he did for making the daily Dnyanprakas popular and a literary paper. Mrs. Mathurabai too is fond of writing and speaking in Marathi and she too has done good work in the line of Marathi literature.

Krsnaji Ganes Limaye

Krsnaji Ganes Limaye was born in 1892 at Pandharpur district Sholapur, where his father Ganpatrav was a teacher in the local high school. His primary and secondary education was done at Pandharpur. But he came for his matriculation study to Nutan Marathi Vidyalay from where he passed his matricu tion examination in 1909. Then he joined the Fergusson College and successively passed his B.A. in 1913 and his M.A. in 1915, his voluntary subject in both examinations being History and Economics. Afterwards he went to Bombay and passed his LL. B. in 1917. Thus Krsnajipant had a very successful career in the University. Immediately he began to do social work for which he had a great liking. So also he began to write in Dnyanprakas. He was made the editor of Dnyanprakas in 1919 a position he is still holding. After his period of probation was over he formally enrolled as a member of the 'Servants of India Society'. Limaya introduced many a new features such as well arranged foreign news, interesting news, letters from Marathi-speaking parts of the country, sympathetic support to women's problems and last but not the least a weekly literary column dealing with detailed but fair criticism and appreciation of new Marathi publications. By these new features Dnyanprakas became both popular and influential and its circulation increased enormously and it reached nooks and corners of Marathi-speaking country. So it has now become a paying concern and both the press and the paper have become a good source of income to the 'Servants of India Society.' This is no small achievement and great credit is due to Limaye and Vamanrav Patvardhan who is the manager of the press. Here it would be appropriate to give some account of Vamanrav Patvardhan as he is intimately connected with the press, and he was the sole founder of another weekly paper called 'Samsthani Svarajya' (Self-rule in States).

Anant Vinayak alias Vamanrav Patvardhan

Anant Vinayak Patvardhan comes from Sangli-Miraj, his family being distantly related to that of the present Patvardhan rulers. He was given in adoption and so he has a double name 'Anant' and 'Vaman'. He was a contemporary in the Deccan College of Messrs. Kelkar and Khadikar. After passing his B.A. examination he was looking out for some opportunity to do social work. Gopalrav Gokhale was glad to take Vamanrav as a probationer of his proposed 'Servants of India Society'. Coming to see the administrative capacity and disciplinary sense of Patvardhan Gokhale entrusted the management of the press to him. How well he succeeded in his work is told already. He being in touch with most of the Southern Maratha States and having their true interest at heart he started his 'Samsthani Svaraja' on his own responsibility.

It described and dealt with the real state of administration, pointed out fearlessly though sympathetically the mismanagement, and evil practices obtaining in many a State and made a fair and friendly criticism of the doings of both rulers and their officers. Vamanrav made his paper not only influential but a kind of terror. But Vamanrav is a genial man of simple habits and simple demeanour. So he was liked by the rulers and freely moved among them and gave them sound and wholesome advice. Unfortunately latterly he is not keeping good health. But he is bearing his chronic ailment with patience. His sons are well educated, one of them continuing the good work of his father in managing the Aryabhusan Press.

The literary activity of Messrs. Dravid, Limaye and Patvardhan is journalistic. They had no time to write or publish academic or imaginative literary works. But all the same they have done good service to modern Marathi literature by adding the journalistic type of literature.

Bapuji Martand Ambekar

Bapuji Martand Ambekar, a journalist by profession, was an Attache of the 'Servants of India Society' and worked on the editorial staff of Dnyanprakas till his death.

Bapuji was born in 1875 at Wai, district Satara. His primary education was done at Wai, and his secondary education in Poona New English School from which he passed his Matriculation examination and then he went to Baroda for his higher education. While he was a student in the Baroda College, Venisambar drama was staged by its students in which Bapusaheb acted the part of Duryodhan the hero of the drama and by his sweet singing and fine acting he elicited the applause of the assembled audience consisting of educated men and college students. But Ambekar could not finish his college course, because he fell constantly ill and the climate did not suit his constitution. Though he did not succeed in his main object during his stay in Baroda, he got a valuable experience in the business of editing and conducting a newspaper. For, he was taken on the editorial staff of Sayajivijaya, a weekly started by Damodar Savalaram Yande, an enterprising publisher and press manager. After his return to Wai Bapurav became a teacher in the local English school. An interesting incident showing both boldness and ready wit on his part is worth telling. Some busybody in Wai sent a written complaint to the Director of Public Instruction that the School managers were corrupt. So he gave a surprise visit to the school and openly scolded the teaching staff for their misconduct. This bold charge was unbearable to Ambekar and he told the Director that it was not his business but that of a judge or a magistrate to inquire into criminal charges against teachers.

He saw his mistake and expressed regret for his indiscretion. While in Wai Bapurav began to write short articles, essays and lives of Indian heroes in the local papers. By this amateurish writing he was laying the foundation of what was to be his life work later on. Such an opportunity soon offered itself. For, he left Wai and came to Poona with a view to secure some job. Fortunately for him he met Nates Appaji Dravid, the then editor of the daily Dnyanprakas and in his first interview with Mr. Dravid he made a good impression about his being well read and his having experience of writing in newspapers. So he was immediately taken up on the editorial staff of Dnyanprakas. He soon became a valuable member of the staff and this work, which was to his liking, he did from 1907 to the end of his life.

For he died in harness. His writing ability, his general efficiency, his careful study of current problems and lastly his consciousness in the discharge of his duties came gradually to the notice of Gopalrav Gokhale. So he was recommended for a membership of the Servants of India Society though he had no academic qualification. Bapurav was a genial man full of hospitality. He had a large circle of friends. His friendship with Haribhau Apte was close and intimate. As an act of pious duty to his friend, Ambekar wrote a short biography of Haribhau Apte. A bigger and more detailed one was written later on by Miss Panse, a daughter of Prof. Panse, another close and intimate friend of Haribhau. Now to turn to Ambekar's literary work. As in the case of all journalists and editors Ambekar's main literary work lies buried in the columns of the several newspapers in which he wrote.

His criticism of books and views was trenchant and sometimes even biting. But he never bore ill-will against his opponents—on the contrary he kept cordial relations with men of all parties in Poona. He had developed a characteristic style having the qualities by clearness, sobriety and attractiveness. His works are the following: 1. Apte Caritra (Life of Hari Narayan Apte); 2. Apte Athavani (Reminiscences of Apte); 3. Pancatantra (Adaptation); 4. Hitopades (Adaptation).

Krsna Mahadev Ciplunkar

Krsna Mahadev Ciplunkar is the younger brother of G.M. Ciplunkar, a life-worker of Karve's University. An account of him is given already and so his younger brother's account may be given here.

Krsna was born in 1890. All his education from A.B C. to B.A. was done in Poona and its several institutions After graduation he did the work of a teacher and within a very short period made a name as an excellent teacher of English. Then he went to Bombay for the study of law and in due course passed his LL.B. examination. Since then he has been practising in civil and criminal courts in Poona. He has specialised in criminal law and has become well known to the court-going public as an expert criminal lawyer. As to his literary work, besides writing short stories and short essays in several magazines he has independently published four novels. They are as follows :

1. 'Vratapalan' (Fulfilment of a vow) ; 2. 'Nirmala' (The pure); 3. 'Papace prayascitta' (Penance for sin); 4. 'Dos Konaca' (Whose fault ?).

Ganes Gangadhar Jambhekar

Ganes Gangadhar Jambhekar comes from an old historical family of Karhada brahmins. It appears that Jambhekar's family along with those of Kirloskar and Gadre migrated to Karnatak about 1800 from its village Pombhurle, taluka Rajapur, district Ratnagiri. Gangadharpant, the father of young Ganes, went to Hubli, a village in Soundatti taluka of Karnatak and rose to the position of a first class magistrate. He was known for probity and strictness in his work. During his service he secured a lot of money and brought a house at Dharwar. However, Ganes was born in 1889 at Bagalkote where his father was then a first class magistrate. Ganes primary and secondary education was done at Dharwar.

But Gangadharpant died at the age of 50 when Ganes was only 14 years of age studying in the High School 5th standard. But his father's death did not disturb his education and he passed his Matriculation examination in 1907. For his University education he went to Indore and studied for the B.A. and got the B A. degree of the Allahabad University in 1914. Then he went to Lahore and joined Government College there for his M.A. study but had to leave the place an account of cholera raging in the town. On his return to Maharastra he looked out for some useful public work for which he had a keen desire and he started the Amalner Education Society in 1914 with the help and cooperation of a few like-minded graduates. These young men and particularly Jambhekar were a nationalist at heart and wanted to conduct the school in a manner to foster a similar spirit among their students. Jambhekar lived and worked for the Amalner society and its school for 7 years from 1916 to 1923. In 1920 he made the school a national institution. But other members did not like the idea for fear of incurring Government displeasure and so they denationalised it and made up their mind to conduct their school as an ordinary High School. So Jambhekar left it. For about 2 years he could not do any work on account of his long continued illness. Then he made an attempt to go to England and lost two years in preparation for it. At least he made up his mind to restart J.V. Oka's magazine named Lokasiksan (Education of the people) and came to Poona towards the close of the year 1927. From January 1928 he began to publish the magazine. In the first issue he assured his readers that it would be conducted on the lines and in the spirit in which Janardanpant Oka conducted it. Jambhekar has kept his word. His magazine is solely devoted to writing on serious subjects like history, economics and social science. It severely excluses stories and novels and what is called light literature intended for mere amusement.

But for such a magazine there is no sufficient demand, there being comparatively very few people prepared to spend money for what is neither useful nor interesting. So, though Jambhekar is publishing a high class literary magazine the only one of its kind in Maharastra he has neither been able to make it a self supporting nor a paying concern. On the contrary he has sunk during five years about 10,000 Rs. Finding that he was unable to conduct magazine on his own account he transferred its financial responsibility to a limited company called Lokasiksan Mandal in 1934 and he is now working as a paid manager and editor of Lokasiksan. It would be really a misfortune if such a fine magazine is allowed to die for want of pecuniary support. Jambhekar's literary work like that of a journalist is confined to what he writes in and for his magazine. He has not written any independent work.

Sankar Vasudev Kirloskar

Sankar Vasudev Kirloskar is a nephew of Laksmanrav Kirloskar. He was born in 1891. He is a highly educated man. Laksmanrav Kirloskar is the founder of the first indigenous factory of iron ploughs located at Kirloskarvadi. It was Laksmanrav's idea to start a magazine called Kirloskar Khabar (News about Kirloskar factory). It was started under that name and the management and editorship were entrusted to Sankarrav He turned out to be the fittest man for the job. For, he very soon converted the magazine (with slight change in its name, the change being an omission of the word Khabar i.e. News) into a literary magazine giving short stories, interesting lives of men successful in some business or other and other interesting matter. Very few articles appeared on serious subjects. Such a magazine was in great demand especially because Manoranjan a Bombay magazine of a similar nature was dwindling and dying on account of its irregularity and mismanagement.

So within a very short period Kirloskar magazine became very popular and its circulation rose by leaps and bounds. Where other magazines could utmost count their subscribers by hundreds, 'Kirloskar' counted its subscribers by thousands and tens of thousands. No doubt credit is due to Sankarrav for his wonderful regularity, his good printing but above all his fine choice of stories and other literary matter. With the assured success of his first adventure Sankarrav added two more magazines, one called 'Manohar' devoted to nothing else but the publication of short stories and the second named Stri (Woman) dealing with the difficult and urgent problems concerning the welfare of Indian women. Of course as a shrewd man Sankarrav did not make Stri purely a serious magazine but was careful to enliven it by publishing interesting stories along with serious topics. His policy was the advocacy of radical social reform and the new morality. Accordingly stories were designed to preach these reformed ideas and views without making them too didactic. In time Sankarrav may make a great reputation as a great editor and literary written of modern times.

Gajanan Visvanath Ketkar

Gajanan Visvanath Ketkar was born in 1898 at Poona in the house of Balvantrav Tilak, who was his maternal grandfather, Visvanathrav being Tilak's son-in-law. His primary and secondary education was done at Nasik. But for his higer education he came to Poona and studied there for two or three years and then he went to Baroda and passed his B. A. in 1918 from the Baroda College and his LL. B. from the Law College, Bombay. Being so intimately related to Balvantrav Tilak he was at once taken up on the editorial staff of the Kesari where he soon acquired a prominent positionwhich he is still occupying. As one of the editors of the by—weekly paper having big circulation he has to study public questions and write articles and notes on current topics. By his literary writings he has been able to maintain the high level of Kesari. This is really not one man's doing but a co-operative work of the whole editorial staff consisting of more than half a dozen graduates. His independently published books are the following:—1. Gita Bij; 2. Lokamanya Tilakanci Bhasa Saili.

Dinkar Vasudev Divekar

Dinkar Vasudev Divekar was born in 1897 at Vasai (Bessein) district thana. After passing his Matriculation examination he came to Poona and joined the Fergusson College and passed his B. A. examination in 1918 and his M. A. after an interval of a few years. Dinkarpant was soon taken up on the editorial staff of Kesari and Mahratta. For, Divekar seems to be Savyasaci (one who can shoot from both hards) i. e. he could write well both in English and Marathi. He wrote in English and published a series of articles on free trade and protection. His Marathi books are the following :— 1. Svabhav Citre; 2. Rastriya Siksan. Messrs. Ketkar and Divekar are still young and have to make their name in Marathi literature. But in time they may come to the front and may write finer books.

A big newspaper concern like a daily or even a by-weekly has to maintain a large staff on its editorial side doing different kinds of writing work required from day to day. But only the names of the senior or more educated members of the staff come to the knowledge of the public. The names of others remain quite unknown and unless they write and publish something on their on account their literary work lies buried and concealed in the columns of the newspaper where they are working. Of such people one deserves to be referred to in this History.

Ramkrsna Gopal Bhide

Ramkrsna Gopal Bhide comes from Wai, district Satara. He has been on the staff of Kesari for a very long time He now about 50 years of age. Of course during all these years he must have written on a variety of topics. It seems his work was found satisfactory. His independently published book is 1. Ingrajani Hindusthan Kasa ghetala ? (How did the Englishmen seize India ?).

Narayan Bhikaji Parulekar

Narayan Bhikaji Parulekar was born in 1897 at Gadaci in Torgal, a feudatory State under Kolhapur. His early education was done at Dharwar. He came to Poona for his secondary education and passed his Matriculation exmination in 1916 from the Nutan Marathi Vidyalaya. Then he joined the New Poona College (Now called Sir Parashurambhau College) and passed his B. A. examination in 1920, he being among the first batch of graduates of that College. His voluntary subject for the B A. was Philosophy. Since his graduation he worked as a teacher in the Anath Vidyarthi Grha and Tilak Mahavidyalaya, Poona for three years. In 1923 he went to America where he stayed for full six years from 1923 to 1929 At first he joined missouri University but he stayed there only for one and one half terms and then he went to the Columbia University of New York. He took both M. A. and Ph. D. degrees from that University. His subject for these examinations was Philosophy. He worked under the guidance and supervision of John Dewey a famous professor of Philosophy. In the latter part of 1929 he travelled to Europe. During his stay in America he not only did the work of a correspondent of Kesari sending American news to that paper but worked as a correspondent of three papers i. e. 'New York World' of

New York, Vossische Zeitung of Berlin and Le Matin of Paris, supplying Indian News to those papers. By this journalistic work he made money which he utilised for his stay and his education in America and for his travels in Europe.

This shows how Dr. Parulekar was a self-made man, how he mastered the difficult art of a correspondent capable of writing in English, French, German and Marathi while he was still studying. This is indeed an admirable versatility ! After completing his higher education in America and after getting experience and knowledge about European life and ideals Dr. Parulekar returned to India by the end of the year 1930. After his return home he continued the work of a correspondent to those papers and for getting accurate news of Indian affairs he travelled over the whole of India from 1930 to the end of 1931. During all these years he was thinking of starting in Poona a newspaper on the American model and accordingly he announced his intention to start a Marathi newspaper and in the American fashion advertised for an appropriate name for his paper, promising a prize of Rs. 150 to one whose suggestion would be approved of Accordingly he received suggestions and proposals about the name from many persons.

The present name 'Sakal' (Morning) was suggested by a student of the Fergusson College who, therefore, received the promised prize of Rs. 150. On the first of January 1932 Dr. Parulekar published the first issue of his Sakal (Morning) in which he declared the policy and the peculiar features of his paper. By strenuous efforts and by the new and novel features introduced by him he has made his paper successful and it has now an established position in Poona and in Maharastra. Now to refer a little to his domestic life, Dr. Parulekar, like Dr. Ketkar remained unmarried till they became financially capable of maintaining a family and felt the need of a life-companion Both of them married European wives, Dr. Ketkar marrying an English lady while Dr. Parulekar marrying a French lady. This marriage took place in 1934 and was of course registered. Now to turn to his literary work.

As I have remarked before that journalists and editors form a separate class of literary writers. Their writings are not regarded by the common people as literary works being on current and temporary topics of the day. But there is no doubt that they and their writings do form a valuable contribution to literature in time. Take the case of Balvantrav Tilak who is rightly regarded as one of the masters of modern Marathi literature. In all his life he did nothing else but write articles for his Kesari. His only independent book is his Gitarahasya. But that too, as is well-known, was only an accidental production. Because he was imprisoned for six long years and because he was prevented from writing on political and current topics, he took to writing on the academic subject of the Gita which was, no doubt, a favourite book of his and about which he had a mind to write. But all the same Tilak's writings and those of Messrs. Agarkar and Paranjpe are now considered good Marathi literature. It is this consideration that has led me to include almost all journalists and editors in my history to Modern Marathi literature.

Dr. Parulekar has a facile pen. He writes in clear and simple style and on a variety of topics. His writings are quite readable and interesting.

Sivram Laksman Karandikar

Sivram Laksman Karandikar comes from the virile land of Ratnagiri Kokan. His family belongs to the class of Khots (landlords) having Khoti rights over the hilly village Maldoli, taluka Chiplun, district Ratnagiri. Sivram's father Laksmanrav with his brother Ganespant migrated to Central Provinces, the father becoming a pleader at Hinganghat and the uncle becoming one at Vardha.

Sivram was born in 1899 at Hinganghat. But unfortunately he lost his father when he was only four years old. He was taken to Parasuram a town of pilgrimage to his maternal grandfather where he received his primary education and also according to old custom, he learnt by heart the Vedic lore. His maternal uncle Vaman Parasuram. Patankar kept Sivram at Mahad, district Kolaba for his secondary education. There he completed his sixth English standard. Then for further studies he was sent to Poona. He passed his Matriculation in 1916 from Nutan Marathi. Vidyalaya, his B. A. in 1920 from the Sir Parashurambhau College. It was sometime after i. e. in 1925 that he passed his M.A. examination and after five years from them he passed his LL. B. in 1930. Thus Karandikar required in all 14 years to complete his University education. But during this period he worked as a teacher in the Maharastra Education Society's High School (Bhave's School) and in the Nutan Marathi Vidyalaya High School. On learning about Dr. Parulekar's plan of starting a daily paper in Poona Karandikar joined him for about six or seven months, worked first as a colaborator and then as a co-editor of Sakal and then left it. Though he formally secured his connection with Sakal he used to write regularly for it. On the occasion of the 60th birthday celebration of Tatyasaheb Kelkar Sakal published a special number to which Sivrampant made a good deal of contribution.

In 1933 for a month or two only he was taken on the editorial staff of Kesari. Karandikar made up his mind on Tilak's Anniversary day to start a newspaper of his own. In the month of November 1933 he did actually start it under the name 'Trikal' (three times) first as a weekly and then from January 1934 as a daily paper. Like Dnyanprakas and Sakal, Trikal has attained a name and an established position in Maharastra by now. Karandikar belongs to the Lokasahi Svarajya party of Maharastra and on behalf of it he contested the last election of the Bombay Legislative Assemby and succeeded in it and is now one of the active members of that body. As to the literary work of Karandikar it is all contained in the columns of Sakal and Trikal for which he wrote a dozen short stories and short essays. Later on he may publish them in a book form and thus got himself formally entitled to be called a literary writer. He is still quite young and may in time write independent books also on his favourite subjects of study.

Dr. Kamalabai Despande

Kamalabai Despande is the daughter of Tatyasaheb Kelkar. She was born in 1898 at Miraj which is the ancestral residential place of her father Tatyasaheb. After the primary and domestic education usually given to girls in these days, she was married to a young and bright boy from the famous family of Despande's of Satara. But unfortunately that young man died a sad and premature death. Since then Kamalabai took to higher education both at home and in the school. She was taught Sanskrit at home and became a good Sanskrit scholar. She passed in 1917 her matriculation from the Huzur Paga Girls' High School, Poona. Then she joined Karve's Women's College and received in due course the Grhitagama Degree (G. A. —Graduate in Arts) in 1920. After completing her education she became a life-member of Women's University of Prof. Karve and began to teach in the Women's College, Hingne. In 1929 she went to Europe for higher study. She found it difficult to get admission in the English and French Universities as her G. A. degree was neither recognised by the Bombay University nor by the Bombay Government. (The Congress Government recognised the degrees of Women's University in 1938).

But with great difficulty and through the efforts of Prof. Hari Ramcandra Divekar who was then living in Paris for his D. Lit. degree, Kamalabai at last succeeded in securing admission in the University of Prague, Czechoslovakia. She selected the following subject for her thesis for Ph. D. degree: 'The child in ancient India' (A comparative study in ancient Indian customs). She was helped in the preparation of her thesis by Prof. Divekar, well-known for his Sanskrit scholarship. For, during vacation times she could go from Prague to Paris where Prof. Divekar was staying. After the approval of her thesis Kamalabai was given the degree of Ph. D. and she returned home in 1931. Then she resumed her work in the Women's College. Sometime after she was appointed Principal of the College, a position she is holding at present. Kamalabai is a quiet and grave sort of a lady who creates a good impression upon a visitor coming to see the College. Now to turn to her literary activity.

Literary talent seems to run in the Kelkar family. The sons and a daughter from Kelkar family have all done literary work to a greater or lesser extent, of course the father exceeding all the literary men of modern times with his huge pile of 12 stout volumes and with his big autobiography called 'Jivanyatra' published in January 1939. Kamalabai had fondness for writing poetry. From her very childhood about which she has memory she longed for being a poet and a journalist. She wrote in 1908 her first poem on Balvantrav Tilak. From that time she has been writing stray poems and prose essays whenever she was in a mood to write. She has written a fine prose poem named 'Hasat Karma Karave' (One should do something laughing) and a collection of poems by name Gita Dvidal (two petals of song). But Kamalabai is still comparatively a young lady and with leisure and suitable opportunity she may produce more and finer literary work.

It would be quite appropriate to refer, in this place along with Dr. Kamalabai, to a budding new writer. He is no other than her son. It appears from his early literary activity that not only literary talent runs in the Kelkar family but flows down to the descendents both on the parental and maternal side.

Sridhar Gopal Despande

Sridhar Gopal Despande is as stated presently the son of Kamalabai Despande. He was born in 1912 at Poona in Tatyasaheb Kelkar's house. He was educated in Satara upto the matriculation standard. He then went in for naval education with a view to join naval service newly opened to enterprising Indian youths. He took his naval education both in theory and practice on the Dufferin steamer, lying in the harbour of Bombay, making occasional trips to other harbours for giving practical training of the naval art to the students on the Steamer and for inuring them to the hard life of a sailor. Young Sridhar went successfully through this ordeal and passed the examination entitling him to get at once an officer's post in naval service. Soon after the course of his naval training was over he was appointed a second officer in one of the ships of the 'Sindia Steam Navigation Company'. He has also learnt the art of flying and has got A licence in that line. Thus Sridhar seems to be one of the most enterprising youths of Maharastra of the present and of coming generations. Now to speak about his literary activity. He has written so far two articles and one novel.

1. Kharavara (Saltish wind). This series of articles is published in Kirloskar magazine and deals with the interesting but exciting subject of life on the sea. It is a creditable performance for a new and young writer. 2. His second series of articles under the name 'Vimanvidyevaril' (About the art of flying) was published in Sahyadri magazine and as the significant name of the series tells, deals with the subject of flying. 3. The third is an independently published novel called 'Sahara.'

Vagbhat Narayan Despande (1892-1935)

Vagbhat Narayan Despande comes of the famous Despande family of Satara. He was adopted by Narayanrav, his uncle, who was a retired Huzur Deputy Collector and built a bungalow near Shirval, an important town in Bhor State. Young Vagbhat was educated at Satara, in the Deccan College and in Bombay and became B. A., LL. B. and began his practice at Satara and soon became moderately successful in his profession. He was fond of writing from his college days and wrote very fine stories in the College magazine. Then he wrote similar stories in Manoranjan and critical articles in Vividhdnyanavistar. When Aikya (Union) weekly was started in Satara by Ravsaheb Kale Vagbhat became its first editor. His independent books are:

1. Reminiscences of Haribhau Apte; 2. Critical articles on the social novels of Haribhau Apte.

B. M. Gore

B M. Gore comes from the family of Gore, the famous poet Candrasekhar of Baroda. Young Gore was born in 1908 at Baroda. He received his education at Baroda and Poona. He was a fellow of the Baroda College and after taking his M A. degree he joined the Fergusson College, Poona as a permanent servant. He has been working in the Department of English in the Willingdon and Fergusson Colleges of the Deccan Education Society since 1932 and has proved a valuable addition to the staff.

His contribution to Modern Marathi literature is his pioneer volume named 'Navi Palavi' (New blossom). This is a small book of about 70 pages and contains 13 very very short stories. This is the latest fashion in the literary field of today. Gore's stories describe a single incident or the revival of a past event in clear and simple language. This form of literature may become popular in time. Gore's second book named 'Adhunik Angla Vangmaya' gives a brief history of modern English literature. It is a slightly bigger book than his first book and consists of about 145 pages. The history begins with an account of the poet Robert Bridges and ends with that of A. G. Gardiner. Gore is still a young man and may in time write better and finer books in Marathi.

Madhav Damodar Altekar

Madhavrav was born in 1890 at his maternal grandfather's in the village of Kale, taluka Panhala. Kolhapur State. Damodarpant was a State servant in the revenue department and became ultimately a Mamledar. Young Madhav was educated at Kolhapur upto his Inter Arts examination and then he joined the Fergusson College, Poona and passed his B. A in 1915 and M. A. in 1917. After a chequered career for some years, he got in 1935 a professorship of Marathi in the Wilson College for which he was eminently fit by his previous study and work. He has now a settled and honoured position and can devote his leisure time to literary work.

He is a popular professor, possessing a good command over languages both English and Marathi and having a fascinating power of speech. Now to refer to his literary activity. Before publishing his independent books Altekar received training in and experience of writing by serving in Dnyanprakas daily, Poona, by becoming an editor of Indu-prakas, Bombay, by serving as an assistant secretary of the Bombay Presidency Association, by working in the Associated Press and lastly by doing the job of an assistant editor of the Indian textile journal.

His independently published books are the following:

1. Aparadh Konaca? (Whose fault?); 2. Lalita; 3. Mukta-bandha; 4. Antarang. All these are social novels depicting the middle class life in Hindu society. 5. Agarkarance Vivecak Caritra (A critical life of Agarkar); 6. Kalidasaci Srsti (World of Kalidas); 7. Pane va Phule, Parts I & II (Leaves and flowers); 8. Dnyanesvarivaril Vivecanatmak Nibandh (A critical essay on Dnyanesvari); 9. Artha Sastra. The last two books are ready for publication.

Narayan Kesav Bhagvat

Narayan Kesav Bhagvat is one of four brothers. They are all well educated and are at present occupying honoured positions in different walks of life, one being a Huzur Deputy Collector, another an Inspector in the Co-operative Department and the last two being professors of different subjects in two separate colleges. N. K. Bhagvat is the last brother. He seems to have been educated mostly in Bombay, taking his M. A. degree in Sanskrit and Pali. He studied Pali under the famous Pali scholar and prosessor Kausambi. Then he became a professor of Pali in the St. X'aviers College, Bombay. In about 1920 Marathi was introduced as a voluntary subject in the curriculum of the B. A. degree. Prof. Bhagvat who was known to be a careful student of Marathi literature and who used to write in Marathi for magazines was asked to teach

Marathi to the B. A. students who took up that voluntary. Thus it was that Professor Bhagvat became a professor of both Pali and Marathi.

In time he came to be regarded as a scholar in Marathi literature. So he was taken up as a member on the Board of Studies in Marathi of the Bombay University, a position which he is still holding. Now to refer to his literary activity. As stated already he has written articles and essays in Marathi. They are mostly about Buddhism, not that he has never written on other subjects. They are not as yet published in a separate book form. Further, he has made selections from old and new writers for higher standards of High Schools intended to serve as rapid reading books for F Y. classes of colleges also. He has written one or two independent books about Buddhism. One is this: 1. Pali vangmayatil tera bhiksuni ratne (Thirteen jewel-like Buddhistic nuns in Pali literature).

Mahadev Pandurang Oka (1874 1930)

Mahadev Pandurang Oka was born in 1874 at Varsai near Pen, district Kolaba. While he was studying in the vernacular school, Mr. Kondopant Chatre, Deputy Educational Inspector of schools, came to observe his intellectual powers and so gave him in marriage his second daughter when he was just only 14 years of age. After his marriage Oka came to Poona, his father in-law giving him money for his expenses. He had received his early Sanskrit lessons from his maternal uncle Pandurang Sastri Londhe and was in the habit of composing verses in Sanskrit even while he was a boy. He passed his Matriculation examination in 1893 but having lost his father in 1895, could not completete his college education. So he had to take to some job in order to meet the expenses of his large family. He worked as a teacher in Pen from 1895 to 1901. Prof. Haribhau Limaye, an influential life-member of the D. E, Society, Poona and the then Superintendent of the Poona New English School, took Mahadevrav Oka on the teaching staff of the school Soon after he was made a permanent servant of the D. E. Society.

He was the most successful teacher of Sanskrit among contemporay Sanskrit teachers in Western India. His private Sanskrit classes, which he was allowed to conduct as not interfering with his class teaching, were very popular, his method of teaching Sanskrit being very engaging and interesting. His Abhinav Ratnamala, Subodh Pathavali, Sulabh Sanskrit Praves and the Suktisudhatarangini, as also his treatises on Aorist and Desiderative have all contributed to create a liking for Sanskrit in the minds of young students. He was in a way a great linguist, having a deep knowledge of Sanskrit, English and Marathi. Not only had he this threefold knowledge but had a quick and ready power of versification, so that any passage simple or difficult from any one of the three languages he could at once translate (in verse or prose) into another language. This was indeed a wonderful power. And Madhavrav possessed a fine gift of versification in Marathi, so that his inclusion in this history is justified. Though most of his literary work was concerned with Sanskrit studies and Sanskrit literature he has to his credit some Marathi poems and translations. One short poem in a dialogue form is neatly done.

It is a sweet and striking song about an interesting story appearing in school books. It is as follows: A confectioner had made a parade of a large number of shining plates overflowing with sweets of strong though pleasant smell. A villager passing by the shop was attracted by the sweet-smelling condiments. So he lingered at the shop to enjoy the smell.

The crafty and wily shopkeeper after allowing the villager to linger for a while demanded payment of money in exchange for having taken the smell of his sweets. The villager knowing the cheating propencities of selfish men proved a match for the shop-keeper. He took out a few gingling coins from his money-bag and produced for a few minutes, a pleasants sound by shaking them in his closed fist. Then he asked the shop-keeper with a cunning smile whether he had not got the full price of what he gave him. This is the humorous end of the story. Madhavrav has composed a beautiful poem consisting of dialogue-songs in a flowing and fascinating metre well-fitted for the homorous story. The demanding song of the shop-keeper and the retorting one of the villager are simply superb. This dialogue-song sung by sweet-voiced boys at the time of school gatherings is known to hold spell-bound vast audiences of young and old. Madhavrav has written a number of such Marathi songs and stray poems which await publication.

Ghanasyam Balkrsna Ciplunkar

Ghanasyam Balkrsna Ciplunkar was born in 1883 at Bhalaval, Peta Bande, Savantvadi state. He had a garden land as a source of income for his maintenance but it was destroyed by locusts. So immediately after his thread-ceremony at the age of 9 was over Ghanasyam went in 1892-1893 to Nasik for education to his maternal aunt's son Mahesvar Narayan Devadhar who was the first assistant teacher in the Nasik High School. But uufortunately for young Ciplunkar he died in 1896. From 1896 to 1901 he studied upto his Marathi 6th standard, maintaining himself on madhukari (system of begging cooked food from door to door). Savarkar brothers lived at Nasik at that time, Narayanrav being his fellow student. Young Ciplunkar formed intimate friendship with Savarkar brothers which led to his joining the secret society started by them.

It is this association with persons of radical views that created in the mind of young Ciplunkar a spirit of patriotism and a keen desire for social reform. Moreover, reading of Nibandhamala of Visnu Sastri Ciplunkar gave him a new and wide vision about life and its duties. In 1901 he came to Poona and joined the Poona Training College. There he lived six months by securing vars (daily dinners) at houses of charitably disposed people. Poona was affected by plague in 1901 so he had to leave it without securing a certificate from the Training College. In 1903 he became a teacher in the Navin Marathi Sala of the D. E. Society, [Poona, his monthly salary being Rs. 7. But the Society seeing that he was a promising teacher sent him to the Training College by giving him a scholarspip. After passing the final certificate examination of that College Ciplunkar became a permanent teacher.

He faithfully and efficiently served the Society for about 23 years from 1905 to 1926 during which period he worked in Navin Marathi Sala, Ramanbag Sala and New English School (Nana Vada School) teaching all non-English subjects from the infant class to 5th English standard. Sometime after retirement he was appointed a teacher in 1926 in the Training College of the Seva Sadan Society of Poona. There he served for 13 years till the end of 1938.

Thus Ciplunkar did in all 36 years service in the teaching line. As he had radical views on social reform both his marriage and remarriage were on the reformed lines. He believes that unless the rigid caste rules are loosened to a considerable extent Hindu society would not progress. He feels perfect toleration for all religions. According to him a person who lives in India and has his permanent home there should be a Hindu be he a Parsi, a Musalman or a Christian. Among Marathi teachers such liberal and radical views on social and religious matters are very rarely met with. But Ciplunkar had imbibed these ideas from Savarkar brothers as stated already.

Now to turn to his literary work. He got good experience while engaged in teaching in the different schools and he made use of it in writing books useful principally for primary school boys. In all he wrote 12 books. Out of these the following are books of general interest: 1. Narayanravaca Khun ani Savai Madhavravace lagna (Murder of Narayanrav Pesve and marriage of Savai Madhavrav Pesve); 2. Maharani Laksmibai Zamsi (Account of Laksmibai Rani of Zamsi); 3. Nibandh Kase lihave (How to write essays); 4. Marathi bhaseca abhyas (study of Marathi language); 5. Lahan mulance prasangvacan (occasional reading for small children).

Pandurang Mahadev Bapat

Pandurang Mahadev Bapat was born in 1880 at Parner, district Ahmednagar. The original home of Bapat's family was Pule, a small but beautiful village on the sea shore in the Ratnagiri district where there is a famous Ganapati temple. God Ganapati was naturally the family God of Bapat's family, young Pandurang's parents being sincere devotees of Ganapti. The family migrated to Parner during the closing years of Pesvai rule over Maharastra. Young Pandurang's primary education was done at Parner. For his secondary education he was sent to Poona where he lived with Cintopant Dev, an intimate friend of Madhavrav. He joined the Poona New English School. He remained in the school from 1892 to 1897 when plague made its appearance in Poona. So Cintopant Dev sent away young Bapat to Parner. Young Bapat had great talents which he had showed by winning scholarships and prizes throughout his school career. For his matriculation study he was sent to Ahmednagar where he joined the local society's High School, then under the superintendentship of the famous sanskrit scholar, Mahadev Malhar Josi. Young Bapat passed his matriculation examination in 1899 and won the second Jagannath Sanskrit scholarship and then joined the Deccan College.

He became a graduate in 1903. By his brilliant University career Pandurangrav had won golden opinions from his professors who strongly recommended him for Sir Mangaldas Nathubhai scholarship for technical education in England. Bapat got the scholarship and with the supplementary pecuniary help on the loan system of the Hindu Education Society he was able to go to England in 1904. There he joined Harriet College, Edinburgh and took up the Mechanical Engineering course. But while studying in the college, he was requested to deliver a lecture in the winter lecture series organised by the Independent Labour Party, about the then state of India. In his enthusiasm he agreed to deliver it and in order to make a thorough preparation of his lecture he asked for a loan of books from Syamji Krsnavarma who gladly supplied him with books containing extreme views expressed in violent terms.

The lecture was delivered and was immediately published. Of course it was admired by the left wing of the Labour Party. But it brought trouble upon young Bapat. For, his scholarship was stopped by the Bombay University for his violent speech. About this time Vinayakrav Savarkar had gone to England. So Bapat met Savarkar and with his advice went to Paris to Syamji Krsnavarma. In India too a violent agitation was going on all over the country due to discontent in general and the partition of Bengal in particular and Bapat longed to go back to India. But before doing so he wanted to learn the art of bomb-making from his terrorist friends in Paris. After knowing the secret of bombing and after secretly printing a confidential pamphlet about it he returned to India in 1908 and immediately went to Calcutta to see his friends who had returned to India before him. Bapat did not like the plan of killing individual Englishmen which the Bengal terrorist party had resolved upon. But while in Calcutta he had an attack of malaria and so had to return home hurriedly. After meeting his wife and children he came to Poona. But the police were after him.

As soon as he came to know of this he resolved to abscond and remain disguised, thereby eluding the police. But during this period of about 5 years Bapat had to suffer constant anxiety and trouble and had to stoop to do even low and disgusting work, had to remain without food for days together, and had to pass his days in the jaws of death as it were, in deep forests full of wild animals. But inspite of his concealment and disguise he was at last caught by the police and brought to Bombay and kept in prison but was very well treated. In the searching interviews which the C.I.D. officers had with Bapat they saw that Bapat was not concerned in any terrorist plot but that on the contrary he was against the murder of individual Englishmen. So he was let off. From 1913 to 1925 he remained free and during this period of 12 years Bapat could do some literary and useful work such as writing in Citramay Jagat, in the Mahratta weekly of Balvant-rav Tilak, and in Dnyankos of Dr. Ketkar.

In 1920 he had the domestic calamity of losing his wife, leaving behind her a son named Vaman aged 10 and a daughter named Kamal aged 2. In 1921 began the Mulsi agitation against the acquisition of land in Mulsi Peta by Government for Tata's great dam and reservoir for storing water and leading it through a tunnel to Bhira in Kokan for producing electricity. Bapat took a prominent part in this agitation. In fact, he was the inspirer and soul of the movement. He was often fined and restrained for days together. But he again and again disobeyed Government or police orders. At last he was brought before a magistrate on a criminal charge, was tried and sentenced to six years' rigorous imprisonment. This was the first serious punishment inflicted upon Bapat. Bapat received the honorific name of Senapati (army general) since his starting and leading the Mulsi agitation. He was released in 1931. But very soon he received his second punishment for six years.

Thus out of his total public life of 30 years Senapati Bapat had to remain without doing any useful work for about 17 years (12 years of imprisonment and 5 years of Adnyatvas, i.e. life in concealment). Now Bapat has become comparatively an old man of about 60. With the long suffering and trouble in his 17 years of idle and unbearable life he has lost his youthful vigour and energy. However, he is a man of high courage and determination and has expressed his resolve to die for the cause of the country. Now to refer to his literary activity; compared with that of Barrister Savarkar Bapat's literary output is inconsiderable. He has a poetic vein and has done some poetic work. His important book is his (1) autobiography written in verse form. The versification is easy and flowing and in simple and clear style and the story is full of stirring incidents; 2. Versified translation of the Bhagvatgita and 3. Some stray articles and essays.

Ganes Sadasiv Marathe

Ganes Sadasiv Marathe was born at Nadiad in Gujarat, his father being then in service in Public Works Department of the Bombay Government. Young Marathe's education from A.B.C. to M.A. was all done in Poona, he passing his matriculation examination in 1897, B A. in 1902 and M A in 1905 with Mathematics as his special subject. He was a moderately successful student throughout his school and college career. But he was fond of reading all manner of books. The problem of what to do faced Marathe after the completion of his education.

He was influenced more by the nationalistic teaching of Balvantrav Tilak than by the liberal views of Messrs Gokhale and Paranjpe who were his teachers and who had a kindly heart for young Ganapatrav. Gokhale even asked him to be a member of the Servants of India Society after his passing M.A. examination. Marathe had almost promised to be a member of the said society. But about that time the agitation against the partition of Bengal has just begun in Bengal. But it soon spread over the whole country. Balvantrav Tilak took up that agitation with his characteristic zeal and vigour.

In order to compel the British Government to repeal the partition of Bengal and to wrest 'svarajya' (A word for self Government which now came into use and became the cry of the whole country) the following remedies were suggested i.e. national education, boycott of British goods and svadesi (Vow to buy goods manufactured in the country) and young Marathe was captivated by these ideas and he tried thrice to do national work, by starting a school of his own or by taking over an already existing school or by joining as a life worker such an institution. Instead of remaining idle he accepted a teacher's post in 1907 in the Poona New English School.

But he remained there only for a year. For 8 to 9 months he was a tutor to Prince Sivajirav Gaikavad of Baroda, getting that post through the strong recommendation of Wrangler Paranjpye. Some time in 1908 and 1909 he worked under

Balvantrav Tilak when he toured through Khandesh and Berar. Marathe took part in the picketing agitation in Poona against drink and was fined Rs. 30. But about this time a founder of Hindusthan Cooperative Insurance Company came to Bombay and blamed educated young men, especially Maharastriyans, for not taking to Insurance work which was a very lucrative business. Further, he said that he was prepared to take into the company's service an able young man. Marathe was recommended and he got in 1909 employment in the newly started Bombay Branch of the Hindusthan Insurance company.

Dr. Bhajekar who was a director of the local Board of Directors of the Company suggested to young Marathe to learn actuarial science. In order that he might be able to study without interruption and with sufficient leisure Marathe gave up his appointment in the Bombay Branch after 8 months. In those days the examination for actuarial science took place only in Calcutta and very few students appeared for that very difficult examination. But Marathe ventured to study and appeared for the examination and passed the first part of the examination in 1910. He got confidence and next year he passed the second part of that examination, thus becoming a full-fledged actuary.

But he had so far only a theoretical knowledge of the science and in order to get practical training he had to go to England. So Marathe made up his mind to go there. His father hesitated at first to give his son a large sum required for his going and staying in England. But on seeing that he had passed both the difficult examinations of the actuarial science and that he had got ready employment in the Insurance Company Sadasivrav agreed to incur the necessary expenses for his son's education in England. Accordingly he went to England in 1911. But he could get no entrance in any Insurance Office. Fortunately for him he found a liberal-minded practising actuary named Mr. George King who agreed to take Marathe as a paid apprentice in his office.

This happened in 1912. There he worked for nearly a

year. During the vacation of August 1912 Ganpatrav travelled to Europe and visited Belgium, Germany, Austria, Italy and Switzerland. He remained with Mr. George King for a year and got all the practical knowledge of the actuarial business. He came home in 1913. On his voyage back he saw the town of Barcelona in Spain, and a few cities in France. As a traveller he stopped for a few days in Egypt and saw the famous cities of Cairo and Alexandria.

Immediately on his return he was appointed a manager and an actuary in the newly started Insurance Company named 'East and West' on a monthly salary of Rs. 250. His father was glad to see that his son was well settled in life. After 3 months his salary was raised to Rs. 300 a month. But Marathe came to see that the actuaries in actual practice made far more profits than what he got as his pay. So after 8 months' Indian experience Marathe made up his mind to start independent business of his own and so he opened his office in Poona about the end of 1914. The rest of Marathe's tale is soon told. From the first Marathe's business became a paying concern though he did not make any very large profits. But gradually his practice increased. Being the first Maharastriyan actuary he began to get large practice. Moreover, as he did his work most conscientiously and gave sound advice to companies, company after company sought Marathe's advice and made him their actuary. Thus in a few years Marathe made huge profits.

Where he at first employed one clerk he now employs 30 and still it is difficult to cope with the growing business. But Marathe is neither very fond of money nor pomp nor luxurious life. So he feels that he has made more than enough of money and he thinks of retiring from business as he is now over 57 years of age and looking forward to his Sastyabdhi-purti (A ceremony performed when one completes 60 years of age). His friends celebrated in a public manner the anniversary of his 50th birthday and published a fine 'Souvenir' volume in which a brief account of his life and life-work, a number of appreciative articles about him and other short essays about different aspects of Insurance business are given. Now to turn to Marathe's literary work.

The output consists of only two books. But they are literature of a high order and especially in a line which is very meagerly represented in Marathi literature. Marathe, though looking grave and serious, is a genial man full of wit and humour. His conversation is lively and interesting and he enlivens it by telling interesting incidents and anecdotes of which he has a good store ready at this command His first book was written in collaboration with Mr. Sadasiv Narayan Thosar. It was published in 1908 when Marathe was in a way idling away his time. 1. It is named 'Natyakala Rukkuthar' (Hatchet of the histrionic Art); 2. His second book is called 'Thalipith' (Bread prepared with flour of 3 or 4 kinds of grain mixed with salt and spices). This gives an account of Marathe's travels in Europe. Both are very humorous writings and are quite readable.

Anant Kakaba Priyolkar

Anant Kakaba Priyolkar comes from a Sarasvat family. He was educated in a town in Portuguese territory where in its primary stage Portuguese is the only language taught. So he had to learn English and Marathi (his mother tongue) privately and at home. For his college education he went to Dharwar and joined the Karnatak College and passed F.Y. and Inter Arts examinations and studied in the junior B.A. class. When the Willingdon College Sangli was recognised for B. A. courses with Marathi as one of the voluntary subjects he came to Sangli and joined the senior B. A. class. He passed his B. A. examination in 1923, being one of the first batch of graduates from the Willingdon College. He went to Bombay and there got a teacher's post in a municipal school. Thus he is permanently settled in Bombay.

Anantrav had fondness for writing in Marathi from his young age. While he was still in the college he wrote articles on a variety of subjects in Svayamsevak, (which was edited and conducted by his brother) in Vividhadnyanvistar and Manoranjan. This practice of stray writing and publishing. Anantrav continued after he was settled in Bombay. His writings in this line are too numerous to mention here. He seems to have a liking for scholarly and antiquarian work about Marathi language and literature. He has the advantage of knowing Portuguese and Kokani (a dialect of Marathi) in addition to the languages which educated Maharastriyans generally know. These literary efforts of his are of great value and besides form interesting reading. So I refer to some of them here.

1. Dhruvakhyanaca Khara Karta (True writer of the story of Dhruva). This is an interesting and informing little essay; 2. Nala-damayanti Svayamvar (Critical edition of the famous poem of Raghunath Pandit in which the problem of the real author is discussed and solved This book received Tarkhadkar prize in 1935 from the Bombay University); 3 Marathi Vyakaranaci Kulkatha (Full and complete story of Marathi grammar). This book is partly historical and partly comparative. Firstly, it gives an interesting account of Marathi grammars made by European writers before the so-called first grammar of Dadoba Tarkhadkar was published. Further, it compares Father Stephens' grammar of Kokani language with those of other vernaculars. This is probably the most interesting and informing book of Priyolkar. 4 Gomantakaci Sarasvati (Learning of Portuguese Territory). This is a historical book. It tries to give how Marathi language from Dnyanesvar's time, had contact with Gomantak and its people. Further, it gives a brief account of the puranas (chronicles) written in Marathi by English, French and Portuguese writers. This book has proved how Kokani language is only a sub-dialect of Marathi and not an independent and separate language as some biased persons try to make out. 5. Siva va Gova (Sivaji and the Province of Gova). This is again a historical book. It gives an account how Sivaji tried to conquer Gova territory and how and why he failed in his attempts. 6. Sikhancya adi granthatil pade racanara Namdev (Namdev the composer

of the songs in the Granthsaheb of the Sikhs). This is again an antiquarian and scholarly book. It shows how Namde the composer of Sikh songs is a different person from the famous Maharastriyan Saint-poet Namdev.

Lastly, it may be mentioned that, besides the above literary output, many short stories, stray poems, humorous titbits and critical essays are published by Priyolkar in several magazines. This recital shows that Priyolkar is a prolific writer. He is a middle-aged man now. But still his literary talents do not show signs of abatement.

Vitthal Vaman Hadap

Vitthal Vaman Hadap is the most prolific novelist and story-teller of this period. So his account ought to have been given at the top of the class of novelists just as Dr. Ketkar's account tops that of prose-writers of the period. But in spite of my keen desire to get an account of him so as to enable me to put it in its proper place, I did not get till the last week of January 1939. So I now give Hadap the last place, justifying my procedure by reference to the phrase 'Last but not the least'. Hadap's life is worth reading. From extreme poverty in his early days he has risen to a position of comparative ease and comfort and that too solely on the strength of his pen. His is probably the first example of a literary man making literature his whole and sole profession and getting a fairly decent yearly income from it. Let me give in brief an account of his life and his life work.

Vitthalrav was born in 1900 at Kotkamte, taluka Devgad, district Ratnagiri. His primary education he received at his birth place. For his secondary education he came to Bombay and studied there upto the Matriculation standard. But he was so poor that he could not live in Bombay unless he became a madhukari (A receiver of cooked food by going from door to door). In fact, for 7 years from his 7th year to his 14th year he remained a madhukari. Since then he made money by writing and maintained himself and educated himself. What a hard life Hadap had to lead from his early age! He spent almost all his life in Bombay. Only two years back he went to live at Satara and there has started a Press of his own by name Adarsa Mudranalaya (Model Printing Press). Vitthalrav seems to be a man of spirit, feeling keenly insults given by others. On account of insulting treatment received from people he tried to commit suiside thrice but ultimately better counsells seem to have prevailed and he lives still to do such a useful and valuable work as production and publication of interesting and informing literature.

He has very radical and almost extremist views on social, religious and economical matters and he had to suffer from the difficulties and troubles due to the social boycott of the orthodox people. But he did not mind such persecution from his ignorant brethren. A man of such views naturally found it difficult to secure a life companion by a suitable marriage. However, he did marry at last and has a wife and three children.

Now to refer to his literary output. As stated already he had literary talents of high order and began to use them from the age of 14. Since then he has been continuously writing. In 1920-21 he started a newspaper named 'Lokasahi' 'Popular Government) in Bombay. But on account of seditious articles having appeared in his paper he was hauled up by the police, was brought before a magistrate, was tried, found guilty and was given one year's rigorous imprisonment. In his absence his weekly paper disappeared. His published books small and great will form a home library by themselves. All told they are more than fifty volumes.

The first important class of Hadap's literary works is that of novels. He has written about 20 social novels. They are almost all novels with a purpose. In them he has described how men and women suffer because of the unjust customs in our society and also because of the foibles inherent in human nature. Hadap has developed a style of his own and he is therefore able to interest the reader by his writings. The second class of his novels are historical. Here they are not promiscuously written. They are designed on a systematic plan. His object is to give the origin and expansion over the whole of India of the Maratha Empire during the times of the Pesavas.

This he wants to do in about 6 novels. Then in the second series consisting of about 6 novels again he wants to show how and why this superstructure built up so laboriously by the Pesavas in their early career toppled down so suddenly at the time of the last Pesava Bajirav. Hadap has been able to write so far only half dozen historical novels out of 12 that he proposes to complete the series. Hadap's scheme is similar to that of Nath Madhav. He also thought of writing about a dozen novels on this very subject though he died before he could fully and completely execute his plan. Let us hope that Hadap succeeds in his plan.

Hadap's short stories are again divided into two classes: those that he published independently and on his own account and those that he gave to other publishers for being included in their four anna series.

The very fact that Hadap's novels have become popular and have given him large profits shows that they are very interesting and fascinating. Thus they are a valuable addition to modern marathi literature. Hadap has find and fertile imagination and a facile and forcible pen. He is now a middle-aged man. Still he may write and publish many more books on varied subjects unless his imagination wanes and his pen fails him.

Before I conclude my long labours I must not omit a duty which I owe to myself and my family. This is not done out of vanity or self-laudation but as a fitting conclusion to a literary history which gives an account of the life and life-work of hundreds of Marathi writers. Having read these interesting accounts readers would be anxious, I believe, to get similar information about the writer who entertained them so far. It is convenient to give this account in the usual impersonal form rather than in the first personal form which may seem egoistic.

Bhate Brothers

Bhate family's original home was the small village of Kasemurbad in the Ratnagiri district, its family god being the famous Ganpati at Pule.

Govind's father was entirely a self-made man of great intelligence and of fine gentlemanly character. After completing his vernacular education he had to seek some service on account of the straightened circumstances of the family. So he accepted the post of a postman and runner in the Postal Department, on a salary of Rs. 5 a month quite inadequate to supply even the urgent needs of himself and family. So he borrowed money sufficient for a year's stay in Bombay, went there and studied very hard for the district pleaders' examination which was to be held in marathi language for the last time that year.

Fortunately for Cimnajipant and his family he passed the examination in 1869. He made up his mind to practise at Mahad, district Kolaba, and came over there with his family. Here his eldest son Govind was born in 1870. Cimnaji soon made his name in the profession and in time he was recognised as the ablest and cleverest pleader in the district. His practice grew rapidly. So his children could be brought up in comfort and could be given higher education. He had five children; 2 sons Govind and Gopal and 3 daughters. All of them are still living. To refer first to the younger brother of Govind. For he has done a bit of literary work though as a busy lawyer and an active public worker he did not and does not find time to devote his time to literature though he has great desire and capacity to write.

Gopal Cimnaji Bhate

Gopal was born in 1878. After his vernacular education at Mahad he was sent to Poona for his secondary education and he joined the New English School, Poona. He passed his Matriculation in 1896-97 from the New English School his fellow students being Messrs. Bhopatkar, Bapat, Naik and Marathe. About that very time Cimnajipant had a serious attack of piles and though he recovered from it he grew weak, requiring the help and companionship of some one. For he was then a widower; so he asked Gopal to remain with him permanently and to study for pleader's examination. Gopal was a bright boy and had a keen desire for university education. But he had to accept the decision of his father in a self-denying spirit and he reconciled himself to his fate and applied his mind zealously to the study of law and passed the pleader's examination in 1899 when he was only 22 years of age. Cimnajipant was so glad to see his son becoming a pleader and coming to take over his practice. Gopalrav was so young that he still looked a boy and so he was nick-named 'boy pleader'.

After six months or so Cimnajipant had an attack of fever which carried him off in 1900 at the age of 60. Gopalrav shifted to Roha, district Kolaba when a new Subjudge's Court was established there. His practice there grew rapidly and he soon acquired the reputation of being the ablest lawyer having up-to-date knowledge of law and law cases. He has by now practised for full 39 years. He has been taking part from his young days in public activities especially connected with the local Municipality of which he was president for over 12 years, with the District Local Board of which he was vice-president and lastly with the Kokan Education society, Alibag of which he has been Chairman from its establishment in 19i6. With such practice and with such public work he finds very little time for literary activity though he has a literary talent of a high order. He has written one fine Marathi drama based on the novel Pride and Prejudice of Jane Austine.

It is a fine piece of literary work better than an English drama written by an Englishman. It is named 'Vicarvilasit' (Play of thought). He has also written half a dozen short stories and they are all published in Manoranjan. He has with him almost ready two dramas for publication. Gopalrav is a great social reformer. He married a widow when he became a widower. He is now 60 years old.

Govind Cimnaji Bhate

Govind Cimnaji Bhate the elder brother was born in 1870 at Mahad. After his vernacular education was over there he was sent to Poona for his secondary and college education and he joined the Poona New English School. He passed his matriculation in 1888. He then joined the Fergusson College and passed the P. E. examination (the F. Y. of present days) in 1890 having lost a year through illness. Then he joined the Deccan College passing his first B. A. examination (corresponding to Inter Arts examination of these days) in 1891 and his B. A. in 1892 and won the Ellis Scholarship for Proficiency in English. Then he was appointed a Daxina fellow in the College for 2 years. He passed his M.A. in 1894 and won the Kasinath Trimbak Telang Medal. His voluntary subject both for B.A. and M.A. was Philosophy. Govindrav was a favourite pupil of Dr. Selby and of Dr. Bhandarkar. Immediately after passing the M.A. examination Govindrav joined the Deccan Education Society, Poona and became a professor of Philosophy in the Fergusson College.

He soon made a name for himself as a successful teacher of the difficult subjects like Metaphysics, Psychology and Ethics (all being included in the term Philosophy). Though he had not studied Indian Philosophy during his College days, that subject not being included in the curriculum of those days. But later on he privately studied Indian Philosophy. So later in his professorial career he used to teach both European and Indian Philosophy to B.A. and M.A. students. In 1919 the Deccan Education Society started the Willingdon College at Sangli and Professor Bhate was appointed the principal of the College where he remained for about 10 years.

He had to work strenuously to build up the College. He collected about 6 lacs of rupees and was able to erect a pile of fine buildings for the accommodation of the college and for the residence of students. Prof. Bhate finally retired in August 1933, thus putting in a total service of 38 years in the two colleges together. During 1929-30 when he had taken a year's privilege leave he had been to England where he collected materials for his projected 'history of modern Marathi Literature' (This history). Now to turn to his literary work.

Bhate is neither precocious nor has he poetic talent. But from his coming to Poona he was inflneuced by men like Messrs. Tilak, Agarkar and Gokhale though the influence of the latter was greater. Love of marathi language and literature and a keen desire to study them were created by Ciplunkar's fascinating advocacy of marathi. Especially his statement 'it is the sacred duty of every educated man to impart to his ignorant brethren, knowledge of western science and literature by writing books in Marathi' made an abiding impression upon Bhate's mind. Since he was settled in life he has been writing stray articles and books for the last 30 years.

His first essay named 'Prem-mimamsa' (Philosophy of Love) was published in Haribhau Apte's Karamanuk in 1895. About that time Haripant Gokhale a close friend of the members of the D.E. Society bought the concern of Aryabhusan Press and Dnyanprakas paper (then an Anglo-vernacular paper). He induced Bhate to write for his paper. Bhate readily agreed and began to write leaders and notes in the weekly paper on a variety of subjects. Sometime after Gopalrav Gokhale bought these concerns and Dnyanprakas was made a daily Marathi paper and Nates Appaji Dravid was appointed an editor of the paper. From this time he began to write more regularly. By this news-paper-writing Bhate got a valuable training and soon became an expert writer in Marathi.

He wrote his first big book on Economics by name 'Arthasastraci Mulatative' (Principles of Economics). This book consisting of over 500 pages was written within five or six months' time and Bhate had to do strenuous work for it.

At that time he was teaching that subject to the B. A. class in the Fergusson College. This first work of his was highly spoken of by men like Messrs. Gokhale, Josi and Mahajani. He received the prize of Rs. 500 from the Deccan Vernacular Translation Society. The book was published in 1910. That very year Govindrav took his first trip to Upper India visiting Agra, Delhi, Mathura and Haridwar. This was the beginning of his travelling hobby. He published an interesting account of his travels in Manoranjan. Since that time he has travelled off and on throughout the whole of India and has written accounts of these travels of his.

As stated already he had gone to England and visited the western countries of Europe in 1929-30. After his retirement he had more leisure and he utilised it in visiting distant countries. In 1933 he went to Ceylon and stayed there for 3 months. On his way back he visited the beautiful country of Malbar (Keral its old name). At this time he had written much about his travels. So he formed the plan of publishing a uniform illustrated edition of all his travels in ten volumes covering over 1500 pages and executed it by 1934—1935. Thus he made the most valuable contribution to Modern Marathi literature and in fact added a new wing to it. By his vast travelling for over 20 years Bhate got the name of 'Traveller Bhate.' He was frequently consulted by would-be travellers and tourists. His other literary works are the following:

12. Tin Tattvadnyani (Three Philosophers); 13. Sir Walter Scott; 14. Kant and Sankaracarya; 15. Lalitakala mimamsa (Philosophy of fine arts); 16. Karlail va Hindu Caliriti (Carlyle and Hindu manners and customs); 17. Maza Mhaisurca Pravas (My travels to Mysore); 18. Prem ki laukik, a novel (Love or respectability).

4

Selections from Marathi Literature

MARATHI PROSE SECTION (TRANSLATION)

1.	The Letter of Commands	:	The Royal Strategy of King Siwaji.
2.	Vishnubhuva Brahmachari	:	An Essay on the Welfare State.
3.	Vishnushastri Chiplunkar	:	Elocution.
4.	B. G. Tilak	:	The Gita-Dharma.
5.	S. M. Paranjpe	:	The found casket.
6.	N. C. Kelkar	:	The Description of Simla.
7.	R. G. Gadkari	:	Punyaprabhava
7a.	V. D. Savarkar	:	The God of the Man and The God of the universe.
8.	Acharya S. D. Javadekar	:	The Immortal Principle of Indian Culture.
9.	Acharya Vinoba Bhave	:	Maharashtra's Saraswati.
10.	P. K. Atre	:	Mahatma Gandhiji immocial.

MARATHI POETRY SECTION (TRANSLATION)

1.	Jnanesvara	:	'The Grace of God'
2.	Ekanath	:	'Bhagwata—a great field'

3. Tukarama	:	'Bodily disappearance of Tukarama'
4. Ramdas	:	'The description of The Uttama Purusha'
5. Moropanta	:	'Kekavali (The crying of the peacock)
6. Ananta Phandi	:	'. . . piece of Advice'
7. Keshavsui	:	'No rose without thorns New Sepoy (Soldier)
8. Balakavi	:	'Audumbara'
9. B. R. Tambe	:	'People will say for a moment, 'Alas! Alas!!'
10. Yeshwant	:	'The method of worlds behaving'
11. B. B. Borkar	:	'O, they have realized the life!'
12. Kusumagraja	:	'This immortal Banner'
13. Indira Sant	:	'Rise up soon, O God Sun'

The letter or Commands

OR

'Adnyapatra' (1666 A.D.)

'THE ROYAL STRATEGY OF KING SIWAJI'

The Navy is a separate entity of the kingdom. Just as one who possesses the strength of horses, controls over the Earth as his subjects, similarly, he who maintains Navy, becomes the master of the sea. With this view-point, Navy should be necessarily built up. The speedy yachts should be constructed of a mediocre size i.e. not big, not small. On the same basis, ships also should be made. There is no purpose in building the weighty frigates which do not work without winds. However, in order to create terror one or two frigates may be constructed; but whatever Navy is required, it should be built up with full equipment such as fighting man-power, daggers, vessels, rifles, ammunition, marinar's compasses etc. This should be divided into parts (subhas). Every 'subha' should be allotted five speedy yachts and fifteen ships. These 'subhas' should be brought under the control of one command (Sirsubha). All these 'subhas' should act in obedience to this command.

Vishnubhuva Brahmachari (1825 A.D. to 1871 A.D.)

'AN ESSAY ON A WELFARE STATE'

O Gentlemen, Listen to me :

(1) The king should persuade his subjects living under his Rule, to understand that all the subjects are the members of my one—single—family I am myself the Head of the family. The whole of land in my kingdom is just like my garden. Therefore, I must make an arrangement for the livelihood of all the members of my family on this soil itself, and see that all of them are happy. Thus, at first, the king should start thinking like that. And it should be the feeling that, the whole kingdom itself, is one house and all the subjects thereof, are in one family.

(2) Thus, all the people (subjects) in this kingdom have constituted one family and as such, all of them should request the king who is busy with the work of making his family happy, that "all of us are fully prepared to act according to Your orders".

(3) Then the whole land should be got cultivated by the subjects in this way that the plants should be cultivated in such a land wherein they will prosper. Dams and tanks should be so constructed that the land can be provided with sufficient water-supply through bunds, for all the twelve months, to produce various fruits, vegetables, food-grains, etc. and grass for the use of buffalos, horses, asses, camels, etc. Store-houses should be kept filled with, in villages, from which villagers should take as much foodgrains and grass as they want. This production should be made throughout all the seasons, in all

sorts of land, and the same should be supposed to be the property of all and for all. It should be entrusted to one person from whom people should take away, ample quantity of food to eat. The king should establish industries and install factories and mills for preparing clothes of cotton, and wool. These clothes should be stored in the Government store-rooms in villages from which people should take as many as they require. When there is a drought for twelve years, water-supply to the land should be made by constructing dams in the region where there is ample rain-fall. Thus the land should be always kept fertile. The king should get the ornaments made of gold, silver, pearls and jewels and they should be kept in village treasuries. They should be used by villagers—men and women—when required. The broken ornaments should be returned to the treasurics and new ones should be taken again by them. All sorts of weapons and machines should be manufactured in the factories installed in villages. Various games should be started; Railways and wireless telegraphy should be introduced. Marriages should take place through the Department specially established for the purpose. The children above five years of age, should be entrusted to the king. They should be properly brought up and educated in all fields; and according to their liking and aptitude, employment should be given to them.

In old age, men and women should earn their livelihood without doing any job.

Thus, one-single family means all the subjects. The general code of the conduct should be just in accordance with what is described so far. If this is done, no one will come to know as to what is meant by theft, quarrel, murder etc. Then by all means, there will be no necessity of the court of law. Nobody will understand the meaning of a famine, and thus all beings will obtain what they desire. Such should be the relations between the king and his subjects.

Vishnushastri Chiplunkar (1850 A.D. to 1882 A.D.)

ELOCUTION

The Rise of the gift of the gab requires a particular form of Government in the Nation. This particular form exactly means a Republic State. In the Parliamentary system of Government, when the administrative machinery is always run by the Majority-Party, or the community, the intellectual personages have to attract the minds of such parties or communities towards them, to take decisions . . . no other powerful weapon like Elocution.

It should be always understood that, all the people have come under the thumb of that personage who is well-versed in the Art of Elocution, and that, after having done according to his own wish, he has established his Rule over the whole of the state. Thus, amongst all other forms of Government, the Republican State is the only form which is favourable to the Rise of the Art of Elocution; because, in all other types, the Governmental Administration is not run by the majority party; and therefore, the Art of Elocution which concentrates the attention of the Majority, on the orator's opinion, is not at all required. Thus, it becomes quite clear, that the Art of Elocution, being nipped in the bud, is not in the least, likely to be developed.

B.G. Tilak (1856 to 1920 A.D.)

'THE GITA—DHARMA'

Thus, the Religion of the Gita, which is a combination of Spiritual knowledge, Devotion, and Action, which is fearless and comprehensive in all respects, and is further absolutely equable, that is, which does not keep any distinction between classes and castes and countries or any other distinction, but gives the same Release to everyone in one and the same measure and at the same time, which shows proper forbearance towards other Religions, is seen to be the sweetest and immortal fruit of the Tree of the Old Vedic Religion. In this Vedic Religion more importance was attached, particularly in the beginning, to the sacrifice of wealth or of animals, that is to six, principally to Action in the form of rituals, but when the knowledge expounded in the Upanisads pointed out later on that, this ritualistic religion of the Srutis was subsidiary and inferior to knowledge, the Samkhya Philosophy arose out of it; but this knowledge also being unintelligible to the common man, and specially inclined to Abandonment of Action, it was not possible for mediocre people to be contented merely with the Religion of the Upanisads or with the Unification of the Upanisads and the Samkhya philosophy in the Smrutis.

Therefore, the Gita Religion fuses the knowledge of the Brahman contained in the Upanisads, which is cognisable only to the intelligence, with the king of Mysticisms' (Raja-Guhya) of the worship of the Perceptible which is accessible to the Love. And consistently with the ancient tradition of ritualistic Religion, it proclaims to everybody with loud voice, though nominally to Arjuna, that, "Perform your several worldly duties according to your respective positions and abilities in life unto the last, desirelessly, enthusiastically and with a self-identifying vision for the universal good; and thereby, worship perpetually the deity in the form of the . . . .which is Eternal and which uniformly pervades the Body of all created things as also the Cosmos; because therein lies your happiness in this world and in the next;" and on that account, the mutual conflict between Action, Spiritual Knowledge (Jnana) and Love (Devotion) is eliminated; and the single Gita Religion, which preaches that the whole of one's life should be transfused into a sacrifice (Yajna) has got the essence of the entire Vedic Religion.

Prof. S M. Paranjpe (1864 to 1929 A D.)

'THE FOUND CASKET'

And the Brahmin exclaimed these words! "Oh, this is the real casket! What a divine comliness this is! The Earth is the lower compartment (case) and the Sky is its upper lid. What a miraculous, expansive and divine casket this is! The same is this casket described in the Vedas and Upanishads is the form of the Heaven and the Earth! God Himself has created this casket with His own hands and has handed it over to the Human-being; but I have not so far looked at it! And I sat lamenting because I had lost my casket! Just like my casket, my idols therein, are quite similar to it! When the casket was lost, my idols also were lost! O God, are You ever lost ? But how will you be lost, when You are omnipresent ? But this is not at all understood by ignorant people! However, this much is quite true that due to my ignorance I had surely lost something! To-day, by Your Grace, O God, I have found it all! O God, I have got my casket which I had lost! But being charmed with ignorance why should I lament in vain when the casket constituted by the Earth and the celestial sphere is there, when my venerable deity incarnate is therein like the rising sun, and when the starlike golden lotuses are present here ? The Supreme Soul is just confined to this casket! The Eternity has also space to live in it! What will not be available if that Supreme Soul which is manifested, is adored, worshipped, venerated, meditated, and intensely contemplated? While in deep meditation of this, man will assimilate with it; and who so-ever will do this, God will shower down His Grace upon him! God will make all of his desires fruitful and in the end, he will be gifted with God-Realization!

N.C Kelkar (1872 to 1947 A D.)

'THE DESCRIPTION (PANORAMA) OF SIMLA'

It is said that in the Himalayas, the ranks of the peaks which are higher than each other are attached, one behind the other; and we witnessed its specimen while coming to 'Simla'. When we started climbing up, at Kalka, we thought that after reaching the top of the big hill 'Simla' will appear but only to see 'Simla' we had to spend six thousand feet out of its seven thousand feet-height. And while doing this, the train had to take so many turns that no direction was left out, to which we had not turned our faces. At so many places, we felt that as if, we are going ahead, putting 'Simla' itself behind our back! A simile of the serpent's access is used to describe the turns.

taking. But the complete circular way of our going, proved this saying to be quite false. As scon as one row of curves was over, first valley being healed up, a new valley and a new row of curves used to be seen; and therefore, much height from the sea-level was not perceptible to eyes! It is just like that, when new calamities take place, old ones should be forgotten! After having adjusted the innumerable compartments of vallies and curves into one another, the structure of the "Himalayas' seems to have been done like a tuberous row of lamps or just like a garland of flowers full of petals.

The Mountain of 'Simla' is a single flower amongst hundred ones of the whole garland. Each one, out of these high spires is equalized to one flower. Probably, all these mountain-tops have been purified by the name of God 'Siva'. The pinnacle which is seen in front of us, is called 'Chudeshwar' (The Name of God 'Siva'). And looking at the disorderly big heap of ice upon that pinnacle, it seems to be the holy Mountain of Ashes, as if, reminding of the desireless splendour of that anchorite 'Yogeeshwar' (God of 'Siva'); and naturally from that, the other favourite Abodes of God 'Siva' such as—Kedar, Kalias, Kanchanaganga, Dhavalgiri etc. are recollected. And when I read in today's newspaper, the description of the attempt to climb up Mt. Everest, I felt some-what relaxed at the thought that there is at least one place of God's Abode which 'Saheb' (Englishman) has not so far touched.

R.G. Gadkari (1885 to 1919 A D)

'PUNYAPRABHAVA' (The Might of Virtue)

Vasundhara:—No, no! Vrindavana, do not consider the value of the woman so much less, who is giving you birth as a mother, who is presenting you a life-long company as a wife, who is drawing birth as a daughter, who is giving you the actual experience of a tender love at three stages in your life and who is raising you to the position of a son, a husband and a father. Woman is standard bearer of victory of the sole essence of Love, Purity, Softness and sanctity in the world.

Each and everything on the earth will prove her dignity. At a single glance of a woman a pleasing park (oasis) has made a dwelling in a barren desert. The name of the woman has given holiness of the conning of the Vedas to the rattling noise of the rivers! Woman has attached tenderness to lustre! And she has made the truth well equipped with Beauty! With the floods of . . . of the genius of great poets have flown; and in order to portray only the shades of colours of the beauty of the woman in the form of reflections, the brushes of an expert painter are engrossed in their colours. In the sanctuaries of the beautiful temples, the idols of the woman-deities are sitting; and the weapons of the brave warriors, causing the human beings to dance at the sharpened edges of their swords, are brightened with the water of the lustre moving in the eyes of woman. For her sake, mountains have danced on the back of the sea! Even the God has actually taken the form of woman! Vrindavan, a happy union of the excellent sentiments of the men and God—Devotees and 'Bhagavanta'—has taken place in the Abode of woman.

The farthest limit of the uttermost holiness of men ends with the devotion of saintliness! The virtuous persons who worship God—'Bhagvanta' disinterestedly are seated in the highest rank in the state of men! And, such a single saintly man will not be found amongst a lac of men like you; but amongst the women, like us, saintly women (chaste) doing ingenuous service of the godlike husband according to his own wishes, giving oblations of their own desires in their self-sacrifice, will be found in each and every house! Similarly, the mother bringing up the children with disinterested affection of the offspring—the devotion of God—with which God loves all beings innately and brings them up, convinces the people, in the world! Thus in the same womanly body, man and God, manifest their excellent qualities! God has created the woman to shoulder the responsibility of Faith and Development of the man who is called the climax of God's own achievement. God has appeared as a loving incarnation of womanhood, in order to maintain the regular succession of men! Man is the celebrity of God! But woman is the Idol of God! and as such, Vrindavana, God will have to rush, hearing the cry of a faithful woman, even if, he is deeply meditating the idea of creating a more delightful world than that of human beings! Vrindavana, see the truthfulness of my words! Look at this garland in my hands! Will you please bow down your head ?!

V. D Savarkar (1883 A. D. to 1966 A. D.)

"THE GOD OF THE MAN AND THE GOD OF THE UNIVERSE!"

To understand these particular laws and regulations by which, this Initial Power prevails and to utilize them as much as possible, in the happiness and welfare of the mankind is the only thing which is agreeable to a human being! What is favourable to the human welfare is good and what is contrary to it is bad; such a distinct definition of morality and immorality should be made by the man. What God likes is good and what is useful to the human interest .... For they are false! We are living in the universe; but the universe is not ours. In a very few respects, the universe is for us; but in most respects it is adverse to us! To know this state of things properly and boldly, and to face it defiantly is the genuine humanity; and that is the real and truthful worship of the God of Universe (Brahman)!!

Acharya S. D. Javadekar (1894 to 1955 A. D)

'THE IMMORTAL PRINCIPLE OF THE INDIAN CULTURE

The Dualism in the portraying of the Future Indian Culture coming in the line of vision of both—the Socialist Leaders of the Present India who are inspired by the current history of other nations in the Modern World, and the 'Satyagrahi' (Truth-persistent) leaders like Mahatma Gandhi who are proud of the old Indian Spiritual Culture and who are respected by the whole world—can vanish. This dividedness will be absolutely nullified in as much as the predicted culture in the Independent India takes a substantial form; and its enviable Nature will be able to satisfy the Material and Spiritual desires of the whole human race. And this very Indian Culture, we trust and believe firmly, will spread all over the world as a culture of the entire mankind.

Acharya Vinoba Bhave (Birth—1894 A. D.)

'MAHARASHTRA'S SARASWATI'

The River 'Indrayani' has conferred innumerable obligations upon Maharashtra. The blind eye of Geography will feel 'Indrayani' as a petty river; and if its length is measured, it is so; or does it seem to be a river ? You may better call it as one of the big springs of water! But this is not a spring of water only; this is a spring of spiritual Inspiration.

The water which is sweet to taste and digestion even when wood is eaten, is the best. The water of 'Indrayani' has stood this double trial (Test). Nothing can be shown which is digestive like 'Knowledge' and delicious like 'Devotion'. The history shows that the water of 'Indrayani' has got abundance of digestive knowledge and delicious devotion. Jnaneshwar—the Preceptor of the wise and Tukarama—the chief (crest) of devotees—had become plump by drinking its water. The water of 'Indrayani' has produced this great incantation, 'Jnanoba – Tukarama', fascinating the pious mind. 'Dehu' and 'Alandi' are situated in the 'Panchkroshi' of each other (A group of five villages within a circuit of five kosas: 10 miles; on the bank of 'Indrayani'. Jnaneshwara's 'Alandi' has founded the basis for 'knowledge'; and Tukarama's 'Dehu' has raised 'the Dome of Devotion'. There it was formed a rare occasion that the two great men of such and immense height of fame, were resounded in the same 'Panchkroshi'. The neighbouring district of the river is probably fertile; but the land on the bank of 'Indrayani' made the climax of fertileness Jnaneshwar lived his life to take out the Essence of knowledge; and Tukarama was the flavour of Devotion incarnate. The worthiness of that water which had stored so uch essence and so much flavour, must be said to be unprecedented!

P. K. Atre (1898 to 1969 A. D.)

"MAHATMA GANDHI IS IMMORTAL!"

Gandhiji departed his life! Mahatmaji passed away! The Father of Independence has disappeared! Thirteen days have elapsed after his death. That was the death of a hero : the Martyr's death it was! It embraced him in the evening on the holy prayer-ground in the Capital of India on 30th of January (1948). At last his own life was sacrificed in the pit enraged with malice which spread up in the nation. This lofty light-house weaving the light of Love and Peace over the world, tumbled down within no time. The next day, on the banks of Jamna, with the witness of the setting sun, lakhs of people with their eyes shedding tears, bade farewell to the earthly body of Gandhiji and from that place, they warned these crores of Gods in the heaven, of his immortality saying, "Mahatma Gandhi is immortal!" Each and every bright particle of his body, mounting on the perfumed blazes of the funeral pile, was merged in the five Elements (Earth, Water, Fire, Air and Sky). Tomorrow, crores of people of this Nation will offer oblations of reverence with tears in eyes, while his bones are being immersed in the 'Prayaga sangam' (The place of the union of three rivers—Ganges, Jamna and Saraswati) and while his pyre-ashes are being scattered in the holy waters of rivers and seas of India. Oh! how finished! The great and noble incarnation of this Epoch was terminated! Five months back, this expansive India was cut into pieces! and now the Creater of her good fortune has passed away!!

POETRY

Jnaneswara (1275 A. D. to 1296 A. D.)

THE GRACE OF GOD

In this passage of the epilogue of the Jnanesvari, Jnanesvara asks grace from God. He says, "O Saints, it is seen after repeated and constant thinking, that the obligation you have conferred on me, by composing this treatise, is incomparable in the whole world. What more shall I describe! The narration of the Religion you have done, is also ended by your hands. What is my own share here is only the service I have put in." Then he further prays, "Let the Lord of the Universe be pleased with this literary sacrifice of mine, and then being pleased, let Him give me His grace : May the wicked leave their crookedness and have increasing love for good! Let universal friendship reign amongst all beings. Let the darkness of evil disappear. Let the sun of True Religion rise in the world. Let all beings obtain what they desire. May the company of the devotees of God, who shower down blessings incessantly, meet the beings on earth! They are verily moving gardens of wish-trees; they are living mines of wish-jewels; they are speaking oceans of nectar. They are moons without any detracting mark; they are suns without any tormenting heat. May all beings be endowed with all happiness, and have incessant devotion to the Primeval Being. Let all those, who live upon this work, have victory in the seen as well as the unseen! God said to this, 'Amen! this shall come to pass' and Jnanesvara became pleased to hear those words". (Jnanesvari XVIII 1791 to 1801).

Ekanath (1533 A D. to 1599 A. D.)

BHAGAVATA—A GREAT FIELD

Ekanath uses the simile of a great field to depict the history of the Bhagavata. "Sri Bhagavata" he says, "is a great field. Brahma was the first to procure the seed. Narada was its chief Proprietor. And it was he who had monopoly to do this wonderful work of sowing the seed. Vyasa secured protection for the field by erecting ten scientific bunds around it with the result that there was the unusually excellent crop of divine bliss. Suka worked as a watchman to guard the crops; and with simply discharging the sling of God's name, he made the sin-birds flow away. Uddhava thrashed the ears, heaped them together in the form of the Eleventh Skanda and winnowing the corn, separated the grains in the form of the weighty words of Sri Krishna. From these were very skilfully prepared several questions—dishes with an immortal flavour. Parikshit succeeded Uddhava. He kept himself aloof from the world to listen to the Bhagavata from the lips of Sukadeva and achieved divine bliss. Following the same path, Sridhara illuminated the hidden meaning of the Bhagavata in his Bhavrthadipika and brought blissful peace for himself. The favourite fly of Janardana namely Ekanatha with the two wings of the Marathi Dialect, flew straight upon that dish and enjoyed it to its hearst's content, as it was left there unmolested by anyone. Or otherwise, it might be said that Janardana's favourite cat happened to see the delicious preparations through the light of the Bhavarthadipika. Smelling the dish to be pure and tasty it ventured to approach the plates. When it mewed, the merciful saints were pleased to offer to it a morsel of the remnants of their dish. The favourite cat of Janardana was simply overjoyed to lick the unwashed vessels of these saints and it enjoyed the dish as a heavenly ambrosia."

Ekanathi Bhagavata (XXXI; 443 to 454)

Tukarama (1606 A.D. to 1651 A.D.)

THE LAST SCENE OF TUKARAMA'S LIFE

Bodily Disappearance of Tukarama

Tukarama had now reached the summit of his spiritual power. As a great saint, his name had become known to all. From the life of an ordinary Vaishya Wani he had risen to be the spiritual king of the world. Now he was waiting only for the final scene. When the time arrived, he tells us. God came in person to take him to heaven. He says, "See, God comes there with the conch and the disc in His hands. The eagle, His favourite messenger, comes with ruffled pinions and says to me, 'fear not, fear not'. By the lustre of the crown of the gems on God's head, even the Sun fades into insignificance. God has a form blue like the sky, and is infinitely, handsome. He has four hands, and down His neck hangs the garland called Vaijayanti. By the lustre of His lower clothes, the quarters are filled with light. Tuka is filled with gladness that the very heaven has descended into his house".

And when God Himself came to invite Him, Tukarama did not think it proper to live and longer in the world. He bade good-bye to the people and said, "I go to Heaven. Let the compassion be on me from you all. Tender my supplications to all. God Vithala is standing up for a long time and is inviting me to heaven. At the last moment of my life, God Panduranga has come to take me away and Tuka disappears with his body."

Ramdas (1608 A.D. to 1681 A.D.)

"RAMDAS'S ADVICE TO SIWAJI i.e. THE DESCRIPTION OF THE BEST MAN OR THE UTTAMA PURUSHA."

This is the advice imparted by Sant Ramdas to a ruler like Siwaji, who had to carry on his kingdom in the midst of Mahomedan. . . clothes and ornaments and his mind by various thoughts of political wisdom." He further tells that if his body is lustrous and adorned with various clothes and ornaments but if his mind is lacking in political shrewdness then he will not shine." He further says to him, "God feels proud of you and particularly the Goddess Tulja Bhawani. You should undertake your enterprises with great care. The Mahomedans have been spreading oppression throughout India for a long time." Hence Siwaji should be always on his guard. When God once calls a man as his own, one cannot imagine what he may do. His justice, his forethought, his ready-wisdom and his knowledge of other people's hearts are all the gifts of God, says Ramdas. Again he tells him that his efforts, his alertness, his courage in the nick of time and his great prowess are the gifts of God. His fame, his power, his greatness and his incomparably rare qualities are the gifts of God. His discrimination between matters pertaining to this world and those pertaining to the other world, his perpetual wakefulness about all matters and his forbearance are the gifts of God. So, those persons in fact, who re-establish the kingdom of God are really the incarnation of God.

—Dasabodha—18 x 6, 2 to 20.

Moropanta—(1729 to 1794 A.D.)

'KEKAVALI' (CRYING OF PEACOCK)

The old age has started to appear just like the banner of the army of the God of Death. The body is exhausted after having faced the leading diseases. There is no other able companion except you. If I do not become impatient, this enemy of mine (Death) will cut my throat.

Let me happen to get always a good company. Let words of the virtuous men fall on my ears. Let the stain on my mind get emaciated. Let me have absolute dislike for all worldly objects. Let my mind hide itself in the toes of lotus-like feet of the pious men; and if it is reluctant to, then let it be made to stay there. Let it weep, when separated from you; and as such, may my mind be infatuated with your story.

O God Hari, You, who are like a cloud of the nectar of compassion, turn your face to this pea-cock (Moropanta). When the child cries out, its mother picks it up and embraces with intense affection. Will such an unexpected guest (like me) available to you who is worshipped and highly praised by religious persons? O God, You will not find it difficult to rescue this devotee from this ocean-like world (for final salvation).

Ananta Phandi (1744 A.D. to 1819 A.D.

A PIECE OF ADVICE—'PHATAKA' VERSE

A difficult way should not be always used. Leave not the conventional way; have this worldly life; but do not wander for no reason whatsoever. Be modest and do not tell a sweet lie; be always humble but do not get angry with anyone. Don't give room to be blamed by the people for your having accepted Atheism; make a lucrative achievement; but do not follow a sinful way. Don't be displeased with parents; do not be lonely and do not get yourself deceived in daily practical life. Never sit idle; and only for the sake of bread and butter, do not make strange and precarious transactions. Do not find fault with others. Don't make contemptuous speeches to make others shameful. Do not try to be malicious with others to deprive them of their treasures. Do not be proud of it, supposing yourself to be the wisest and the richest one. Do not advertise your greatness as there are many others in upgraded superiority. Do not growl at the poor and the weak by means of the power of your assistance. This very short-lived mastership will elapse and therefore, do not take the burden of the failure.

Do not lose your prestige on account of your being lost in debt. Spend for your friend from your own pocket; but do not give surety for him. Do not wage a bet; do not weigh with defective balance-scales; do not sink a pawn; do not beg when you possess; but when you don't possess, why ask? do not show regard for anybody, as the whole village is yours. For your own interest, neither slander not praise anybody unnecessarily. To flatter a wise man is good; but to make friendship with a fool is not advisable. The bread earned by labour is quite tasty; but the theft of Ghee and sugar is not admissible. Do not hesitate to give a handful to an unexpected guest who has come to you. Be contented with what you have got; do not be fed up with it, Save something from what you are earning and spend for the cause of good deeds, without any hesitation.

Now I tell you one thing that you should not be indifferent to good deeds. If you do this, then rest assured, that your glorious fame will undoubtedly get wide publicity. Do not be afraid of having good thoughts; do not abandon good company. Do not trust in dividedness. Forget not, to worship God.

Keshavsut (1866-1905 A.D.)

'NO ROSE WITHOUT THORNS!'

No rose without thorns; bear in mind this truth.
Then the despair will never perturb you.
Thus the happiness and sorrow are always commingled together in this world.
While striving for happiness, sorrow comes to our lot.
Has anyone ever seen light without shadow!
The picture gets ready when the shadow assimilates with light!
What is admirable in this world is only one thing ;
and that is Love! Nay, what is disheartening?
Certainly the same! Love!
There is nothing authoritative; this worldly life is perverted and loathing. Realizing this, give up the lamentation and grief, though unavoidable.

Keshavsut

A NEW SEPOY (SOLDIER)

I am a brave sepoy with a new spirit and a new stamina in this new age; and I want to see as to who dares to bring me into the state of obedience! I am not a Brahmin, not a Hindu; I do not belong to any particular sect. Really those who draw up (contract) the province of completeness are depraved! My hunger is glutionous; a small piece (of bread) does not bring me happiness. I am not a frog in a pit (parochial). I do not at all bear to see the fencing put up around my orchard! I want to see as to who will make me obedient!

Wherever I go, I find my brothers and sisters. Everywhere I find the signs of my house. Wherever we go, we see the ground beneath the foot, covered with green grass. Go anywhere, you will find the blue sky overhead! These delicate and lovely children look like pleasing flowers in the sunshine; and when I see them, my mind nods with joy. They are mine; I am theirs and the same current flows within us! I want to see who can bring me round!

Whom do I worship? Of course, I worship my own self! I see the whole universe within me and therefore, I adore the same. The word 'I' does not apply to me. See how these people, putting it into the casket, invite calamities of any type to fall on their heads. I do not realize the small and great, little and big. The dualism between the good and the mean droops down; and the feeling of closeness and remoteness runs away! Each and everything seems to me to be great, big, good and close! I have remained to live, after having pervaded all these things! Let me know now, as to who is going to check me up!

Just as, while preparing the sweet meat (halva), the particles of the sugar-liquid are raised on the sesamum-seed, similarly, the covering of the sluggish, dull and hard is adhered to the centre of the Egoist inspiration all-around, and therein lies the mole of the sesamum-seed without attributes; but outwardly there seems the liquid-sugar which is like and with attributes. But each of the particles holds thorns to prick others! Such is the state of affairs among the people in the world! But how will this strife be ended? This is the anxiety staying in my mind! We will establish the Empire of Peace so long as we are alive! I am the divine missionary! I am a brave soldier—Sepoy with new spirit and staminal !

Balakavi—(1890—1918 A. D)

'AUDUMBARA' (TREE)

There flows a blue dark spring of water carrying the green grass grown on his side and the opposite bank, from islets to isles. Yonder dwells a tiny village of a very few houses towards the hill. In front of it, therc appear many green and dense plantations. In them, stretches a whitish, zig-zag trodden path which goes through green meadows to a black narrow pond. The water therein, is darkened with sweet blackness, spreading on the waves.

Putting the legs into this water, there sat this 'Audumbara' (tree).

B. R. Tambe (1874—1941 A. D.)

PEOPLE WILL SAY FOR A MOMENT "Alas, Alas !"

People will say 'Alas ! Alas !' for a moment. If I depart, will the work stop ? Sun will shine; moon will glitter. Stars will follow their own routine. Winds will blow on and on, as usual. Will there be any obstacle in this ?

Clouds will pour down, and farms will grow crops. These rivers will carry on with impudence. Who cares whether the same steps will be distinct on their banks ?

The friends and relatives will shed tears and again they will start their work. They will get up, sit down, laugh and romp about. And if I die, what are they going to lose ?

Gods like Rama and Krishna were born and then they disappeared ! Is the world forsaken without them ? Who has observed mourning for ever ? Has the daily life been held up in my absence ?

Should we sulk for such a world? Why should one be indulged in anybody's temptation? Why should we be unpropitious to the messengers of God ? Why should we not make ourselves soaked in peace ?

Yeshvant (Birth—1899)

'THE METHOD OF THE WORLD'S BEHAVING'

O World, the whole of your method is always adverse ! I desired that you would offer me at least a single flower from the garden, with admiration but in vain: and now the bier is drowned in a heap of flowers !

While walking on foot, I was made to fall down at each and every spot; now what a good deal of haste they are making to give shoulder to (the bier) and they are marching pompously in the bazaar !

Nobody spoke a worthless word sweetly and properly; and a thrashing of bitter criticism was lodged against me; but now cemetary is resounded with words of praises and admiration !

With the same desire to get a call from anywhere, I had trodden the three worlds; but now the kinsmen have flocked together to embrace the corpse !

During the whole life, not a single drop I could get to extinguish the fire-blazes; but now, how many water-jars have been made empty to renounce !

The collation of friendship (Sneha-gatha) was built up, but only dry blades came into hands. The head was knocked with spikes; and now there appear temples over the bones on the river banks !

To get the warmth from anywhere, thresh-holds were made to waste away; but now prayers (Dhooparti and Shejarti) are being offered day and night !

Having been harassed till the end, I had crossed the outskirt of this life (died); and now they express the feeling of love for me !

Really blessed is the method of your appeasing, O World !

B. B. Borkar (Birth—1910)

'O, THEY HAVE REALIZED THE LIFE !'

O, they have realized the life ! whose
egoism has, like a ripened fruit dropped
(perished); Whose mind is clear like
water, who have become one with what
they met; Who have become the life of
the animate and inanimate : Who have
kindled with the feeling of friendship;
Whose oceanlike hearts have comprehended
all the sentiments together; Who are
diverted; like clouds, towards the needy

persons in their adverse times; whose
vision has burnt the sin being enchanted with.
By whose rise, the merit is flowered and
richly perfumed; Who have weighed the
glory of the stars with their self-knowledge;
Who have found the Eternal Brahman (Supreme
Power) at home without any efforts;
. . . . Who have realized it at heart;
(It is they who have realized the life !)

Kusumagraja (Birth—1912)

THIS IMMORTAL BANNER

This immortal Banner,
This forlorn Flag,
Will ceaselessly flutter !
This gets wet with the blood of the brave
It sprouts in faith of the saints.
This fearless tri-coloured Banner
Will pour down the new life through
the dark-blue sky.

This white Himalaya Mountain gives shelter.
The vast oceans give oblations of water
And like the rising Sun on the
Mountain in the East, will shine
this immortal Banner.

The dreams in the injured heart of the
Earth will be fruitful here;
and to protect the wealth of humanity,
this immortal Banner will be vigilant
and will make others to be.

This is the protection of the weak and
the trampled.
It will march pompously as the king of
equality.
The blind but great power of the inhuman
will crack against this immortal Banner.

And where-so-ever this blue wheel will go
through the divine pathway of the stars
and the gate of the Rainbow,
There will blossom a new world,
and this immortal Banner will ceaselessly
flutter !

Indira Sant : (Birth—1914)

'RISE UP SOON, O GOD SUN'

O God Sun, rise up soon,
Come on, come early,
With golden steps, adorn this abode.

The arena is given a cow-dung wash
The mark of 'Swastik' suggesting
sacredness, is portrayed on it,
With turmeric-Kumkum-powder.

The open apartments are eager to
Welcome you, O God Sun,
Rise up soon, and come early.

O God Sun, You have come in the
centre of the sky, and the
earth glitters in the down-power
of the lustre.

Let the stream of rays come to my
house, Like the hands of my luminous
father full of affection.

May the silvery rays coming through
the open window-panes, and the
tiled air-holes, linger on, in
my house.

And while bidding good-bye
O God Sun, come into the court-yard
through the golden gate.

15